HENRY ROOT'S **A-Z** OF WOMEN

HENRY ROOT'S A-Z OF WOMEN

'THE DEFINITIVE GUIDE'

WEIDENFELD AND NICOLSON LONDON

Published in Great Britain by
Weidenfeld & Nicolson Limited
91 Clapham High Street
London SW4 7TA

ISBN 0 297 78593 1

Printed in Great Britain by
Butler & Tanner Ltd, Frome and London

139 Elm Park Mansions,
Park Walk,
London, S.W.10.

C. James Anderton Q.P.M., F.B.I.M.,
Chief Constable's Office,
Chester House,
Boyer Street,
Manchester, M16 0RE.

18th June 1984

Dear Anderton,

You'll want to know that to balance Miss Anna Ford on men I am to write on women for Lord Weidenfeld of Nicolson. That being the thrust of it pro tem, I need a deputy for a month or so to stand in re my other interests. It was between you and Buster Mottram, and you just got the vote. I am mailing the membership apprising them of your appointment and instructing them to liaise with you until otherwise informed. You'll be flat to the boards with this and that, so lean on young Mottram if you judge the lad up to it.

Keep an eye on Worsthorne. He wants to arm the membership and take on Scargill. He means well but I'm not sure if he's got both oars in the water. Ditto Johnson.

By all means ring me if a wheel comes off, but don't pester me with details.

What Manchester thinks today, Hampstead will think in ten years time! Well done!

Yours for policing by confession.

Henry Root

Henry Root

MONDAY 18 JUNE

'Had to clear the decks, do you see?' said Root. He stood on his toes and flexed his barrel-chest. 'Give ourselves a clear shot at the target. Can't be diverted from the job in hand.'

'That's important, Mr Root.'

'Needed to appoint deputies *re* my other concerns. My pressure groups, my flying vigilantes. Can't sideline them merely to accommodate Lord Weidenfeld. They must carry on.'

'That's right, Mr Root.'

'Had to be Anderton, do you see? Chief Constable of Greater Manchester. A sensible man. A man with bottom. A man with a small moustache. Worked with him closely in the past. There were other contenders, of course. Buster Mottram? An invaluable lieutenant on many of my enterprises, but a bit of a hot-head, a bit lacking in experience. He'll measure up. His time will come. Harvey Procter MP? An ideal choice, but socially stretched after hours. The Major from 138? Been with me a long time, but a few bananas short of the bunch if you want my candid opinion. Falklands business affected him badly. Brain shot out at the Upland Goose. Took it well. "No hard feelings. Just a professional doing his job. Shot my brain out. Luck of the draw." Shouldn't have been there at all, of course. Hitched a lift privately. Old General Sir Walter Walker? Fine man. You've read his book? *The Bear At The Back Door*. Another to be affected badly by the Falklands business, though. Assembled his men and marched them up and down Salisbury High Street. Attitude right, timing wrong. It must be Anderton, with Buster Mottram as his number two. My monitors in the suburbs will liaise with him. We'll need to mail the membership. You're gaping, lad.'

'No no – I was just wondering how many there are. Members, I mean.' I was being interviewed for the job of Root's assistant. If I got the job I was in for a lot of typing.

'At the last count, 3,879. Not bad, eh?'

'I've got to write to all of them?'

'Of course not! We'll get a firm to do it for us. Same people as do the monthly news-letter. So – where were we?'

'Women, Mr Root.'

Root recoiled, his eyes on stalks. 'Women, eh? Is that it? Well well well.'

'What a coup. For him, I mean.'

Root squinted suspiciously. 'Coup eh what who? What coup, lad? We'll not have coups.'

'For Lord Weidenfeld, Mr Root.'

'Lord Weidenfeld? He's had a coup?'

'The book, Mr Root. He must be pleased.'

'He will be, lad. He will be. Once he knows about it. Only had the concept last week, do you see? Anna Ford was here. Interviewing me for her book on men. A book about the bedroom, that's my guess.' Root pursed his meaty lips and scowled with distaste. 'She used – er – *words*, lad. Said "masturbate" in the early afternoon. Sat where you're sitting now and said "masturbate" as cool as mustard. While ejaculating her into the common parts I had this concept. Two birds with one stone, I thought.'

'Two birds with one stone, Mr Root?'

'You have it, lad. It so happens that I am currently raising the wind for the Home Secretary. Discreetly, of course. The Establishment's way of doing things. We look after our own, you understand. You read the allegations? Against the Home Secretary?'

I said I hadn't. I was becoming confused, but I tried to look alert. What had the Home Secretary to do with Anna Ford and Root's book on women?

'In *Private Eye*, lad. You read *Private Eye*?'

What! I thought of explaining that only wrinklies read *Private Eye*, but decided not to. I nodded vaguely.

'Inferences', said Root. 'Between the lines stuff. I'm forming a fund to finance an action, do you see? Weidenfeld will be a trustee. Good name to have on the writing-paper. A man of influence. A man with impressionists on his walls. A man to shape up well at the top end of a dinner-table. A word here, a word there. A man to have on your behalf. As a *quid pro quo* I'll write for him on women. But he'll need to be informed. A letter!'

Root, thumbs in waistcoat, chest out, a beefy forefinger occasionally removed to prod the empty air in emphasis, strutted importantly between the cocktail cabinet and three-piece suite, dictating, without pause for thought, into a tape-recorder sitting on the coffee-table.

139 Elm Park Mansions
Park Walk
London, S.W.10.

Lord Weidenfeld,
Weidenfeld (Publishers) Ltd.,
91 Clapham High Street,
London, S.W.4.

18th June 1984

Dear Weidenfeld,

Be so good as to keep your authors on the leash. Lastweek Miss Anna Ford - writing for you on men, or so she claims - said 'masturbate' in my lounge-room. To oblige you, I'd granted her an interview, but 'masturbate' is not a word I'm accustomed to hearing in my lounge-room in the early pm. "Kindly wash your mouth out, madam," I said, and she went head-first down the backstairs with her tape-recorder.

Once shot of her, I had this concept. To balance her on men, I'm prepared to write for you on women. I know what you're thinking. You're thinking: Women, eh? What's there to say on women? The bedroom and the kitchen. The duvet and the blender. The corset and the rubber glove. That covers it, you're thinking. And you're right, of course. But Root on women, that's different, that's one the mugs will go for. Your marketing men and PR girls will get the gist. Root and Ford, yoked together for publicity purposes. Front and back ends of a panto horse. A whistle-stop tour. Pebble Mill At One. Good Morning Manchester. Tyneside At Six. The signing sessions. The literary lunches. Two for the price of one. Root and Ford. Could take the curse off hers, do you see?

Here's the quid pro quo. I save your chestnuts re the Ford debacle and you sit on the board of 'The Friends of Leon Brittan Fighting Fund' - currently being formed by me - and contribute generously thereto. (Don't worry. You don't really have to be a friend of Leon Brittan's. There'd be precious little in the kitty if that were a contributing condition.) You'll have read the allegations in Private Eye. Unsubstantiated stuff, of course, but the party can't afford another scandal after the Parkinson cock-up. To say nothing of the matter of Heseltine's man caught two to the cubicle. Luck of the draw. Could have happened to anyone in the Tory Party, but there you are. I have decided that the inferences against Brittan must be nailed in court. But court cases cost money, and Brittan isn't a wealthy man. He'll have his pride too, no doubt. He'll not be one to set forth himself with the begging-bowl. Into Hambro's in a bowler hat. "Brittan's the name. I'm raising the wind re Private Eye." Can't see it. The Home Secretary. Wouldn't do. I've taken it upon myself to do it for him.

Telex your offer for Root on Women by return. We're talking about sums in the region of £50,000. Let's move on this one.

My commiserations re your autumn list.

Yours sincerely,

Henry Root

Henry Root

'So – it's women here', said Root, when that was done. 'That's the size of it. That's our thrust. You're on, lad?'

I was on all right, this was the opportunity of a life-time, my chance to work with a really famous author. It was important, however, that I remain cool. I mustn't appear too keen. I must discover the terms and conditions of my employment. I'd say 'perhaps', suggest there were other possibilities in the offing.

'I'm on', I said.

'Excellent!' cried Root. He seemed delighted. He clapped me on the back 'Right! Off you go!'

He prodded me towards the hall. Something was wrong here. Half-way across the room I realised what it was.

'About money, sir?'

'Money? Of course. Four hundred pounds a week for a morning's work. We stop at lunchtime. Other matters to attend to in the afternoon.

Matters that take precedence over a mere chart-topper for Lord Weidenfeld. My pressure groups. My flying vigilantes. There are rising tides, lad, enemies within. What's Scarman up to, that's the point?' Root went to a desk and produced a shoe-box from a drawer. 'Here. Two weeks' money in advance. In cash.' He pushed me towards the door. I remembered something else.

'About my duties, sir?'

'No idea!' said Root cheerfully. 'No plan yet. It's finger-tip stuff here. A matter of instinct. I drive by the seat of my trousers, do you see? Just a question of opening up the right flap in the brain and out they come. The concepts. The letters. The *aperçus*. There'll be *aperçus* here, lad, I tell you that.' He tapped himself on the forehead. 'Open up the right flap in the brain and we'd be inundated. Ideas. Initiatives. Insights. Perceptions. There'd be a flood, lad. The tapes will catch them.'

'The tapes, Mr Root?'

'Tape everything in the ops-room, lad. Tomorrow I'll show you the ops-room. Your job, I'd say, to correlate and transcribe a copy-tape at the end of the day. You can type?'

I said I could, which was true, more or less.

'Good. Good. I've done some letters, have I?'

'Just two, as far as I know, sir.'

'Just two?' Root scowled. 'Below average that. Got to keep the letters coming. They like to hear from me, do you see? Who to? The letters?'

'The Chief Constable of Manchester, sir, and Lord Weidenfeld.'

Root was astonished. 'Lord Weidenfeld, you say? Whatever next! Well well well.' Suddenly he beat himself on the side of the head. A smaller man would have knocked himself clean off his feet with such a blow, but Root's stumpy, sawn-off tree-trunk legs withstood the shock. 'I have it!' he cried. 'Women, was it? Root on women? That was it! What a concept, eh? Type the letters and bring them in tomorrow. You have a machine? To play the tapes on?'

I said I hadn't. I have my music-centre, of course, but I don't see why I should use that, and anyway the tape might not fit it.

'Better take this one. Any questions?'

'No sir.'

He handed me the tape-recorder, together with the day's tape and bundled me into the hall.

'Off you go, lad. See you tomorrow. Eight o'clock sharp. Don't be late. It'll be curry for breakfast.'

I came home and counted my money. I'm rich! I can afford the Charlie Allen suit I've had my eye on *plus* a pair of canvas high-top boots from Willi Wear. This arrangement with Root suits me brilliantly. I'll work for him in the mornings and if that doesn't lead pretty quickly to my becoming a successful writer I'll take the money in the shoe-box (it could be thousands by the time we've finished – it's a big subject, women) and bog off to Thailand or Bali or somewhere to think things over. When I get back to England I'll have some photographs taken (while I have a tan) and then I'll get some film parts. And I could write some great songs in Bali. I can't write so well in London due to the harassments of a capital city and people, like my father, interfering with my head.

My father telephoned, in fact, while I was counting my money. We've had our differences, Gay and I, but I keep the lines of communication open because he's surprisingly good in an emergency. There was the time at Eton, for instance, when I very naturally declined to take part in the silly Wall Game thing on the reasonable grounds that if I did I'd get my hair wet and Gay came down to the school and reasoned with my rebarbative housemaster. One never knows when there could be another emergency, so it's worth keeping in touch. I told him about my exciting new job with Henry Root.

'Henry Root?' said Gay. 'Isn't he that right-wing loony who writes crazy letters to important people like Alexander Chancellor?'

I explained that being left-wing – being into compassion and social justice and all that stuff – wasn't a fun idea anymore, that it simply wasn't fashionable, but he didn't seem to understand. He's hopelessly stuck in the so-called sixties.

'What happened to the group?' he said.

'It broke up.'

'I'm not surprised!'

I thought that was rather unnecessary. 'A natural consequence', I said coldly, 'of our being musically years ahead of our time. It was Henry Jr, in fact, who introduced me to his father. That's how I got the job.' Henry Jr had been our bass player.

Gay snorted and rang off. Then Ned telephoned suggesting a drink, but I didn't fancy sitting around talking about coffee futures all evening. Ned in any case is not the sort of person I'll have a lot of time for in the future. From now on I'll be meeting artists and intellectuals, which will suit me brilliantly. I preferred to stay at home in case Charlotte rang. She's strange, Charlotte. She's obviously interested, but she keeps me guessing. I think she may be an old-time type who doesn't see it as the woman's role to make the running. She certainly didn't make the running on Saturday. I was looking really good, but she didn't make a move. She just sat on the bed smiling mysteriously as if she expected *me* to do something. I wasn't going to humiliate myself like that again, so I considered ringing Melissa. Melissa takes the initiative all right, she's dead keen, in fact, but she seems to think the whole thing's funny. She giggles and squeaks and telephones her mother in the middle to check on the weekend arrangements. And afterwards she clings and says: 'Tell me a story.' Then Charlotte *did* ring! She didn't say she wanted to come over, but she's got Thursday afternoon off from Parrots so I've made a date to go shopping with her after lunch. She can help me choose the accessories to go with the Charlie Allen suit. She'll enjoy that. If that doesn't turn her on nothing will.

I tried to write a song, but was too distracted by thoughts of Root On Women. I find when composing that inspiration shies away like a startled deer unless the brain is absolutely still and welcoming. I reckon I can be a real help to Root. I noticed that he shuddered every time he mentioned women. Not surprising really. At his age it would be highly disagreeable to have to think of such things. He'll need my knowledge of the current mores.

TUESDAY 19 JUNE

I arrived for work a little late due to a long-standing appointment to have my nose pierced in Oxford Street (not too bad, but I will be watching out for two infectious dangers: blood poisoning and hepatitis B – both all too common according to a very useful article in *The Sunday Times Colour Supplement*). I was let in by a quaking Filipino boy who pointed me towards what Root calls his lounge-room. 'I don't care to go any further,' he said, and off he scuttled. From the other side of the door came the sound of a family fracas. There was a sudden, indignant, high-pitched cry of: 'It's *not* a Laura Ashley, you ignorant man! It's an Arabella Pollen original.' There followed a terrible throaty gurgle, and then a choking noise.

Wife-bashing was happening here. Mrs Root was undoubtedly being murdered. I was tempted to make a run for it, like the Filipino help. There are, after all, professional people from the council, trained to deal with matters of this sort on the rates. But I wasn't going to abandon my job so easily, so I pushed the door open and peered inside. A scene of amazing domestic violence was being acted out between the cocktail cabinet and three-piece suite. Henry Jr, indeed dressed in an Arabella Pollen original (any fool could have seen that), was caught by the scruff of the neck in a stranglehold, up in the air, held at arm's length by my employer, his little feet in black high-heels (Charles Jourdan, I'd have guessed, and pretty nice) pathetically beating the empty air. In a bird-cage, hanging from the ceiling, a bull-terrier yapped dementedly. It was the first time I'd seen a bull-terrier in a bird-cage. The day before, as I recalled, there'd been a canary in it.

I acted with great presence of mind. 'Fire!' I shouted, not too loudly.

Root, eyes bulging with surprise, turned his enormous head and stared in my direction. His moustache bristled angrily on his butcher's face. A cigar the size of an Indian club, clamped between meaty lips, swung rocket-like to lock on target, menacing me between the eyes. Then he gave a little grunt and padded across the room towards me, still holding Henry Jr in mid-air, still at arm's length. He must be incredibly strong. His shoulder muscles bunched massively under the jacket of his bookie's suit. He has the upper-body of a gorilla. He looked me up and down and then, with his spare hand, removed the cigar from his mouth.

'And what can I do for you, madam?' he said. 'It's women here for Lord Weidenfeld. Every aspect of the matter. What do you know of women, madam? What of Irma Kurtz?'

I think Irma Kurtz is absolutely great, as it happens, her advice being invariably valid and caring, but before going into all that it seemed best to remind Root that he'd engaged me yesterday as his research assistant.

'I'm Kim Kindersley, sir,' I said. 'You hired me yesterday to help you on your new project.'

Root came closer. He stood on tiptoe to squint into my face. His bruiser's nose was within inches now of mine. Sprouting from it, I noticed, was an abundance of ginger bristles.

'Yes? Is that the case? Well done indeed!' He suddenly beamed. His face was transformed at once into that of a pier comedian or cheeky chappie, suggesting that his bow-tie might light up and revolve. He was much less alarming now. He planted the cigar back in his mouth, held out a hand the size of an oven-glove and seized mine in a crushing grip, while continuing to hold Henry Jr up in the air with the other. 'So – what do you know of women, then? That's the matter in hand.'

In my confusion at his not having recognised me I replied a little pompously, perhaps. 'About normal for my age, I think, sir.'

'Yes? And what is that?'

Henry Jr, still suspended at arm's length in empty air, had stopped moaning, so Root shook him briskly, like a rattle. The moaning started up again.

'Twenty-three.' I said. I'd told him all this yesterday. Then, foolishly, perhaps, I tried a little joke. 'A difficult age, sir. Too young for Joan Collins, too old for Britt Ekland.'

Root glared. He breathed heavily. He blew out his cheeks, suggesting that his cigar was about to be launched, stunning me between the eyes. He angrily rattled Henry Jr. Then – suddenly – he let out a great bellow of laughter. I was overwhelmed, almost swept off my feet by a huge eddying gust, a swirling wind, a powerful hurricane of garlic, haddock, Brut, cigar smoke, ripe stilton and strong beer.

'Ha! A joke! Isn't that right? Well done! We shall get along famously.'

His shoulders heaved. Henry Jr bobbed up and down, the yo-yoing motion causing his high-heels to drum a death tattoo on the carpet. Root prodded me delightedly in the ribcage with a forefinger the size of a Polish sausage. I was winded, but I didn't go down. Then, suddenly, he struck his forehead a tremendous blow, the fleshy thunderclap causing the bull-terrier in the birdcage to yap and scrabble at the bars.

'I have you now!' cried Root. 'The CV comes to mind. Kim Kindersley. You were here yesterday. A friend of the boy's. That could go against you.' He rattled Henry Jr. 'Still – Eton, wasn't it? You have an entrée here and there? There are trust funds in offing? That was the point of hiring you, yes?'

I was quite offended by this revelation, but I nodded urgently. That seemed best. If he took me to be well-connected perhaps he wouldn't prod me. Another prod and I'd go over.

'Good. Good. Henley, is it? "Up Leander!" "Pardon me, madam, but that's my Pimms, I fancy". Royal Ascot? Polo, is it? You have a horse?'

I kept up my enthusiastic nodding.

'And what since Eton?'

My breath was gradually returning. I found I could speak again. He'd liked my last joke, so I tried another. 'Oh, you know, sir. The usual employments available to Old Etonians in Mrs Thatcher's Britain. Waiting at table. Busking. Tea-boy. Toy-boy. Boutique salesboy. Bunny at the Embassy. Associate Editor of *Ritz*. Ha! Ha!'

An ominous silence. Root stepped back another pace. He squinted angrily. He rattled Henry Jr. Then he let out a great bark of approval.

'That's right! Splendid woman! Advancement by merit in Mrs Thatcher's Britain. Glad you approve. Splendid woman, eh?'

'You have to admire her', I said. Then, because we seemed to be getting on so much better, I thought it might be in order to refer to the domestic outrage happening before my eyes. I couldn't allow such wanton violence to pass without comment. 'Excuse me, sir,' I said, 'but is that bull-terrier all right?'

Root spun round as though under attack from the rear, the sudden move through ninety degrees causing him to crack Henry Jr's head against the cocktail cabinet. 'What bull-terrier, where?' he cried. 'Is the little bugger loose again?' The cocktail cabinet, meanwhile, went into operation on its own, activated by Henry Jr's head. The lid rose, the front came down, a light went on and it started playing the title song from *Hallo Dolly*.

'Up in the cage!' I shouted.

'Phew!' said Root, fanning the air with relief. 'Keep treading on the little bugger, do you see? Put it in the cage when Mrs Root's not looking.' With his spare hand he shut down the cocktail cabinet. 'What do you think? A present from the Michael Parkinsons. Plays excerpts from *Hallo Dolly*, do you see? Original cast recording, if I'm not mistaken.'

'Very nice,' I said.

'So! It's into the ops-room, then. We'll leave the boy here.'

He let go of Henry Jr so abruptly that he sprawled on the floor like a broken puppet. Then he led me down a long passage to a kind of reinforced pass-door, which he unlocked with a variety of keys from an enormous bunch.

'My private quarters.' He beamed proudly. 'Don't care to bump into the family during the week.'

I nodded sympathetically. A working man and so forth. An artist must have his privacy. I'm the same way myself. The slightest interruption and the creative chain is broken.

'Nor at the weekends, come to that,' said Root. 'Get out of London at the weekends, that's my advice, lad. A change of air. A complete break. Come Friday I'm into the Rolls and bowling down the M4.'

'The country cottage, sir?'

'The Cunard Hotel, Hammersmith. Spend the weekends there. Away from the family. Have my own suite and credit arrangements, do you see? The Lord Matthews a personal friend of mine. It's a cocktail in The Hawaiian Lounge and then into the Gay Paree Rib-Room for the *à la carte* and international cabaret. All top turns in there, lad. Shirley Bassey. Frankie Laine. Johnny Matthis. Remember her, do you? "Oh Danny bo . . . y . . . y. . . ." Here we are.'

We were in a large, carpetless room which was almost without furniture. There was a huge computer, a row of filing cabinets, two tape-recorders, one portable, the other of the sort you see in a sound studio, and, dominating the whole, an imposing desk, perched on a rostrum, with, above it, photographs of the Queen and Mrs Thatcher. In one corner of the room was several thousand pounds' worth of exercise equipment – a bicycle, a rowing machine, one of those revolving belts on which you run in place and some sort of power-lifting contraption. As we passed it, Root pushed lightly down on a bar and a weight that would have knocked a house down swung easily to the ceiling.

'Like to keep fit', Root explained. '*Mens sana in corpore* whatsit, eh?' Then he switched on a tape-recorder. He checked the time on a huge half-hunter chained to his waistcoat and cleared his throat importantly.

'Ahem. Testing testing testing. Tape number HR/38765/KP. Eleven hundred hours on Tuesday 19 June. Present in the ops-room Henry Root and one Kim Kindersley, research assistant. We'll try you for voice level, lad. Say something. Mind your language.'

'Hullo', I said.

'That'll do. Don't want to waste the tape. Right! We're off and running, then.' The conducted tour continued. Next stop was the bank of filing cabinets. 'Dossiers', Root explained. 'We have folk under investigation here. Working closely with the Home Secretary, do you see? Needs back-up at street-level. They're all in there.' He paused and cocked an ear. 'Did you hear something, lad?'

I had, in fact. A muffled banging on a door at the end of the room, as though someone was trapped behind it and trying to get out.

'Over there', I said.

'A moment, lad. To the broom-cupboard!'

He crossed the room and opened the cupboard door. He went inside and closed the door behind him. There was the sound of a short, decisive confrontation. Two heavy thumps, followed by a shrill, Caribbean cry of protest. Root emerged from the cupboard massaging a ham-like fist.

'Who was that?' Was it impolite to ask?

'Who was what?'

'In the cupboard, sir.'

'Him? Captured by two of my men last night. Holding him in

communicado for ninety-six hours as per the new law. Short sharp shock. Where were we?'

'The filing cabinets, sir.'

'That's right, the filing cabinets. They're all on file. Community lawyers. Workshop types. Lunchtime mimes. Sociologists. Bishops. Perverts. Belgrano Bores. Alternative comedians. Defaulters. Oh yes, there's folk to be informed on there. Man O'The People can't do it all, you know. You read *The People*, do you, lad? "Exposing rogues has always been our business". A fine campaigning paper. Who revealed that Ron "Tank" Atkinson had dumped his wife and taken off with his fancy woman? Who blew the whistle on the methodist minister who turned his vestry into a massage parlour? Who ran the headline: "Oh Brother! Nude Tessa Stuns Monks!"? Who revealed "The Saucy Secrets of the Kisso-gram Girls"?'

'*The People*, sir?'

'*The Sunday Times*, lad. A relevant paper once again.' He marched me across the room. 'And what do you suppose this is? A lift, lad! Our *personal* lift. Oh yes, we have our privacy in here.' He pressed a button and the lift-door slid open. 'From the basement garage to the ninth floor without stopping. A secure entry and exit without meeting others. Don't care to bump into Mrs Root in daylight, do you see? Nor in the dark, come to that.' He paused in mid-stride, and passed a hand across his eyes. Then he shook his head briskly as if to dislodge some awful picture conjured up of fleshy collisions with the lights out. 'And here's the bathroom. Like to take my ablutions after work on the heavy weights.' He opened another door. 'And here's the kitchen. Oh yes, we'll be self-supporting here, you and me. Had it put in for the celebrity lunches. Idea I got from Archer. Nice little man. Can't write, of course, but bags of go. Understands hype. You've read the *Mail* today?'

I said I hadn't.

'He's got the Potter woman working for him.' He picked up a copy of *The Daily Mail* from a pile of papers lying on his desk, opened it at the Lynda Lee-Potter interview and handed it to me. 'Read that. First paragraph.'

He stood over me as I read, beaming and nodding with approval, chuckling and breathing heavily, the queasy combination of haddock and stilton and Lee-Potter's prose being well-nigh asphyxiating in their impact.

' "Perfection for me", I wrote in *The Daily Mail* a few weeks ago, "is solitude, a glass of champagne and an advance copy of the latest Jeffrey Archer." Later that morning his smashing secretary arrived with a basket filled with fruit, flowers, a bottle of champagne and an advance copy of *First Among Equals* with the inscription: "Now all you need is solitude." It was a lovely, glamorous, stylish gesture, but then Mr Archer is a stylish man. In his wondrous flat with a Henry Moore on the glass coffee-table, laden with glossy books, he gives monthly literary lunch parties for eminent men from the world of letters. Next week his guests will be King Constantine, Ernie Wise and Laurie McMenemy and they will be greeted, as his guests always are, with a glass of chilled Krug, followed by a gourmet lunch with the finest wines money can buy.'

'Stylish, what?' said Root. He was looking as pleased as if he'd written the piece himself. 'And the cost to Archer? Fifty pounds top whack. You have to hand it to the little monkey. Potter isn't as stupid as she looks but a bunch of bananas and a bottle of pop and she's doing Archer's PR for him. Head turned completely. Gone at the knees. Simpering. Wet-lipped. Doggy. Bent to his masculine will. But that's women for you.' He winked heartily and gave a saloon bar chuckle, but suffered a crisis of confidence almost immediately. He cocked his great head enquiringly. He was about to defer, to seek a second opinion. 'Isn't that women for you?' He needed confirmation. It was an exciting moment for me, indicating that when it came to our set task – writing on women for Lord Weidenfeld – he was far from sure of his footing. For the moment I would reassure him; as the project progressed he would lean on me more and more, affording me opportunities to take the lead.

'That's women for you!' I said, returning the saloon bar wink with interest.

He beamed. He was greatly reassured. 'That's right! Put Potter on the list.' What list? Should I be taking notes? I felt myself urgently about the chest as though I might be carrying a reporter's pad under my Katherine Hamnett blouson jacket. 'A sexual woman, do you suppose? The Potter woman?'

I considered the possibility – flinchingly – but I couldn't handle it. A safety device in whatever part of the brain it is which handles such things simply blew a fuse.

Root swept on. 'She'd like the up-and-under, that's my guess. Comes from the north, do you see? Mrs Root comes from the north.' He swayed backwards and, as before when a picture of Mrs Root had come to mind, he passed a hand across his eyes and moaned softly. For all his great virtues, Root doesn't seem to be a man of the most delicate aesthetic tastes, so it occurred to me that Mrs Root, to cause him such pain, must be truly frightful. 'Never mind', said Root. 'Put her on the list. We'll write to her. Send her a crate of Thames eels and ask whether she likes the up-and-under. My guess she does. We'll write to Foyle's too. Coffee-table books, that's what we need in here. For the literary lunches. We'll draw up a guest list when we have a moment. Get the mix right, do you see? The mix is everything. Archer had it. King Constantine. Ernie Wise. And Lawrie McMenemy. Not bad, not bad at all. How about this? Frank Delaney. Dickie Davis. A. N. Wilson. Cannon and Ball. And Lulu. What a top table, eh? Take a seat, lad.'

He gestured me to what was really a high-chair of the sort in which children sit at table. He must have had it specially made to disconcert his guests. It was so tall that when I had managed to clamber on to it my feet were left swinging in the air. You're at a silly disadvantage when your feet can't get a purchase on the floor. Root sat behind his desk. He stared down at me – high off the ground though I was – from the little stage on which his desk was placed.

'So. Where were we?'

'Women, sir. Women for Lord Weidenfeld.'

'Women, eh? Is that it? For Lord Weidenfeld, you say. You're right, of course, but first I've other matters to attend to. My pressure groups. My flying vigilantes. New legislation to be monitored. What of the Police and Criminal Evidence Bill? Raises questions, does it not?'

He had me there. He'd moved too fast for me, his strange mind racing and boiling, hopping from subject to subject. My legs swung stupidly off the floor. 'It does?'

'It does. Stop and search and anal probes. That's the point. Does the right extend to my vigilantes? You look surprised, lad.'

'Anal probes, sir?'

'Of the essence, lad. When the Bill was before Parliament, Eldon Griffiths – a personal friend of mine as well as being an expert on such matters – reported to Parliament that provincial police forces had been carrying out random anal probes throughout 1982 and 1983. What do you suppose they found, lad?'

'I've no idea, sir.'

'According to Griffiths, they recovered as a result of these probes drugs with a street value of £55,000, three vibrators, a police truncheon, explosives, £2,000 in bank notes, a gardening glove, a detonator and a radio transmitter that had relayed a confidential interview between the Thames Valley Police and an informer, as a result of which chummy had had it away on his toes.'

'Good lord.'

'Precisely. Then there's the matter of holding a suspect for ninety-six hours incommunicado. Has he the right to phone his solicitor? Are we exceeding the mark here? Have we violated the safeguards *re* our coloured friend?' He jerked his head in the direction of the broom-cupboard. 'I'll admit I have a doubt, lad.'

I was a bit uneasy myself. I'm no lawyer, but might I not in these circumstances be a party to racism, kidnapping and GBH?

'If you have a doubt, sir, perhaps you should let him go.'

'Let him go, eh?' Root considered the point. He drummed his fingers on the desk. He frowned. 'You may be on to something, lad. Give him a cuffing and let him go, is that it? We'll seek a ruling. We'll address ourselves to 'B' Division on this one. A letter!'

139 Elm Park Mansions
Park Walk
London S.W.10.

The Commander,
'B' Division,
Chelsea Police Station,
London S.W.3.

19th June 1984.

Dear Commander,

I seek your guidance re the Home Secretary's Police and Criminal Evidence Bill now before the Lords.

As per the present law, the responsible member of the general public has the right and obligation, as I understand it, to effect whenever possible a citizen's arrest. Here's my query. Will the powers given to the police under the new law - viz stop and search and anal probes - extend also to the citizen?

I have a team of flying vigilantes here, Commander, and now seek guidance as to stopping and probing and holding incommunicado for ninety-six hours of suspicious types after dark as per the new Bill.

Last night a contretemps occurred when two of my men - Glidewell and Major Snipe, to be precise - 'felt the collar' of one of our coloured friends outside a King's Road disco and stripped him down to his boots and half-hose in search for substances. The lad transpired to be 'clean', but my men, confident in the powers now residing in them thanks to Mr Brittan's initiative, elected to hold him incommunicado for ninety-six hours anyway, and thus bundled him back to operational HQ, where he is currently being held in a broom-cupboard.

What are the lad's rights re one phone-call and contacting his solicitor (not that he has one)? What of habeas corpus? Does this still apply in Mrs Thatcher's Britain? He is our first prisoner, you understand, and we don't wish to exceed the safeguards. Kindly advise.

We all know what goes on at 'B' Division, Commander (and nothing wrong with that), but I wouldn't be so foolish, of course, as to put anything in writing re 'buying you a drink' personally. I enclose a tenner on account, however, pending 'a meet'.

Here's to policing by confession!

Yours sincerely,

Henry Root

Henry Root

'Where were we, lad?'
'Women, sir.'
'Women, eh? You're right! I've been thinking, lad. How long will this

take us, do you suppose? To cover the subject comprehensively? A month? As long as that? Other matters to attend to, do you see?'

I was quite surprised. I'd assumed that a book of this importance would take much longer than that, but I hadn't seen him working yet; no doubt when his great brain began to concentrate we'd devour the subject, biting and tearing into it. I said that a month should be ample.

'Just as I thought,' said Root. 'So – what now?'

'Shouldn't we make a start, sir?'

'A start? What on, lad?'

'The book, sir.'

'The book, eh? Not a bad idea. I tell you what, though. We'll make a start tomorrow.'

He got up and bundled me towards the lift, on the way handing me the day's tape. He also gave me one of those punch-cards by which CIA agents gain access to top security establishments.

'You'll need this', he said, 'to avoid entry via the family quarters. The lift will carry you straight to the ops-room from the basement garage. Security, do you see?' He winked and touched the side of his nose with a slab-like finger. He pushed me into the lift. 'Type the letters and bring them in tomorrow. Don't be late.'

I went home and typed Root's letters, the one to 'B' Division reviving uneasy memories of our prisoner in the broom-cupboard, eyes rolling in terror, no doubt, under his woolly hat. Root is by any standards a literary figure of the first rank, and working for him is a great opportunity for me, but in many respects he is something of a monster. Is this relevant? I have managed to convince myself that it isn't. It is the literary Root for whom I'm working; his robust way of doing things is neither here nor there. Evelyn Waugh, the famous author of *Brideshead Revisited*, was from all accounts a brute in his private life, but for a literary apprentice to have refused to work for him on that account would have been absurd. I do still have this lurking fear, however, that we might be breaking the law with regard to the black man in the broom-cupboard.

Henry Jr rang. He left home after the violence this morning and is now living with a religious community in Deptford. I met him for a drink in the Chelsea Potter. He told me about his new guru, who used to be a mini-cab driver in Peckham.

'He has amazing powers', said Henry Jr. 'He can be everywhere at once. He is in outer space one minute, in a fish and chip shop in Deptford the next. With one bound he can be on a distant galaxy. He has the x factor – IT. IT takes the place of ego, availing itself of a facility and dexterity that can neither be understood nor laid hold of. It is everything and nothing, everywhere and nowhere. It's really great. One day I will experience IT. Meanwhile can you lend me twenty pounds?'

Then we had a brilliant conversation about music. Henry Jr explained why I keep hearing my songs played on radio, attributed to other composers. Every time I write something really good, I turn on Radio One and hear *my* song introduced as someone's latest hit! It's a real downer. Henry Jr explained it like this:

'What you've got to understand is that up there, up above us, there is a realm of pure creation where the really great ideas float around waiting to be used. Truly creative people are able to plug into this realm of pure creation and tap it for inspiration. Naturally, there's only a limited supply of really great ideas up there, so you're bound to get the same ideas as the established song-writers. And, of course, being established, they can get your songs performed before you can. The fact that you keep writing the same songs as them proves you're plugged into the same inspirational source. That's great.'

I think this is a brilliant account of the creative process and explains my bad luck to date. Obviously I must just keep going and the breaks will come.

WEDNESDAY 20 JUNE

There was a more encouraging start to the day, in so far as Root recognised me almost immediately, but he still seemed reluctant to confront our task.

'It's women, eh? Is that it?' He motioned me to my high-chair. He stared unhappily at his fingertips, then shuffled the papers on his desk, playing for time. 'Nothing wrong with women in their place, of course. But they must yield to the big debates. Isn't that so? There's full participation here in the big debates, lad.' The idea seemed to cheer him up. He left his desk and began to stride up and down in front of me, chest out, up on his toes, puffing at his huge cigar. 'There are books to be written on the big debates, lad, that's the point. Books of purport. A book on Our Sad National Decline. How's that for a concept? That's an idea with bottom, eh? Better than a book on women, eh? A letter, lad! A letter to André Deutsch!'

139 Elm Park Mansions
Park Walk
London, S.W.10.

Andrew Deutsch Esq
105 Great Russell Street
London, WC1B 3LJ.

20th June 1984

Dear Deutsch,

Here's one! Our Sad National Decline by Henry Root. Examples:

The Americas Cup: Three Spaniards in a bucket would have done better.

Law and Order: It is estimated that 78% of the single men in West End cocktail lounges, sipping the house white with their zips undone, are members of Sir Kenneth Newman's Gay Squad.

Literature: "We aim to be to poetry what Anusol are to suppositories," said Faber and Faber marketing supremo, Desmond Clarke, announcing a tie-in with Boots the chemist. In my day, Andre, a man could buy his denture fixative without bumping into poets.

Etiquette: Daily Mail gossip writers seeking to interview their social superiors now present themselves at the front-door instead of queueing with the odds and sods at the tradesmen's entrance.

Publishing: In the hands of a gang of shifty-eyed middle Europeans who arrived in this country with sixpence in their pockets and a season ticket to the Westminster Library.

You'll get the gist, Andre. Telex your office by return.

Yours etc,

Henry Root

Root returned to his desk, beaming triumphantly. 'What do you say to that eh? A definite chart-topper, what? How are you *re* Our Sad National Decline, lad?'

'My father mentions it from time to time. He's Gay, you know.'

Root slumped in his chair, feeling for his heart. He closed his eyes and made a moaning noise. His face turned purple, like that of a man competitively holding his breath. He clenched his fists and worked his jaw. Suddenly, the pressure of accumulated indignation shot him out of his chair. Growling angrily, he strode towards the broom-cupboard. I averted my eyes. There was the sound of a short, sharp cuffing, a high-pitched squeal, and Root returned to his desk, looking more relaxed.

'Is he really?' he said. 'How sad. How very sad.' He sighed and shook his head. 'But there you are. Not your fault. A hair-dresser, is he?'

'Actually he's a racehorse trainer and he's very far from. . . .'

'Trains horses, does he? Well well well. Still, where were we?'

'Our sad national decline, sir.'

'That's it. Well done. Examples crowd in daily, do they not? Here in *The Sun* this morning.' Root picked up *The Sun* from a pile of papers lying on his desk and scrabbled with sausage-fingers to find the page he wanted. 'Here we are. Frankie Goes To Hollywood. Crooners, it says. You've come across them?'

'Relax,' I said.

Root looked displeased. 'I'm quite relaxed, thank you, lad.'

'No no, sir. That's the name of their current hit.'

'Is that so? Anyway, picture of them here, do you see?' He passed *The Sun* across the desk. 'Perverts, is that your guess? Shirt-lifters? Backdoor men?'

I muttered something non-committal, played for time. A word out of place and it would be another cuffing for our prisoner.

'Well, they're not!' cried Root triumphantly. 'That's the gist of it, do you see? All a PR stunt. They are merely pretending to be perverts! For their image, do you see? Says so here.' He indignantly tapped the picture with a stubby finger. Then, suddenly, he looked embarrassed. He coughed apologetically behind his hand. He raised an arm as if to acknowledge a professional foul. 'Excuse me. Your father. Not your fault. Live and let live. But what do you say to that? To be successful in today's Britain you must *pretend* to be a pervert! Explains everything, does it not?' He was struck by an idea. 'Your father? *Pretending* merely to be a pervert? Necessary in the racing world, perhaps? Make him acceptable to the Queen Mother, God bless her? The Cheltenham Gold Cup? Bums up over the hurdles? The tightening silks? Is that it?' He looked at me hopefully.

It was time to put the record straight, defend Gay's reputation. 'He certainly isn't. His name happens to be . . .'

'Known for it, is he? How sad. Oh well.' He looked me up and down. 'So – the boy's a friend of yours?' The train of thought was all too obvious. He jerked his head towards the family quarters, where only yesterday Henry Jr had lain like a broken puppet on the floor.

'More of an acquaintance really, Mr Root. We've never been close.' For the sake of a good working relationship with Root, some pretence was obviously in order, but this was pretty shameful. Having denied my friendship with Henry Jr, I now felt, guiltily, that I couldn't let yesterday's beating-up pass without comment. I'd reason with Root, get him to talk about his violence, explore its mechanism, steer it into the work in progress, thus helping the project – which I was keen to get on with – and at the same time saving myself, to say nothing of our prisoner, from a cuffing in the future. I'd be tactful, of course. Root would have his reasons. An artist's reasons are not always apparent to the ordinary man.

'Excuse me, sir. Why yesterday did you have him by the throat?'

'The boy? Because he can't take a punch, that's why.' Root snorted contemptuously. 'The boy's got a glass chin. Merest punch – over he goes. Doreen – a different matter. Doreen can take a punch. Puts up a show. You've met Doreen?'

'No sir. I've not had that pleasure.'

'Nor will you if your luck holds.' Root scowled. 'Currently a secondary picket. One of Scargill's best. A bully-boy. Seconded from Greenham Common. Hospitalised two constables the other day in Nottingham. Saw it with my own eyes. *News At Ten*. Tipped one into a ditch with a judo throw and wrestled the other upside down and shoved his helmet up his harris. On TV! A daughter of mine!'

Root looked stricken. He passed a hand across his eyes. He rose slowly from his desk and walked with leaden steps towards the window. He gazed out over the rooftops. There was a long silence which I dared not break. When at last he spoke his voice had lost its resonance. It sagged like his shoulders with defeat under the burden of his sudden, inexplicable despair.

'There's thunder in the air, lad,' he said. 'There'll be thunder by tea-time, I tell you that.' Another long silence, and when he spoke again there was an edge of disgust to the awful desolation in his voice. 'And there'll be Mr Kipling's French Fancies for tea. How do you stand *re* Mr Kipling's French Fancies, lad?'

I didn't know what to say. Was he acting at all? The transformation had been so sudden and so terrible. The cracking voice, the peculiar, contorted posture, the eyes staring madly into space were certainly reminiscent of classical British acting at its best. I was moved.

'It was kippers for tea in the old days, do you see? The whole family round the table. Mrs Root and the little ones. "Another kipper, Mr Root? There's plenty left." There never was. She gave me hers, do you see? "Can Lucy May have another kipper, mummy?" Lucy May was Doreen's doll. She loved that doll. She was so gentle then. She took it everywhere. I can see her now, asleep, my little girl, clutching her doll.' There was a long pause. I said nothing. It was my job to hear him out. I was privileged to have revealed to me this other, deeper side to his extraordinary personality, the side that gave his work its breadth and resonance, that made it accessible not only to those of the most refined literary tastes, but to the common reader too. 'And I can see her in her first party-dress, running towards me with her arms held out. "Daddy! Daddy!" It seems like yesterday. And now? It's French Fancies for tea and my little girl's a flying picket in a boiler suit, bursting with revolutionary fervour. I tell you, lad, it's best not to look back. There's only pain in looking back.' He stared silently over the rooftops for a while and then, with a sudden courageous effort, he squared his shoulders and briskly shook himself, as if unhappy thoughts could be shaken off as a wet dog shakes off water. 'Never hit it off with Henry Jr, though.' The realisation seemed to cheer him. His voice was suddenly firmer. He left the window and, with recovered vigour, walked back towards his desk. 'Couldn't take a punch, do you see? No satisfaction punching a wet noodle. That answer your question, lad?'

It didn't really. 'But why should you want to punch him, sir?'

Root stared at me in astonishment. 'You saw how he was dressed? Auditioning for a girlie show. *La Vie En Rose*. He'll pose. A son of mine. In tights and feathers. On a pedestal.' Root groaned and covered his eyes. 'This at the Windmill, you understand. You remember the

Windmill, lad? "We never closed." A proud record. Six shows a day in spite of Fritz and his doodlebugs. It was Jimmy Edwards and the fan dance then. The scramble over the seats to get to the front row. "Behave yourselves, gents, or we'll bring the comic back." Wouldn't have worried me. To tell the truth I preferred the comics. Those were the days.'

'Jimmy Edwards did a fan dance, sir?'

What had I said? Root scowled and clenched his fists. His knuckles turned white as he fought to keep control. I feared for our prisoner in the cupboard. Root began to splutter.

'Jimmy *Edwards*? A *fan* dance? How dare you! He flew for "Bomber" Harris, lad! If it hadn't been for the likes of Jimmy Edwards we'd all be paying our rates to the Berlin District Council, and don't you forget it!'

'I'm sorry, sir.'

Root was still purple in the face with fury. 'And Henry Jr wouldn't be up West in high-heels and a cocktail frock in the early p.m. They took a dim view of that sort of thing in the Third Reich, I tell you that, lad.'

'Of course, of course.'

Root seemed calmer. His breathing had returned to normal. 'So. Where was I?'

'On why you should want to punch him, sir. Of course, now I understand.'

'No you don't. That wasn't the reason. It wasn't the costume. We've all got to earn a living, right? If he lands the job at *La Vie En Rose* he'll be able to contribute to the family budget. He'll be able to eat again.'

'He doesn't eat?'

'Where would he eat, lad? He hasn't got any money.'

'Well, with *you*.'

Root was flabbergasted. He recoiled in his chair and stared at me open-mouthed. 'With *us*? He can't eat with us, lad. Not unless he's contributing to the family budget. That's fair, surely?'

I was frankly scandalised. There was a limit, it seemed to me, to what I could decently swallow for the sake of our collaboration. 'But he's *unemployed*!'

Root gave a short bark of laughter, and then shook his head sorrowfully, as if dealing with a simpleton. 'Look lad. There are four million unemployed in the country at the moment, but they don't all come here and help themselves to my eel-pie.'

That stumped me. There should have been an answer, something to do with flesh and blood, I suppose, but it didn't immediately come to mind.

'But that wasn't the reason', continued Root. 'It wasn't the costume. Fact is I'd just made a special effort. I'd gone into the family quarters after lunch. Tried to engage the boy in conversation. Tried to communicate with him, do you see? Bridge the generation gap. That's right, isn't it? That's what the books advise? Talk to them as though they're people?'

He looked at me questioningly, cocking his great head to one side, seeking confirmation. I liked it when he did this. It seemed to define my role as that of equal, or near-equal.

'That's right,' I said.

'Of a mind to involve him, do you see? To engage his interest. Give him the benefit of my current thinking. Acquaint him with the work in progress. "Come, boy", I said. "An example of our Sad National Decline. Quickly now!" ' Root groaned. 'My God! The boy was cross-legged in a cocktail frock with his hair in a bun and I'd asked him for an example of Our Sad National Decline!' Root growled and clenched his fists. He looked towards the broom-cupboard. I smiled encouragingly and nodded in that direction. Better our prisoner get a duffing up than that I should be at risk. The moment passed. Root unclenched his fists. 'The boy responded,' he said. ' "Well father," he said – doesn't usually call me father, usually calls me Henry and makes a run for it. I was encouraged. "Well, father," he said, "I've been studying the Police and Criminal Evidence Bill now before the Lords." I was amazed! I could scarcely believe my ears. There was progress here. You follow my thinking, lad?'

'An encouraging moment, sir.'

'It was a trap!' Root snarled and knuckled his forehead in self-reproach. ' "Capital!" I cried. "Let's have it, boy!" The boy got up from the table and backed towards a neutral corner, checking his rear for a means of exit. I should have collared him then. "I see", he said, "that the English police now want ninety-six hours to do what the Scottish police can achieve in only six." I was on full alert now, you understand, yet I walked right into it. "Oh yes!" I said. "And what might that be?" The boy looked me straight in the eye. "Beat a confession out of the wrong man", he said, and he took off like a barnyard hen. It was blatant provocation, do you see? A chase ensued. He had a start, but I cut him off. It was the high-heels. No good in a chase, the high-heels. I had him by the cocktail cabinet. The rest you saw. So. Where were we?'

I'd no idea. I couldn't take these lengthy detours and sudden dislocations. Just when I wanted to seem whippet-smart and on the ball my brain whirred but connected with nothing. My legs swung stupidly off the floor. My perch began to feel unsteady. I had a touch of vertigo. At any moment I could topple backwards.

'Er . . .'

'Women!' cried Root. 'That was it. Women on behalf of Weidenfeld. You all right, lad?'

'I'm fine.'

I wasn't fine. I felt quite faint. I tried to call to mind the details of 'The *Cosmo* Stress Guide for those pressure moments in the life of a *Cosmo* girl' – a type particularly under strain, of course, what with constantly having to redefine her femininity, to check herself for negative self-perception, to discover who she really is, etc. – and all this while holding down an onerous secretarial job as well as occasionally helping her bloke with the washing-up. 'Take the phone off the hook,' – that was it, I had it now, that was the first piece of advice – 'put your feet above your head, empty your mind of all negative thoughts and *relax*.' I couldn't do that, not here in the ops-room. What was next? 'Pamper yourself', that was it. 'Look at yourself in the mirror and repeat over and over again, "I like *me*". Then give yourself a treat. Buy that dress you've been saving up for, or splurge out on avocadoes for your bloke's dinner.' I could do that. Not the avocado dinner, but when I escaped from here I could go to Toni's for a scalp massage and manicure. Thank God for *Cosmo*.

'Glad to hear it', said Root. 'So. I told him. We're back with Weidenfeld, you understand. What is there to say on women? The bedroom and the kitchen. The duvet and the blender. The corset and the rubber gloves. That covers it, does it not? You've met Mrs Root?'

'No sir. I've not had that privi . . .'

Root groaned. 'She's a woman, do you see? Stores toilet rolls and walks around all day in rubber gloves. Not much of a life on the face of it. The mail-order catalogues. The special offers through the post. The brochures. The problems with the washing-machine. Women's lot. Easily satisfied, I suppose. And yet . . . and yet . . .' The sadness was back. The memories were crowding in. 'I remember her at The Coq Sportif. In Greek Street, it was. Run by a friend of mine. Jack "Spot" Comer. Remember him, lad? His knife fight with Albert Dimes in the vegetable shop in Soho. What a do! Crates all over the road. Sprouts were down the next day, I tell you that. Jack was a friend of mine, but I had a pony on Albert at seven to four. Mrs Root worked there. At The Coq Sportif, not the vegetable shop. On a barstool. My God, she could sit on a barstool in those days, lad. Perched on a barstool in gold lamé, she'd be, split to the waist. She had a pair of legs in those days, lad, I'll tell you that. There was a promise then. We had plans. No time for the honeymoon, mind, but it was to be two weeks in Herne Bay when my ship came in, I promised her that. "Take me to Herne Bay, Mr Root", she'd say. She'd been there as a child, I fancy. I never did. Too busy. Too busy to take her to Herne Bay, and that was all she wanted. There were things to be done. I blame myself . . .' He was silent for a while, gazing out of the window, burdened by self-reproach. 'And now it's the fucking washing-maching, if you'll pardon my French, and the surgical gloves. Doesn't do to ruminate, lad. Keep going, that's best. Don't look back. We're on the down escalator, I tell you that. You have to run like hell to stay in place, that's the secret. Keep moving, the upward thrust. Stop pumping the legs and you'll be swept down into the dark depths where the rats breed in the drains. Still, she keeps the place clean, I'll give her that. Where were we, lad?'

'Women, sir, for Lord Weidenfeld.'

'Women, eh? Is that it? I tell you what. We'll start tomorrow.'

He bundled me into the lift with the day's tape, and, since I felt a little shaky, I went straight to see Dr Butt. My dizzy spell had quite alarmed me. Root doesn't strike me as the sort of man who would take kindly to a fainting research assistant, so I asked Dr Butt for some tranquillisers, but he's put me on malt! While sitting in his waiting-room I read a very interesting article in a magazine called *The Spectator* about someone called Wilhelm Reich. Reich argued, apparently, that aggression is a substitute for sex. Or perhaps it was the other way round. Either way, the theory seems relevant to Root. If I could channel some of his aggression away from our prisoner in the broom-cupboard and into the work in progress, what a masterpiece we might come up with! *The Spectator* seems to be a very well-written magazine. There was a particularly brilliant article by someone called Richard West about the absurdity of Arts Council grants. It was so good that I sneakily tore it out and brought it home. Now that I'm a writer I must keep a common-place book of pieces that impress me.

'As long as the Arts Council lasts,' writes West, 'we at The Coach and Horses will have to persist in trying to get some money out of it. This year Jeffrey Bernard and I will apply for grants towards books that might appeal to the Arts Council non-fiction panel. The two titles we have in mind are: *Good-day Sailor! A Sensitive Study Of Homosexuality In New South Wales* and *Male Fascist! An Exposé Of Sexual Harassment At Work In The New South Wales Ministry Of Pensions*.'

West is joking, of course. This sort of irony may be a little elusive for some, but I think it's absolutely brilliant.

Later I read a chapter or two of Jan Leeming's excellently helpful *Simply Looking Good*. She has a marvellous tip called The Jan Leeming Mirror Test.

'Beauty comes from within,' writes Jan, 'but the mirror test helps too! Dress in your normal way and put on your usual make-up, then take a long look at yourself in the mirror. *Pretend this is a stranger you're looking at*. Overall do you look healthy but lack style? Does your hair-style flatter your face? Are your clothes co-ordinated or merely thrown together? Jot down what you see. With an honest list of your bad points it's far easier to work out what to do with them.'

I resolved to do the Mirror Test first thing in the morning.

THURSDAY 21 JUNE

I woke up in a pool of sweat, with pumping heart. At first I thought I'd had a cardiac arrest! I lay there motionless, fighting for breath. Then I realised I'd had a nightmare in which the police had come for me and Root, accusing us of kidnapping and GBH. Root had chortled and hit the policemen's helmets off with a pornographic bladder of the sort with which Mr Punch traditionally, I think, belabours Mrs Punch. Then the police dragged *me* away, on Root's advice, leaving him behind wheezing and cackling with delight. I told myself that this was just a bad dream, that Root was my collaborator, after all, and would never use me thus. Gradually I fought my panic down. Then I checked the time and discovered to my horror that it was nearly ten o'clock. No time for the Jan Leeming Mirror Test or The Celebrities' Crunch-by-Crunch Breakfast Diet recently featured in *Company*. I threw on any old thing, ran out of the house and grabbed a taxi. I arrived, panting, in the ops-room to find Root striding up and down in mid-composition. He seemed to be finishing a letter.

'... so get a grip on yourself, my good woman, otherwise I'll have to hop over to your place and put a cracker up your back.'

He broke off and greeted me cheerfully.

'Morning, lad. Sending Her Majesty a chaser, do you see? Ignored my last. Seeking a clearance *re* speculating in this context on the Royals. The Palace's view. The gossip columns expose the toplessness of Lady Helen Windsor and so forth, but not sure we should. They have nothing to lose, but we have our reputations to consider.' I liked that 'we'. Root definitely thought of us as a team. 'Known as "Melons", do you see? Lady Helen not Dempster, that is. What do you say? Don't want to get on the wrong side of the Palace, eh?'

I agreed wholeheartedly, and then, rather to my surprise, Root suggested that I should meet Mrs Root.

'In my judgement, better to get it over with', he said. 'Do you agree?'

He went to his desk and spoke briskly into an inter-com. 'Mrs Root to the ops-room! Mrs Root to the ops-room! At the double now!'

I braced myself. From Root's description I expected something out of *Coronation Street*, in curlers and surgical stockings. Moments later the door to the family quarters swung open, operated, I supposed, by Root, and Mrs Root came in. Well! She's all right! A curvacious, comforting woman with a barmaid's smile and generous bosom, the latter ballooning ripely over the top of an early-evening cocktail frock. I've never been into older women, as it happens – Felicity Kendal and all that stuff – but it occurred to me that, if I had been, I could have found her quite attractive. Even the red washing-up gloves were a slightly erotic touch, I don't know why, combined with the night-club hostess's ensemble.

She glared at Root. 'Here', she said. 'That bull-terrier's in the bird-cage again! *Poor* little thing. I'll thank you to stop putting the bull-terrier in the bird-cage, Mr Root. And what about the black man? Still in the broom-cupboard, is he?' Root opened his mouth to say something, but she actually cut him short! She, clearly, isn't intimidated by him in the least. 'It's not right', she said. 'Has the poor boy eaten?'

'Of course he's eaten, woman!' shouted Root. 'It's the new law. Only holding him subject to a ruling.'

'*You'll* get a ruling I wouldn't wonder', said Mrs Root. A happy smile spread across her face. 'And no one to blame but yourself.'

'Forget the prisoner, woman! I want you to meet young Kimbersley. He went to Eton, do you see?'

'That's nice!' said Mrs Root. She smiled sweetly and did a little curtsey, which caused her skin-tight skirt to reveal a large expanse of still-firm thigh, enclosed in a black lace garter. This was for my benefit, of course, and – rather to my surprise – I found myself responding with a little butterfly twitch of erotic interest. She removed a rubber glove and held our her hand. 'Pardon my appearance', she said. 'I was up to my elbows in it when Mr Root buzzed.' She wiped a strand of hair from her forehead. 'It's that blasted washing-machine again, Mr Root.'

Root turned to me with a loud 'hah!' of triumph. 'What did I tell you? Obsessed with the washing-machine. Make a note of that. It's relevant, if I'm not mistaken.' He addressed himself to Mrs Root. 'It's women here, do you see? We're studying women for Lord Weidenfeld of Nicolson. Every aspect of the matter.'

Mrs Root seemed very amused by this. She gave me a private smile which said: 'What he knows about women could be written on a postage stamp.' What she actually said was: 'Another of your books, is it, Mr Root? That's nice. On women this time?' She was struck by a sudden thought. 'Here. Say something nasty about Susan Hampshire, will you?'

Root groaned. 'The woman's got a thing about Susan Hampshire. Doesn't like her.'

'Never have', said Mrs Root. 'Rubs me up the wrong way, does Susan Hampshire. It's the eyes for the most part. Don't care for her nose either, come to that. Something funny about her nose. *And* her voice.'

Root was losing patience. 'Enough! Away with you woman!' He went to his desk and shuffled his papers. 'There's work to be done here. We're off and running!'

'Oh pardon me for expressing an opinion', said Mrs Root cheerfully. She gave me another of her private smiles. 'I trust you'll be happy working for Mr Root she said. 'If there's anything I can do...'

There was a promise in this, and in the way she looked me up and down, which was frankly appreciative, though I must have looked a mess what with having dressed in such a rush, just throwing on the first thing that came to hand and with no time to do the Jan Leeming Mirror Test. I didn't feel at all harassed by that appreciative glance and in this respect I suppose I differ from Jan herself, who says in her book that she doesn't want men to lust after her, merely to like her. I don't mind women obviously wanting me, and in this respect I differ too, I suppose, from Henry Jr. When we were jamming at my place the night before last he suddenly said – rather tellingly, I thought, so I remember his exact words – 'You know, Kim, in spite of all the advances men are supposed to have made in the last few years, reality for me is still women telling me how intelligent I am while staring at my crotch.' Perhaps I *could* be into older women. An experienced confident woman, a woman with a past, a woman with a washing-machine, wouldn't sit around *waiting* like Charlotte. Nor would she giggle all the time like Melissa. Mrs Root gave me another private, teasing smile and then withdrew. She definitely liked me, there was no doubt of that, and, more importantly, her attitude to Root had been immensely reassuring. If she wasn't intimidated by him, why should I be? I felt I had an ally, should an ally prove necessary.

'Sorry about that', said Root. 'Seemed best to get it over with. She won't disturb us again. So! It's women here.'

It was an exciting moment. The start of our collaboration. I was daunted, I admit, by the sheer size and complexity of our subject, but at any moment now Root would open up a flap in that extraordinary brain of his and we'd be inundated by the wise aperçus and startling insights of a mature, ordering intelligence.

'You've been at stool today?' he asked. 'You've had a motion, lad?' He swept on before I had time to answer. 'Always start the day with a good clear-out. Lesson I learnt in the Navy from P.O. "Tonker" Taylor. National Service, you understand. Obsessed with his bowels, was P.O. "Tonker" Taylor, and, it must be said, with the bowels of those under him. He'd had a formative experience during the war, do you see? His ship had depth-charged a German U-boat. Blew it clean out of the water. Bits and pieces floated to the surface – bodies, hats, bunks, *plus* a toilet door marked "Engaged". Nasty, what? Fritz at stool – bang! – what a way to go. P.O. "Tonker" Taylor had made a vow that day never to be taken short at action stations. Regularity, that was it. No good our ship attacking in the early a.m., no. 2 gun-crew would have been at stool, lined up like a row of coconuts. But he was right. I'm grateful to the man. Into the bathroom with you, lad!'

Root took me by the neck and marched me across the room. I demurred, of course, and wriggled in his grip, but he had me fast. He opened the bathroom door and pushed me in. It is a measure of his peculiar domination over me that, in spite of my earlier resolve not to be intimidated, I laboriously unpeeled my Calvin Kleins (it takes *hours*, but unless they're virtually a second skin they don't look good) and lowered myself towards the seat. As I did so, a loud, indignant voice from *under* me, from *inside* the lavatory bowl, shouted: 'Watch it! I'm working down here!' I shot upright and, snarled by trousers, fell into the ops-room on hands and knees. Root, to my amazement, was doubled up with laughter. 'Always catches them', he gasped. 'Oh dear, oh dear.' He was choking with laughter. Tears were pouring down his cheeks. He clutched his ribs. At last he had his convulsions under control. He wiped his eyes and beckoned me into the bathroom where he showed me a tiny tape-recorder hidden under the rim of the lavatory bowl.

'Got it in a novelty shop, do you see? Triggered by the descending buttocks. Not bad, eh? Caught the Falkender woman like that. Ugliest woman ever to sit in the Lords, if you want my candid opinion. She was up here once, do you see? In the ops-room was a crowd of celebrities discussing a charity do. Personalities, for the most part, of the type who live on Wentworth Golf Course and are quick to participate in the Pro/Am aspect of things. Cardew "The Cad" Robinson, Fred Housego the Cockney Mastermind, Pete Murray, Jimmy Tarbuck, Jessie Conrad, you have the picture? More amusing bunch than she'd normally meet. Had to go in there eventually, of course. Seconds later she hurtled in here with her knickers round her knees. White as herring-roe.' Root was choking at the memory. 'Oh dear, oh dear. *She's* not been back!'

I failed to see the humour of this and tried to convey as much by my pinched expression. I hoped that no such lavatorial tone would creep into our book on women. I'd have to be on my guard against this. There is, frankly, a crude side to Root that would be quite out of keeping in a serious book. I have nothing against a little humour in its place – indeed I hope myself to introduce an agreeably light-hearted note from time to time – but anything scatological would be entirely wrong. Root, meanwhile, having at last got himself under control, went and sat behind his desk, motioning me to my high-chair.

'So', he said. 'It's women, then.' He squared his shoulders and shot his cuffs. 'That's the project. Women. We're in the starting stalls.'

This was it! We were off at last! I waited expectantly. He said nothing. He stared at me, and I stared back at him. Then he made a deferential gesture with his hand.

'The ball's in your court, lad.'

This was an honour. Far from being a junior partner, I was to serve first. My mind went blank.

'Women', I said.

'That's the size of it', said Root. 'Women.' He frowned. He hummed. He rearranged the papers on his desk. He scratched his nose. I was expecting this, of course. It's known in the business as displacement activity, something all writers indulge in before engaging the creative gears. Sartre, the well-known French philosopher, worked for hours on a model of the Eiffel Tower made from matchsticks, Frank Muir the humorist prunes his moustache with tweezers, Arthur Marshall plays with his balls on the croquet lawn and Benny Green writes a book or two. It was exciting to see it happening before my eyes. Root cleared his throat. Inspiration had come at last. We were off!

'Got your tickets for the Ferret Olympics, lad?'

I was quite startled. I said I hadn't.

'Hm. Just wondered. Well worth a visit.'

He was silent for a while. He examined his finger-nails. He cleared his throat. This would be it.

'What of the big lad, Tavare, eh? He's not dropped the anchor for England in a while.'

He was playing for time, of course. Waiting for the thoughts to drop easily into place. Suddenly he got up and, looking pensive, did his slow walk towards the window. For a while he followed the movement of the clouds across the sky, seeking inspiration, I supposed. When he at last turned round he was, to my amazement, looking bashful. Bashfulness was not a quality I'd have attributed to Root until this moment, but he was clearly struggling now to make a confession of some sort, to admit the hitherto inadmissible.

'I'll come right out with it, lad', he said. 'The doubts crowd in. Women. Can we handle it?'

It must have cost him dearly to say as much, to acknowledge any weakness in himself. As a fellow artist it was my duty to restore his sagging confidence. It was an attack of stage-fright, that was all, a healthy sign, they say, before an enterprise of note, but he looked so troubled – so helpless even – that had I been able to clamber off my perch with ease I'd have crossed the room to place a reassuring arm around his shoulders.

'Come sir!' I cried. 'Surely we can. Your track-record speaks for itself.'

'Thank you lad. Thank you.' He tried to square his shoulders, but the doubts still weighed him down. 'The fact is – well, I'm at a disadvantage, that's the truth of it. I'll admit it frankly – in this particular area, well, I've not had the experience of some. This is not what you might call a sexual household, do you see? For myself I chose not to have a personal life, I eschewed that side of things. Instead, I married Mrs Root. The energies went elsewhere. You follow me, lad?'

'Of course, but ...'

Root swept on. He had to unburden himself. 'It was the struggle upwards, do you see? The push to the top. I make no apology for that. It was three to a shirt where I lived, lad, and the outside bucket. I wanted more. We were in eels, do you see? The family business – a stall, to be precise, down by the docks – started by my grandfather, Henry "Cannonball" Root. Bit of a character, my grandfather. Been a boxer in his day, hence his name. Eighty-six fights, seven convictions. I went to work for him when I was sixteen. After a year he – er – retired for health reasons, and I took over the business. There were rumours, of course, but the allegations were never proved.'

He was silent for a while in thought, and then he briskly shook himself, as if to dispel some lingering, uneasy memory.

'I worked my balls off, lad. Soon I had another stall, and then another. Then my first shop. And then another shop. I was able to persuade others that – how shall I put it? – they might find life more peaceful were they to trade elsewhere. I needed prime sites, do you see? High-street locations. It was the knuckle under the nose. The Pakis particularly couldn't take the pressure. By the time I sold out in '76 my sites alone were worth upwards of three million. There'd been little time for women, do you see? I don't deny that before I met Mrs Root there had been the quick, angry occasions down by the wharves. The dark nights. The available local girls up against a bollard. Later, there were the late nights in the shop, tumbling among the herrings on the slab. Never cared for it much, to tell the truth, but it seemed to be the thing to do. Then there was Mrs Root. For a woman, Mrs Root was unusually interested in that side of things.' The memory caused Root to sway backwards and lean for support against the desk. 'I explained that expertise on top of the duvet with the lights on was unbecoming in a woman hoping to join the middle-class, but she couldn't seem to take the point. Fortunately, after the birth of Henry Jr she discovered she couldn't take a lot of pressure on her left leg. "I'm not a person who can take a lot of pressure on the left leg, Mr Root", she'd say. She got no argument from me, I can tell you, lad. Hell of a relief. No, I'll be straight with you. I've not had the experience of some. I've no fund of knowledge on the subject.' He tapped his forehead. 'No flap to open up, do you see? That compartment empty, lad. If it was eels I could handle it. But women! What a proposition! I'm daunted, I'll admit it. I'll be frank with you, lad. I don't know when I was last within spitting distance of an attractive woman, and that's our subject.'

He looked utterly dejected. It was clear that for the sake of the enterprise I must somehow bolster his morale.

'But Mrs Root's an attractive woman, sir.'

Root took a short pace back as he grappled with the notion. '*Attractive?* Mrs Root? *Attractive?*' He pointed with a stubby finger towards the family quarters. '*That* Mrs Root?' Then he did a sudden panto turn, checking quickly to his rear in case another Mrs Root had materialised from nowhere.

'Yes sir. I'd say she was a highly sensual woman.'

'*Sensual*? Mrs Root *sensual*?' Root was stunned. He felt his way carefully round the edges of his desk, leaning against it for support as if the last ounce of strength had been knocked out of his body by the proposition. He sank with relief into his chair. 'Mrs Root is a woman of

44, lad. Why on earth would she be sensual? Oh dear, oh dear. It's the blind leading the blind here. I'm disappointed, lad. You've let me down. I'd thought to lean on you somewhat, I admit it. No, there's nothing sensual happening here, I can tell you. Last thing to have a sensual experience here was Mrs Root's bull-terrier, I guarantee it. We'll not find inspiration here.' He slumped dejectedly in his chair. Then, suddenly, he was struck by an invigorating thought. 'I have it, lad!' He sprang to his feet. 'We'll seek assistance from the sexual. From sexually active men! We'll pick their brains. What do you say to that?'

'You know sexually active men, sir?'

'I know *of* them, lad.' He winked cunningly and tapped the side of his nose. 'Come! To the computer! They're all in there. The Romeos. The dancers. The keyhole men. We'll have a read-out!'

I followed him across the room, where he scrabbled in a pile of soft-ware like a dog in a sandpit, sending up a shower of rejected discs behind him with a reverse under-arm scoop.

'Need organisation here, do you see? Your job sometime to impose a system. What's this?' He inspected a disc. 'Scarman amendments? Trots? Yoghurt eaters? Rising tides? Insurrectionists? Wets ripe for deselection? Conservationists? Moles? So-called experts? Academics? Pah!' The rejected discs flew around my head like UFOs. He scooped on impatiently, muttering angrily to himself. Suddenly he let out a cry of triumph. 'Ah! I have it! The sexual militants. The bogglers. The afternoon men.' He inserted the disc in the computer and within seconds he had a read-out. 'Let's see. William Deedes. Duff Hart-Davis. A. N. Wilson. Kenneth Rose. Christopher Booker. Godfrey Smith. Paul Johnson. Michael Rubinstein. Max Hastings. Philip Howard. What's this? This can't be right. There's confusion here. We've hit the old farts file!' The old farts flew over his shoulder, causing me to duck and weave. He searched again among the soft-ware and soon came up with another disc. He flicked a switch, there was a busy whirring, and he had a read-out. 'What's this?' he cried. 'Malcolm Muggeridge? This is it! We have them this time. The Lotharios. The sexual activists. Paul Raymond. André Deutsch. Yes, this is it. Ronnie Knight. Geoffrey Dickens MP. John McVicar. Nigel Dempster. David Sullivan. Cecil Parkinson. Michael Parkinson. Noel Annan. Alexander Chancellor. Jim Davidson, the Cockney comic. The Duke of Devonshire. Michael White. Prince Andrew. George Best. Clive James.' Root scowled in disbelief. 'Clive James? What's he doing here? He won't make anyone forget Robert Redford, that's for sure. Won't make anyone forget Walter Redford, come to that. Richard West. Taki, the little Jap. Oliver Tobias. Philip Hodson. Irma Kurtz. What a crew! I tell you what, lad. We'll have a word with Victor Lownes. We'll be visiting Stocks, I wouldn't wonder.' He was struck suddenly by a doubt. 'On the other hand, he's just got married. May have given it up, do you see? We'll contact Dempster. He's at it day and night from what I hear.'

This was all very well, there was no harm in seeking advice, but I didn't see how men could help us. Our brief was women.

'But sir,' I said, 'surely it's women we should talk to.'

'By God, you're right, lad!'

The angry rummaging resumed among the soft-ware, discs flying in all directions as they were rejected.

Root straightened up. 'Hm. Don't seem to have anything on women.' He looked utterly stumped.

I had a brainwave. 'We'll start one, sir! Open a file on women. What do you say to that?'

Root was open-mouthed with admiration. 'Start one, eh? What a concept, lad! But – er – who? That's the question.'

'What about the women you admire, sir?'

'Women I admire, eh? Here's a challenge. There's Lady Olga Maitland. Rachel Heyhoe-Flint. The Queen Mother. Sefton.'

'Not a woman, sir.'

'Is that so? Well, there you are. And Mrs Thatcher, of course. And the woman with the harp.'

'With the harp, sir?'

'That's it. The religiose at 6. On Sundays. Never miss it. Mary O'Hara! A nun, I fancy. Lucinda Prior-Palmer. Una Stubbs. Anna Neagle. Claire Francis. Torvill and Dean, champions of the rink. Grace Kelly, a princess from the moment she was born.'

'All sexual women, sir.'

Root scowled. His face turned purple. 'Grace Kelly a sex . . . how *dare* you boy!'

He shot out of his chair and, rounding his desk, came at me snarling. He raised a hand.

I was inspired by terror. 'To the broom-cupboard, sir. Quickly!'

'You're right, lad!'

Root, with a neck-hold, lifted me easily off my chair and ran with me across the room.

'Not me, sir! Our prisoner!'

'Of course!'

Root dropped me so suddenly that I fell in a heap as I hit the floor. There was a cry of alarm from the broom-cupboard, followed by three muffled thumps. I couldn't look. I told myself that it was in the interests of the enterprise. The broom-cupboard door was banged shut and Root returned to his desk. He was breathing heavily, but he was looking more relaxed.

'Be more careful, lad,' he said. 'I nearly had you with a boxing-shot. I'm sorry, but the conjunction of that sainted woman's name with anything so . . . so . . . below the belt as . . . as . . .' He couldn't make the connection. He hummed and clenched his fists. 'A moment, lad. You'll pardon me, but I must think of other things. Of Goose Green and graves and victory marches. Of church bells and British hurdlers coming sixth.

Of *The Illustrated London News* and Mrs Thatcher's Airforce issue knickers. Of Zola Budd and headlines in *The Daily Mail* – "Queen Mum Tip-Top at 84!" Of have-a-go toddlers and PC Olds. Of tug-of-love cats and certified accounts. Of tax havens and *Stars On Sunday*. Of Sir Patrick Sergeant and the English sausage.'

He went for a little walk around the room, shoulders squared, toes turned out, humming inspirational songs. 'Dreeeeeeam the impossible dreeeeeam!' 'Climb every mount-taaaaaaiiiin. . . .' He levered some weights angrily to the ceiling. He kicked the broom-cupboard door. At last he had himself in hand. He returned to the desk. 'That's better. Where were we?'

'Women, sir. We are to write on women for Lord Weidenfeld. That's our brief.' In spite of my narrow escape, I really felt I had to crack the whip. We were getting nowhere. 'We must confront the matter head on. There's nothing else for it.'

'You're right, lad.' He took a deep breath. He shot his cuffs. 'The mind will have to dwell. But surely on a different type of woman? He looked at me hopefully. 'On jacuzzi girls? Actresses? Topless boxers? On women of Hungarian birth?'

I was relentless. He must face up to it. Actresses and jacuzzi girls could only be part of it. 'We must cover the spectrum, sir, if we're to rival Anna Ford. We must deal with women in the generality.'

'That's so, that's so.' He looked immensely unhappy. 'But we've to conjunct admirable women with the sexual side of things, with that aspect of it?'

'If we're to make the charts, sir.' I was being coldly realistic. 'Root on Women, sir? The punters will expect it.'

'You have a point.' He sighed deeply. 'But I'm at a disadvantage, lad, as I explained. Been too busy. The energies went elsewhere. Into my work. Into the eels. Later into my letters and other compositions.'

I saw this as my chance to impress him with reading of *The Spectator*'s article on Reich. The details, indeed the main thrust, were far from clear in my mind, but I reckoned I had enough to get past Root. Sex as a substitute for aggression, that was the thesis, or possibly the other way round. Clearly, in Root's case, aggression had been a substitute for sex. If I could get him to channel that abundant energy into sex, who knew what masterpiece we might come up with? It was an exciting prospect, and things might go more easily for our prisoner in the cupboard. I could serve literature and appease my liberal conscience at the same time.

'Of course it did, sir. Your aggression, your energies, went into building up your business. There was none left over for the – er – pursuit of women.' I must step lightly here. Root was following with a beady eye. 'But you're an artist now.' Root looked pleased. He nodded. 'Like all artists you have a choice: do you keep your energies – your sexual aggression – separate from your work? Or do you channel that energy into the work in progress, tapping it, as it were, for drive and inspiration?' Root looked impressed. 'Many artists have kept the two rigorously apart. Before they can start work they must release their sexual energies. One thinks of Richard Ingrams, who, it is said, before starting work on a serious book, must first shave his legs in the bathroom while drawing up a mental list of prominent Jews in public life. Or of Clive James, who, I'm told, before sitting at his desk, must first tot up his hard-back sales, comparing them with those of Martin Amis, and then count the invitations on his chimney-piece. Or of A. N. Wilson, who, it is said, first does Evelyn Waugh impressions in front of the looking-glass, complete with monocle, ear-trumpet and waistcoat three sizes too big for him, and then sits heavily on the sharp end of a shooting-stick before praying on his knees.'

Root was goggle-eyed. 'Where did you discover this, lad?'

'From an article in *The Spectator*, sir, an agreeably written magazine of the fun-right, or so its editor says. Many artists, on the other hand, have merged the two – their work and their sex-drives – making it impossible to tell which is which. Sometimes their work is an expression of their utter sexual frustration – Jeffrey Bernard is an example of this, or so *The Spectator* says – and sometimes it is a celebration of sexual satisfaction. With some artists the two are so perfectly fused that they actually have sex while creating.'

Root sprang up and, gorilla-like, leant forward on his knuckles.

'They do?' His eyes bulged with surprise.

'They do, sir. George Gershwin, as is well-known, composed *Rhapsody In Blue* with a negress sitting on his face.'

Root collapsed in his chair. 'Is this so? What you're telling me now? Is this really so? About Gershwin?'

'Indeed, sir.'

'You're saying that I should compose this book – Root On Women – with a woman I admire sitting . . . my God! If Rachel Billington sat on your face you'd know about it! I tell you straight, lad, that would be no laughing matter.' He fanned the air in front of him with a meaty hand, setting up a reviving breeze.

'Indeed, sir. But the point holds. And other examples come to mind. Georges Simenon, they say, wrote a Maigret novel in precisely five days, locked in a cork-lined room no more than ten feet by six. For inspiration, and to satisfy his raging sexual needs, local girls were pressed four times a day into a serving-hatch normally reserved for the passage of his meals.'

'What! Is this so?'

'Quite so, sir.'

'I can scarcely credit it!'

'It is the case, sir. With you, of course, it has not been like this. You have always separated your work and your sexual energies. The latter have not gone into your work. You are with Mr Ingrams and A. N. Wilson. But, like them, you *have* a sexual capacity and now we must tap it. For the first time, perhaps, it is relevant to the work in progress.' I was becoming more confident by the minute. I was on to something here, I was sure of that. I clambered off my high-chair and, with mounting excitement, marched up and down the room. For the first time, I was really taking the lead. Root rose from his desk and padded after me. I turned and confronted him.

'Here's the point, sir. To date your work has merely been a substitute for sex. Now you must ...'

Root exploded. 'A *substitute* for ... how *dare* you, boy! My work a mere ... you've gone too far!'

He growled and assumed a boxing crouch. A hand came up.

'Quick sir! The broom-cupboard!'

Too late. The massive fist, already travelling, downed me with a short jab below the rib-cage. I fell to the floor and lay still. To my surprise I wasn't hurt. Root must have pulled the punch, but now he was seriously alarmed. He knelt down beside me and tried to raise my head. He slapped my cheek. He blew cigar smoke and haddock fumes into my face. That was worse than the punch, but I managed to lie still and keep my eyes closed. I'd make the most of this.

'Come, lad', he cried. 'It was the merest tap. We'll get nowhere unless you can take a tap. The collaboration hangs on it.'

He shook me with increasing agitation. He became seriously frightened. He went to the intercom and summoned Mrs Root. She hurried in.

'That washing mach ...' She gave a little cry. 'What have you done, Mr Root? You've *killed* the boy!'

She pushed him roughly to one side and took me in her arms. She smelt of Tweed and washing powder. She cradled me against her swelling bosom. She smoothed my hair. It was delightful.

Root blustered. 'I merely ... the merest tap ... I ... '

I could have lain in Mrs Root's soft arms all day but it seemed unfair to frighten her. I opened an eye and bravely tried to lift my head.

'It was nothing', I said. 'The merest tap. We'll get nowhere unless I learn to take a tap. The collaboration hangs on it.' I struggled up.

Root whistled with relief. He picked me up and perched me on my chair.

'What did I tell you, woman? He's as right as ninepence. Isn't that right, lad?'

'I'm fine', I said. I smiled courageously.

Mrs Root looked doubtful. 'Well, if you really are.' She gave Mr Root a nasty glance and, with a show of much reluctance, started to withdraw. She stopped at the door. 'Here. Have you said something nasty about Susan Hampshire yet?'

Root exploded. 'I told you! The woman's obsessed! Out with you woman! There's work to be done!'

Mrs Root gave me a sweet, encouraging smile and closed the door behind her. She definitely likes me, and I'm beginning to think I really could be into older women. It's a pity in some ways that she should have seen me spread all over the floor like that, but on the whole my plight will have aroused her protective instincts. Next time, however, she must see me in a more dominant role. That too can sometimes arouse a woman's interest.

'You all right, lad?' Root was still concerned. I had the advantage now. I wouldn't let it slip away.

'Just a little faint, sir.' I swayed on my perch. 'Not been eating.'

'Not been eating?' Root, thoroughly alarmed, hurried to catch me before I could fall to the floor. 'We'll feed you up, lad. Short of money, is that it? Look, I've been doing some thinking here. About our arrangement. Impressed by what you said. Need you here, that's the truth of it. A full collaboration, what do you say? Royalties for you and equal billing.'

'*Billing*? My name with yours? No, I never could.'

'I insist, lad! We shall be a team. We'll halve it all. Money and billing. There'll be no argument.'

I'd be famous! I'd have my teeth capped. I'd be appearing coast to coast on American TV. The Johnny Carson Show was a serious possibility.

'I'd be honoured, sir.'

'That's settled, then.'

'We'd better crack on', I said. I felt I had the initiative. 'We're off and running here.'

'That's right! It's . . . it's . . .'

'Women, Mr Root.'

'You're right, lad! Where were we?'

'We were going to seek the assistance of sexual activists. Nigel Dempster's name was first out of the computer.'

'Of course. A letter! A letter to Nigel Dempsey!'

139 Elm Park Mansions,
Park Walk,
London, S.W.10.

Nigel Dempster, Esq.
The Daily Mail,
Carmelite House,
Fleet Street, E.C.4.

Dear Dempster,

You'll want to know that to balance Miss Anna Ford on men I am to write on women for Lord Weidenfeld of Nicolson.

Here's my problem, Nigel. I am not, as you know, a lady's man like you, my experience in this area being limited to Mrs Root and a back-street lapse in '62 at the hands of a 4th floor masseuse with thin legs and a ginger pubic goatee, who in any case turned out to be a cashiered Major in the Pay Corps on his third suspended sentence. I haven't cared to dabble since - nor, I imagine, has the Major, who, if memory serves, went head-first in his frillies into a Greek Street rubbish-skip.

For research purposes I have hired a staff to do my thinking on retainer (young Kim Kimbersley, to be precise - his father's gay, but there you are) and we have decided to consult with those who, like yourself, have at every opportunity studied available modes and positions - on floors, in doorways, up chimneys - with the sort of woman prepared to go the other way at forty-eight hours notice: actresses, jacuzzi girls, *Ritz* readers, topless boxers, three-in-bed *Star* birds, models - both kiss-and-tell and cat-walk types - big blondes who get the writing bug (Pat Booth comes to mind) and Erica Creer. Your name was first out of the computer, Nigel, after Paul Raymond and Malcolm Muggeridge.

It occurs to us that as a single man you must have kept on file the names and inclinations of the above specified types, in order, quite rightly, to grass them. Now that you're hitched for better or worse to Lady Camilla (it just shows that there's someone for everyone, Nigel) you'll not need these. I am prepared, if the price is right, to purchase your files, since I haven't got time to start from scratch merely to accommodate Lord Weidenfeld.

Another thing, Nigel. We seek advice as to ambience and props. Goings-on could happen here, if you catch my meaning. What do we require on the premises to get the above specified types going without demur? Are Japanese loveballs needed? Is a jacuzzi of the essence? (I live on the ninth floor, Nigel). Is a sauna with plunge-pool a top priority, after which some like a twigging, or so I'm told? Should the latest in video equipment be installed (I gather your pal Polanski, the little Pole, likes to record his doings for later reflection and to encourage others, not least Mynah Bird, the big Ibo). What of coke and kaftans? Does one offer money or is it sex on credit these days? Kindly advise.

May I congratulate you on your sharp rebuke to *Ritz* magazine *re* Arabella Pollen the topless seamstress? 'A favoured dressmaker to the Princess of Wales', you wrote in your column yesterday, 'has issued a writ over a trashy news-sheet's *unauthorised* publication of a topless picture of her, which was then sold on, *equally without permission*, to a Sunday rag'. This was well said, Nigel. *You* never expose the antics of your friends without permission or print unauthorised stories. If only all yellow journalists were as scrupulous as you!

Here's to licensed gossip and authorised saddle-sniffing only in the tabloid press!

Yours,

Henry Root

Henry Root

P.S. I am surprised, I must say, that Princess Caroline of Monaco authorised the photo you print today over the classy caption: 'Mama Mia! It's Curvey Caroline!' She bulges like a napkin filled with junket.

cc. Sir David English

'Should do the trick, what?' said Root. 'Hits the nail on the head, unless I'm much mistaken?'

I agreed whole-heartedly. The letter was great and I was excited, too, at the prospect of meeting Nigel Dempster, whom I admire enormously. They say he is the highest paid journalist in the land, which can't be bad, and if Root can persuade him to hand over the files he keeps on the misdemeanours of his friends (the most exhaustive ever assembled, it is rumoured, outside the FBI's Washington vaults) we will have an amazing store of research material.

Then, rather to my surprise, since it seemed to me we were getting somewhere at last, Root announced that that was it for the day. He got up from his desk and steered me towards the lift. He was still playing for time, of course, but this didn't particularly bother me. There was no point in starting the actual book until he was in the mood. An artist has to be in the mood, as I know only too well myself. Was it George Lyttleton or Rupert Hart-Davis who observed that Dame Creation is a capricious Mistress, likely to gather up her skirts and flee if too assiduously courted?

It was only twelve o'clock and since I wasn't meeting Charlotte until one-thirty I had time to go home and change before our shopping expedition. I had a long, relaxing bath (missed in the rush this morning) and then I pottered about a bit, trying to decide what to wear. By the time I got to Bolton's in the Fulham Road, where I was meeting Charlotte, I was only about three-quarters of an hour late, but you'd have thought it was the end of the world. She sulked for half an hour and then she behaved incredibly badly throughout the shopping expedition, showing very little interest and telling me to hurry up while I was trying to decide whether I could afford a pair of Willi Wear muscle-leggings and a white Body Map hat, which was really great and only £13.50, as well as the canvas high-top boots. 'I am *not* an impulse shopper, Charlotte', I said, but I got flustered and bought the hat rather than the leggings, when I think it should have been the other way round. In the circumstances I thought it best to leave the Charlie Allen suit until another day. With Charlotte yawning and harassing me by turn I'd probably not insist on the correct alterations.

Back at the flat I told her about my exciting new job with Henry Root, but she hadn't even heard of him! Then I described how I'd been beaten up, thinking that this might excite her.

'He beat me up', I said.

'That was silly of you', she said.

If she wasn't so haughtily beautiful, I really wouldn't bother. I did a little fashion show for her and then lay on the bed looking moody, but she *still* didn't make a move.

'I think I'll go into the bathroom and slip into something more comfortable', I said.

When I came out of the bathroom wearing nothing but my new Willi Wear canvas high-top boots and Body Map hat, she'd gone! After a couple of minutes there was a ring at the front-door, so, thinking that Charlotte had had second thoughts, I went to answer it. It was old Lady Huggins, a friend of my mother's. She screamed, I don't know why, and ran off down the street, colliding with another little old lady, whom she knocked for six.

Later in the evening, Gay phoned. He wanted to know why I had opened the door to old Lady Huggins wearing nothing but thigh-boots and a hat. She'd been on the telephone already, it seemed, lodging a protest. I explained that I'd thought it was Charlotte.

'Poor Charlotte', said Gay. He likes Charlotte, and so does my mother, probably because her father's a judge.

Then – foolishly, perhaps, because Gay has a very limited understanding of how creative people work – I told him that Root had beaten me up. He was absolutely furious and immediately threatened to telephone Root. I asked him not to, but I'm afraid he may.

FRIDAY 22 JUNE

Woke up feeling very rough, after another restless night during which I dreamt erotically of Mrs Root. What can this mean? It was one of those disturbingly vivid dreams in which all the details are sharper-edged on waking than reality, quite altering for a time one's perception of the person dreamt about. In the dream I'd come into the ops-room to find Root manhandling Mrs Root. I fought him off with a karate move and Mrs Root, sighing with gratitude, took me fiercely among the filing cabinets. She laid me down. She was wearing rubber gloves and nothing else. Her figure was full. 'Do anything you like with me', I sighed. Now I feel ashamed and rather foolish. It was only a dream, but in my subconscious I'd defiled the ops-room and cuckolded my collaborator. It occurred to me on the way to work that I'd be able to look neither of them in the face, in case they guess my secret. I blame Charlotte. If she stopped being so coy this sort of thing wouldn't happen.

Root greeted me cheerfully, but I could hardly look at him. As I climbed onto my perch the telephone rang.

'Root!' His face darkened. His eyes boiled with anger. He held the receiver away from his ear and glared incredulously into it. I could just hear an angry, undecipherable jabbering coming down the line. Suddenly Root could take no more. 'Listen you monkey!' he roared. 'Hold hard here!'

This was good. Someone was going to catch it! I began to feel more cheerful. I rubbed my hands together and grinned encouragingly at Root, miming my support. 'You tell him!' I mouthed. Whoever the caller might be, I was keen that he should get an earful. I was shoulder to shoulder with my collaborator in this as in everything. Loyalty was all.

'We all know about you,' snarled Root. 'Another call from you and I'll put the police on your tail, you savvy?' He banged the receiver down.

'Who was that?' I asked.

'Your father,' said Root. 'I told him. My word yes. We won't be hearing from him again.'

That was a pity in a way. There'd be another uncomprehending call from Gay tonight, in the course of which he'd probably try to pull me off the job.

'So!' Root was beaming. The confrontation had done him a power of good. 'It's women, then. Chapter one!'

We were off at last. 'I've been thinking . . .'

'A moment, lad.' Root held up a hand. 'Can't keep the Home Secretary in the dark. Been working closely with him, do you see? There's the matter of the allegations in *Private Eye*. Need his approval *re* the formation of a fighting fund. A letter! Henry Root to the Rt Hon. Leon Brittan PC, QC, MP, etc., The House of Commons, SW1.

139 Elm Park Mansions,
Park Walk,
London, S.W.10.

The Rt. Hon. Leon Brittan PC, QC, MP,
The House of Commons,
London, S.W.1.

22nd June 1984.

Dear Home Secretary,

Please note that I shall be taking the next month off from matters that concern us both - viz keeping an eye on Scarman, flying bully-boys, video nasties and rising tides of this and that - to write on women. This, you'll be surprised to hear, transpires to be a full-time occupation and as a consequence some temporary reorganisation is called for here re the various doorstep pressure groups I've headed up for the past few years. I shall be stepping down from the driving-seat pro tem and have appointed Anderton of Greater Manchester to take the wheel on my behalf (Buster Mottram, Harvey Proctor, Old General Walter Walker and Major Snipe from 138 having been designated as unsuitable for one reason or another.) Kindly liaise with him.

Reading between the lines of Private Eye, I infer that M15 are alleging this and that against you. Here was libel if every I saw one and I take it you'll be suing. May I put forward the name of my own lawyer, Peter Carter-Ruck, to handle the action? He fell on his face in the matter of Derek Jameson against the BBC, which, as we all know, is full of Trots but people tell me he is not as stupid as he looks. He's not cheap and since I gather that, unlike the Tory gents old Pym, Whitelaw, Carrington, Gilmour etc - you have no inherited loot, I have taken it upon myself to form 'The friends of Leon Brittan Fighting Fund' to raise the wind re your costs.

In order that we may discuss the details and parameters of this appeal, I suggest that I attend on you in your offices one afternoon between the 9th and 13th of July and would nominate Wednesday 11th in your chambers at 2pm. I'd make it sooner but I'm flat to the boards at the moment what with this book etc. I shall be bringing Buster Mottram (Anderton's deputy) with me so that he can pass on the fruits of our meeting to Anderton. I'll be too busy.

Yours sincerely,

Henry Root

'So', said Root, when that was done. 'What now?'

'Shouldn't we make a start?'

'A start? What on, lad?'

'The book.'

'The book, eh? Not a bad idea. I tell you what, lad. I've given the matter a certain amount of thought. Been considering the form the thing should take. What do you say to a simple A to Z? The punters would know where they were, do you see? Easy to zero in on areas of special interest. Not necessary to wade through the whole thing.'

'A Who's Who of women, Mr Root?'

'In a nutshell, lad. Mugs could skip the letters where the mind naturally recoils, do you see? P could be nasty. Erin Pizzey, Libby Purves, Mary Parkinson, Molly Parkin, Elaine Page. And what of R? Jean Rook, Anna Raeburn, Lady Rothermere, Esther Rantzen, Angela Rippon, Erika Roe, Mrs Root.' Root slumped in his chair and fanned the air in front of him. 'You take my drift? And another thing: before we had to confront the matter of Paula Yates, you and I, the finishing line would be in sight. A consideration, wouldn't you say?'

I think Paula Yates is great, as it happens, and I had imagined something a little livelier than the over-worked A to Z formula, but I agreed with the suggestion, just so we could make a start at last.

'That's really great,' I said.

'Capital!' cried Root. 'We are of one mind, then. So – it's the letter "A". Off we go. *Henry Root's A to Z of Women.*' He sat back and looked at me expectantly. 'Well? Speak up, lad! The tape's running.'

I was caught by surprise. I hadn't realised it would all be down to me. 'What exactly do you have in mind, Mr Root?'

'Names, lad. Let's have some names.'

'Oh.' I marshalled my thoughts. 'Okay. Here goes. Lady Annunziata Asquith, Suzy Arthur, Davina Alexander, Lolicia Aitken, Camilla Aziz, Isabelle Adjani, Amanda Aspinall, Sarah Aspinall, Arabella Ashley, Lady Sarah Armstrong-Jones, Laraine Ashton, the Hon. Joanna Aston-Bostock, Daisy Appleton-Smythe, Princess Alia Ali Khan, Princess Alexandra, Princess Anne, Bridget Astor, Teresa d'Abreu, Selina Attenborough, Anabel Astor, Lucy Armstrong, Pamela Armstrong, Francesca Annis, Maria Aitken, Jane Asher, Abba, Sian Adey-Jones, Jenny Agutter, Laura Ashley, Evelyn Ashford, Jane Abdy, Amanda Atha, Diana Avebury, Lady Elizabeth Anson, Sophie Andreae, Janine Andrews, Julie Andrews, Archduquesa Sophie of Austria, Lady Ampthill, Lynn Arrowsmith, Frances Awdrey, Alice Adams, Margaret Duchess of Argyll. Then, of course, there are categories such as Agony Aunts, Aristocrats, Actresses, Athletes, Americans, Acrobats, Adolescents, Asians, Australians, Air Hostesses, Adultery, Astrology . . .' I could have gone on, but I had to pause for breath. Root was impressed. His cigar, aimed at his mouth when I started, was frozen in mid-air a foot from his face.

'I'm stunned, lad!' he cried. 'Go like rockets, do they, that lot? Known for it, are they? Better take them one by one. Who was first?'

'Lady Annunziata Asquith, I think.'

'Excellent! Run you ragged, would she? Next!'

'Er – Suzy Arthur.'

'Is that right? I'm dumbfounded, lad! Next!'

'Lolicia Aitken.'

'Her too, eh? Next!'

'Amanda Aspinall.'

'Who'd have thought it! Next!'

'Camilla Aziz.'

'Do what?'

'Camilla Aziz, Mr Root.'

'If you say so, lad. Next!'

'Laraine Ashton.'

'What! I can scarcely credit it!' Root pummelled his desk triumphantly. 'I tell you what, lad! This will rock them on their heels! A letter to Weidenfeld!'

"Dear George, we're sitting on a hot potato here. Alert your lawyers. Put Carter-Ruck on a stand-by. There's a time-bomb in the pipe-line. Yours, etc."

'Have that off tonight. Next!'

'Bronwen, Lady Astor.'

'That'll shake them! My word we're getting somewhere now! The book takes shape. We'll have finished "A" by lunchtime, lad. Next!'

'Excuse me, Mr Root, but shouldn't we say something *about* these people? A bare list of names will hardly make the charts.'

'I don't know. Many have. *The Book Of British Lists. The Book of Football Lists. The Book Of Royal Lists. The Complete Naff Guide.* I take your point, though. Trouble is I can't do the dirty on people I've never heard of. Not my way. Fair's fair. Wouldn't be right.'

'Who have you heard of, Mr Root?'

'Babs Windsor, the Cockney Cracker. Sue Pollard, the zany blonde from Hi-De-Hi. We could blow the whistle on her. Maureen Lipman? She's asking for a smack in the mouth. "What's it to be, Maureen? The crisp one-liners or do we do the business?" And what of Tracy Ullman? A mad-cap, would you say?'

'None of them begin with the letter "A", Mr Root.'

'You're right!'

'We must have order.'

'That's true. Next!'

'Lady Sarah Armstrong-Jones.'

A cry of triumph. 'Ah! I've heard of her. A troublesome royal, albeit on the fringes. Runs around the East End as loose as a goose. I blame her mother. It was the Pinters to dinner, do you see, and off to Bedales.

Boxing and basket weaving. Plus the staff smoked pot and taught in the nude. Head and his good lady posed for *Mayfair*. Readers' wives section. Dismissed, of course. Beth Blackwell. My God, she was no oil painting.' Root slumped in his chair and passed a hand across his eye.

'That was Dartington Hall, sir.'

'There too, eh? There'll be trouble ahead, mark my words. We're doing well. We're getting somewhere now. The book shapes up. A letter to Cape. "Dear Cape. There's one in the pipe-line may prove too hot for Weidenfeld. Telex offer by return. Yours sincerely, Henry Root." Options open, that's the game, lad. Next!'

'Princess Anne.'

'Another problem royal. In this case not her mother's fault. Too busy here and there. Royal Ascot. Badminton. The Highland Games. The girl lacked discipline. I'd have sat her in an ice-bucket. Should have gone to Gordonstoun. Cold shower and up a mountain. Next!'

'Ashley, Laura.'

'A man, surely?'

'April, sir.'

'That's the fellow. Met him, as it happens, on a TV show. Late night chat, chaired by my friend Alexander Chancellor. Other guests were Taki, the little Jap, Jeffrey Bernard, looking like a ballet dancer, and this fellow in a ball-gown. Assembled in the hospitality room before the show. Thought I'd put him at his ease. 'Your secret's safe with me, sir. Live and let live.' Took it upon myself to mark Chancellor's card. "A word in your ear. The lady in the corner – it's a man in drag. Don't blow it for him." Ten minutes later Chancellor tells the whole world! Announces him as a fellow, do you see? Queer chap, Chancellor. Always drawn quite well with him, as it happens, but others speak less highly. I recall Bron Waugh remarking that in *Tom Brown's Schooldays* Chancellor would have *watched*. Don't know what he meant, but gathered he didn't approve. Then there were the curious circumstances surrounding his dismissal from *The Spectator*. Apparently he'd been publishing extracts in his column from other people's private correspondence. Not on, what? Surprised he'd stoop to anything so dishonourable, but there you are. Every leopard has his spots. Next!'

'Agony Aunts, Air Hostesses, Astrology . . .'

'Astrology, eh? Men born under Aries are usually fairies.' Root banged the desk and barked with laughter. Then he had himself in hand. 'I'm sorry. Your father.'

'We're on women, Mr Root', I said sternly. I hadn't thought it at all funny. A major problem, I was beginning to think, would be to keep Root's sense of humour out of the book. It is no accident, I think, that by far his most important work – *Henry Root's World Of Knowledge*, a positive storehouse of distilled wisdom – contains no jokes at all.

'You're right, lad.' Root looked repentant. 'Astrology, is it? I have it!

Aquarians. Know something about Aquarians, as it happens. Wore flowers up their noses and went without their knickers in the Sixties. May still, for all I know. I'm not uninformed. I saw *Hair* you know. "This is the daaaaawwwwn-ing of the age of Aquaaaar-iuus!" Oh yes. I was there. Danced on stage with the principals until asked to leave. Transpired one wasn't welcome over the footlights until the end of the show. Martita Hunt. She was typical. Posed nude and sang in the chorus. Then there were others. The little mynx with the hair-do. Dusty Springfield. Wore her brain in the Afro-style. Janis Joplin. *Going Down On Janis*. The mind recoils. Can't come to terms with the proposition, do you see? "I've just made love to twenty thousand people and I'm going home alone". Hardly surprising. And Margaret Trudeau, of course. Never wore knickers on state occ . . .'

'Marsha, Mr Root.'

'Really? You have me there. Marsha Trudeau, eh?'

'Marsha *Hunt*.'

'Her too? Mick Jagger's mother, if I'm not mistaken.'

'No no. It was his *son*.'

'A man, was it? Like the Ashley fellow? A friend of Chancellor's? Should have known. Saw the show too. Built like a bollard. Well well well.'

'*No*, Mr Root. You misunderstand. She *had* his son.'

'Did she really? I'm not surprised. Father and son, eh? Had both of them, is that it? What did I tell you? The Sixties, do you see? The Age of Aquarius. We can be glad that's over.'

'Or was it her daughter?' I was getting confused. 'Yes, that's right. It was his daughter. Karis.'

'Had his daughter, did he? That's more like it. Still, not our problem. Next!'

'Adultery.'

Root squinted with distaste. 'Now available to the working classes as a result of so-called progress. If the left had their way it would be adultery on the rates, I tell you that, lad. Subsidised brothels and flying masseuses. "All the joys of democracy: porn, lawlessness and irreligion." Peregrine Worsthorne in *The Sunday Telegraph*.'

'I'm not sure I see the connection, Mr Root.' Was I being incredibly thick?

'What connection, lad?'

'Between democracy and irreligion.'

'Obvious, lad. Let people think for themselves, first thing that happens they stop believing in God. Can't have that. "Without religious sanctions, what's to stop people enjoying themselves?" Paul Johnson. Next!'

'Er – *Anglais, Le Vice*.'

Root blinked. His cigar, on its way to his mouth, was suspended in mid-air.

'Do what, lad?'

'A whacking, Mr Root.'

'A *whacking*? We're on sex here for Lord Weidenfeld of Nicolson. Don't let the mind wander lad. We'll get nowhere if the mind wanders.'

Should I explain? I was quite surprised by the depths of his innocence. On the other hand, this innocence was possibly the mainspring of his art. Should I tinker with the mechanism, muddy the pool? It was an awesome responsibility. I'd proceed with caution.

'To some, there's a connection, Mr Root. Some are aroused by a whacking.'

'Good grief! A *whacking*? None of that where I came from. The dockers wouldn't have taken kindly to a whacking, I guarantee it.'

'It's an upper-class thing, for the most part, sir.' I was beginning to wish I'd never brought the subject up. 'They say it starts at school. It's supposed to be character-forming.'

'At your school, lad? At Eton? There was the vice anglais? The whacking?'

'Yes sir.'

Root's eyes bulged with surprise. His breathing had become unnaturally heavy. He lent forward on his desk. He seemed curiously interested.

'Describe it, lad. Was it on the bottom, this vice anglais?'

'Er – yes, sir. We were dragged by the bulldogs to a block. The school watched. We were bent over. We were thrashed by the head.'

'Yes? Yes? How many times? How many stripes, lad?'

'Usually six, sir.'

'Six, eh? To the bottom, was it? To the bare bottom, is that it, lad?'

'Yes sir.'

In his excitement, Root temporarily lost his sense of spatial relations. Aiming for his mouth, he stuck his cigar up his nose.

'Shit!' He angrily stubbed it out. 'And it was enjoyable? This whacking? Is that the gist of it?'

'*I* didn't think so.' I thought I'd make that absolutely clear at once. 'Others might have enjoyed it. It accounts, they say, for the number of men who like it in later life.'

'Do they really? The upper-classes, you say? Etonians? The well-born? In Whites, in Pratts, they whack each other? Is that the size of it? "Evening, Minister. Over you go!" Is that it?'

'Well, not really, sir. Not often, anyway. In later life, after school, enthusiasts for this prefer women, or so I'm told.'

'Women, eh? A whacking from a woman. This is interesting.'

He seemed seriously disturbed. He got up from his desk and crossed the room to the exercise equipment in the corner, humming patriotic songs. He levered some weights beefily towards the ceiling, he climbed aboard the rowing-machine. He lent into the stroke, growling angrily. '*Mens sana in corpore* ...' Suddenly he dismissed me. 'We've made progress, lad. A whacking, eh? A whacking from a woman.'

I let myself out, leaving him on his rowing-machine, pumping backwards and forwards, muttering distractedly to himself. I went home and pondered this development. What does it mean? What is Root suppressing? Should I encourage him to let it out? Would this help the work in progress? Would it, less importantly, help our prisoner in the cupboard? I suddenly realised that he'd not been in evidence today. Perhaps he'd been released. While I was pondering all this, Gay telephoned, just as I feared he would. He said I couldn't go on working for 'that madman'. I tried to explain that Root wasn't mad, merely the victim, sometimes, of his own artistic temperament. I said that working with Root was the chance of a life-time. Poor Gay simply didn't understand. To him creative people are alien beings, their work methods a mystery. He told me to let him know if I was beaten up again. I judged it best not to tell him of Root's developing interest in *le vice anglais*.

Later, I sat around wondering whether Charlotte would telephone. She didn't. I then discovered, before dropping off to sleep, that it wasn't Charlotte I was thinking about, but Mrs Root. This is significant. It goes without saying that I find Charlotte more obviously attractive, and yet in many ways I find the thought of Mrs Root more disturbing. How little we know about our *real* sexuality until something happens to bring us face to face, perhaps uncomfortably, with the truth. What then, if the likeness we see has little resemblance to the image we had of ourselves? Do we draw back in alarm, or do we venture into the deep recesses of the perilous unknown? Artists like Root and I owe it to our readers and to the work in progress to follow our instincts wherever they may lead. I'm sure of that. Wasn't it John Mortimer who said: 'The writer is bound to explore all areas of the human experience. The whole of life must be open to his voyage of discovery, he must sail as far as he can and his only duty is to come back with the truth as he sees it. There can be no "no go" areas in the world of art'. Very true. Yet didn't Flaubert observe that 'it isn't the drunkard who writes the drinking song'? (To which his parrot replied: 'yes, but it isn't the tee-totaller either. The writer must wade into life as into the sea, but only up to the navel.') Whatever the truth of the matter, Root, of the two of us, must wade into deeper water. I merely am duty bound to pursue my new-found interest in older women, Root must go down a darker alley, leading who knows where. In his letter today to Lord Weidenfeld, he got it right. We are indeed sitting on a time-bomb.

SATURDAY 23
SUNDAY 24 JUNE

Rather a depressing weekend. It was boiling hot and I didn't want to go home to the country. If I went home I'd just get involved in endless arguments with Gay about Root. I typed up yesterday's tapes, and then tried to sunbathe on the roof, but had to give that up because a lot of silly women opposite insisted on staring. I wasn't going to loll about simply to titillate a crowd of esurient housewives. In fact, I wasn't too disappointed at having to come indoors, because the sun plays havoc with my skin. I don't want to end up looking like Lauren Bacall.

Reading more of Jan Leeming's brilliant *Simply Looking Good,* I came across the following:

'What you wear is an attitude of mind. At one stage when everyone was wearing bright colours, I was in dowdy black and brown – I didn't have the strength of character to wear colour, let alone white. And I hadn't realised that if you have mid-brown hair and mid-blue eyes you can wear almost everything. Now I've learned that lesson. The other day I gave away a depressing brown cocktail dress I knew I'd never wear again.'

I noticed that Jan was wearing a rather nice brown top on TV the other night, so I've written to her asking whether she is thinking of giving this, or anything else, away. If she was I'd be interested, I said. It's a long-shot, I suppose, but you never know your luck, and I'm woefully short of designer separates.

Charlotte didn't ring, so in the end I rang Melissa. She came straight over, of course, and then proceeded to be her usual giggly self, regressing chubbily. It's no good a girl taking her clothes off within minutes of arrival if all she does then is to lie on her back on the bed, wriggling and squeaking and obviously expecting *you* to do something. Women should show consideration. Men aren't machines. They need to be put in the mood. I made a suggestion of a perfectly natural kind and Melissa went quite nutty, bunching her little fists in mock horror and pummelling me painfully in the chest.

'*No*!' she squeaked. 'That's dis*gusting*!! You're *awful*!! *No* one would! That's *foul*! You're a *night*mare!'

Then, before I could stop her, she rang up Charlotte.

'Hi! It's me. *Listen!*' She proceeded to tell Charlotte about my perfectly normal suggestion! I've never been so embarrassed. Charlotte's so straight that she doesn't do it at all. Melissa finished spilling the beans, and then listened to Charlotte with mounting astonishment, her eyes growing wider and wider. 'He *doesn't*!' she gasped. 'He doesn't *rarely*, does he? You poor scrap. Why do you let him?' Her eyes grew wider with surprise. Her classy little mouth formed a perfect o of astonishment, like someone about to blow a smoke-ring. 'You *do*? You *rarely* do? I can't *believe* it! Oh well, live and learn.' They chatted on for a bit, and then Melissa rang off. '*Poor* Charlotte', she said. 'Do you know what? Henry makes her stand around for *hours* wearing nothing but a suspender-belt! Then, dressed like that, she has to cook his dinner for him! Can you be*lieve* it? I *do* worry. She's such a pet. The oddest part is she says she en*joys* it!'

What an incredible downer. While I've been treating Charlotte with respect, letting her define her femininity as per *Cosmo*, letting her discover who she really is, etc., my so-called friend Henry Jr had been using her as an object, standing her in a corner dressed in a suspender-belt! I shall never speak to either of them again.

Spent the rest of the evening thinking about Mrs Root.

❮MONDAY 25 JUNE❯

I arrived at work to find Henry Herbert, a friend of my father's, caught in a wrestling-hold, face down, his body parallel to the floor, held by my collaborator by the seat of his trousers. Suspended like that, he looked like someone learning to swim, an impression emphasised by the fact that his arms were waving around in an untidy breast-stroke while his legs beat the air behind him.

Root greeted me cheerfully. Physical confrontation always raises his spirits and brings his colour up.

'Good morning, lad! This is Herbert Herbert. I'm about to ejaculate him, as you can see.'

My father's friend looked to me with an expression of aristocratic resignation. 'Look here, Kim. Explain things here. Tell this fellow to leave off. Tell him to put me down, I say.'

'There's some mistake,' I said. 'This man is a friend of my father's.'

'I'm not surprised!' said Root. 'He wanted to interview me as an eccentric, *plus* he left his mistress's knickers on a bus.'

With one huge heave, he launched Henry Herbert into the lift, closed the door and punched a button, sending the lift down to the basement garage.

'What was his misdemeanour, sir?' Gay would be on to me about this, so I needed an explanation.

For Root, the incident was already closed. He was now behind his desk, shuffling papers, ready to deal with other matters. He looked up with a puzzled expression. 'Who? What misdemeanour, lad?'

'Henry . . .'

Root scowled. 'Mr Root will do, lad.'

'No no, you misunderstand me. That's his name. *Henry.*'

'Henry Henry? Nonsense. Ridiculous. Whoever heard of anyone called Henry Henry? What sort of name would that be? Herbert Herbert, that was his name, lad.'

'*No*, Mr Root! Henry *Herbert. That's* his name. He's the Earl of Pembroke.'

Root was less impressed than I'd expected. 'That's right, lad. Precisely why I granted him an interview. Don't let any Tom, Dick or Harry into here, you know. When we buy the files from Dempster he'll get five minutes in the pantry and the use of the tradesmen's entrance. He wanted to film me, do you see? Herbert Herbert. Then he had the knuckle to say it was for a series called "Great British Eccentrics!" The nerve! Me! An eccentric! He'd have me on camera, no doubt, with types who squat on poles and live in double-decker buses! I'm mainstream, lad, that's the point. That's why I have the ear of the common man. Do you think Mrs Thatcher would seek the advice of an eccentric? She's common too, that's why she keeps in touch. Me! An eccentric? Pah!' He was seething. He'd been cut to the quick. '*Am* I eccentric, lad? We'll have a ruling here.'

'Certainly not, Mr Root.'

'That's right!' He was greatly cheered. 'I'm ordinary, that's the point. A letter, lad! A letter to Deutsch while I'm running hot.

139 Elm Park Mansions,
Park Walk,
London, S.W.10.

Andre Deutsch Esq.
105 Great Russell Street
London, WC1B 3LJ.

25th June 1984.

Dear Deutsch,

Here's another one. Henry Root's Guide to Ordinary People. Ordinary people live in Essex and cancel their subscriptions. 'Dear Sir, I have been taking your magazine for twenty years, but after your vitriolic attack on the Queen Mother, God bless her ....' Ordinary people believe Selina Scott is the fifth most intelligent woman in the country, that dolphins are fluent in forty-four languages including Chinese and that Gloria Hunniford is a very nice person. Ordinary people say "If you can't be good be careful", "What's yours?" and "fucking nig-nogs". Need I go on, Andre? Telex your offer by return.

Yours etc,

Henry Root

Henry Root

Root thought for a while and then suddenly prodded the air with a meaty finger. '*Plus!*' he roared, 'I was reminded of his unfortunate publicity a couple of years ago in the Hickey column. Left two hundred pairs of his mistress's knickers on a bus. Not Deutsch, I'm back to Herbert Herbert, you understand. On the Knightsbridge route at that, a not immaterial point, lad. It was that which caused the rough-stuff, the matter of the route.'

He'd got it entirely wrong, of course. As it happened, I remembered who'd left his mistress's knickers on a bus. It wasn't Henry Herbert, but another friend of my father's, old Lord Hubert Hubert.

'That wasn't him, Mr Root. It was Lord Hubert Hubert, who left his mistress's knickers on a bus. Another friend of my father's as it happens.'

Root scowled. '*Another* friend of your father's, eh? I might have guessed it. A letter! To your father! "Dear Kimbersley, *re* your friends and their mistress's knickers. Kindly keep them out of the ops-room. It's serious work here." Something along those lines. What do you say?'

'But it *wasn't* Lord Pembroke, sir. It was old Lord Hubert Hubert.'

'A triviality! The point holds.'

'But he's very respectable, sir. He's a noted film producer. He made *Emily*. With Koo Stark.'

Root snorted with such violence that his cigar, as it had been threatening to do for days, rocketed across the room, spearing me between the eyes. To make matters worse, the eye make-up I was wearing must have been made of some incendiary substance because there was quite a nasty conflagration, which I only managed to put out by spitting into my handkerchief and applying it to my smoking eyebrows. I shall write to the manufacturers about this.

'Sorry, lad. Set fire to your mascara, did I? A word of advice from *How To Marry Up*, by Joanna Steichen. Been meaning to mention it. "Over-elaborate make-up is a sign of new money," says Ms Steichen. "The older the money, the plainer the make-up." I'd bear it in mind, if I was you, lad. Always telling Henry Jr, but he never took a bit of notice. Haven't seen the boy for a couple of days, as it happens. I wonder where he is.'

Should I tell him? Henry Jr had asked me not to, but after he'd double-crossed me so disgracefully with Charlotte I had little compunction about grassing him up. And a father surely has the right to know. 'He's living in Deptford', I said.

'Is he really? Deptford, eh?' He made a note of this. 'Where were we?'

'Koo Stark, Mr Root.'

'Koo Stark? What about her?'

'She made a film for Lord Pembroke, Mr Root.'

'Did she really? I'm not surprised. Just threw the fellow out. No wonder he trades as Herbert Herbert. Among such types I'd use an alias myself. Which brings me to the point in hand. A seat, lad.'

I climbed on to my perch.

'On Friday, after you left, I got to thinking. About what you were telling me.' There was an edge of embarrassment. Root looked down. He examined the backs of his beefy hands. 'This – er – vice anglais and such. You recall?'

He was quite unsettled. He looked extraordinarily uncomfortable. Just as I'd thought, the subject had set off bells in his head, there had been stirrings deep in his psyche.

'Perfectly, Mr Root.'

He hurried on. 'I was hit by the sheer scope of what we're doing here. On women, do you recall? The variety and extent of the necessary research. I've much to learn. I admit it freely. A comparatively sheltered life vis-à-vis that aspect of things, do you see? This vice anglais was news to me, you understand.' Whenever he mentioned it, his huge torso trembled slightly, as if hit by private earthquake. 'A bolt from the blue, you might say. We have to investigate it, what?' He tried to appear casual. He examined his finger-nails.

'I'd have thought so, sir.'

'As I imagined. And there'll inevitably be other matters into which we'll probe, isn't that so? Disagreeable matters, no doubt, but our duty to probe for the sake of the work in hand. What I'm saying here, lad, is that we'll be out in the field. Up at the sharp end, right? Looking into this and that. Our main thrust will be up the fairway, of course, the A to Z, but occasionally we'll need to stray into the rough, what?'

'I imagine that will be necessary, yes. For the sake of the project.'

'As I thought. As I thought. And there'll be other practices – like this vice anglais thing – with which we'll need to acquaint ourselves?' A sizeable tremor, spreading upwards, caused his neck to twitch quite violently.

'I should have thought so, Mr Root.' He was rubbing his neck. Our researches would be somewhat handicapped if brooding on *le vice anglais* required him to wear a neck-brace.

'And what are these exactly?' It embarrassed him horribly to have to ask. He casually traced a little circle on the desk-top with a finger.

I was no expert myself, of course, but I probably knew more than him. I'd *heard* things from time to time, and I'd occasionally read *Forum*. This was a chance to impress him.

'I'm not very experienced myself, of course, but inevitably I've read of certain practices.'

'Naturally, lad. Fire away.'

'Well, I've read about something called S and M.'

'S and M, lad? What's that?'

'It stands for sadism and masochism, Mr Root. Some try it, I'm told, particularly in California.'

'I see. I see. I take it the vice anglais would come under this heading, then? Under this M and S?'

'It's a branch of it, I suppose, sir. But it entails other practices in which actual beating doesn't occur. Domination. Restriction. Verbal humiliation. That's what I've heard, at least.'

'I'm open-mouthed, lad! To the heavy-weights!' He crossed the room, humming inspirational songs. He climbed on to the bicycle. His powerful little legs began to pump. 'Proceed lad! I'm all ears!'

I carried on as best I could, competing against 'Climb Every Mountain' and 'Dream The Impossible Dream', vigorously rendered.

'Bondage, sir. A sub-class of S and M, but devotees, I gather, see a difference.'

'Describe it, lad. This bondage.'

'I think they tie each other up.'

'Just that? No whacking, eh?' He seemed disappointed, though the mention of whacking caused his legs to pump more vigorously. 'No one lays it on?'

'I think not, Mr Root.'

'A trifle dull. We're speaking of perverts here. That's all? Trussed like gooses?'

'I'd say so.'

'Hm. Next!'

'Well – there's group sex, troilism and so forth.'

'What's that? This troilism?'

'Three at a time, sir.'

Root was aghast. His legs stopped pumping. He stared at me open-mouthed. '*Three* at a time? My God!' He wiped his brow, and then resumed his pumping. Clearly one at a time was more than he cared to contemplate. 'Next!'

I was running low. 'Cross-dressing. High-heels and so forth.'

'Like the boy, you mean? Deptford, is that it? In a squat? They'll not have seen the likes of it in Deptford. High-heels and Laura Ashley. He'll be duffed up, that's my guess. Next!'

'Rubber, sir.'

'We'll not wear rubber. I draw the line at rubber.'

'Of course.'

'That's it? The well is dry?'

'I fear so, sir.'

'Hm.' He climbed off his bicycle. He shook himself. He crossed the room and sat behind his desk. 'And these practices. It might be necessary, might it not, to visit the type of girl who does these things? Friends of Dempster's? Girls who visit Stocks? It will be up alleys in disguise for you and me, isn't that it? For research purposes?'

'I suppose that might be necessary, Mr Root.' I didn't like the sound of this, but for the sake of the enterprise risks might have to be taken.

'I recall that excellent French photographer – his name, alas, doesn't come to mind – who went with Hasselblad and strobe to the Place Pigalle where he snapped, with exciting consequences, pimps, prostitutes, gangsters, government officials, bent coppers, addicts, and what-have you.'

'How thrilling!'

'That's right. "Smile please! *Fromage*, if you will." Gggleerrgh!' Root mimed a razor slash across the throat. 'Removed his head. Clean off. As he was setting his equipment up.'

'My God!'

'Precisely. We'll be exposed to risk. Literary cover might not impress. "Evening, madam. We're here for the bondage and troilism on behalf of Lord Weidenfeld of Nicolson." Might not be of a literary bent. Might not take our drift.'

'I see what you mean, sir.' I was shaking. There was a danger I might topple off my perch.

'And another thing. I might, for research purposes, have to take a mistress, might I not? Literary folk tend to take mistresses, isn't that so? Must appear to be in the swim, must I not?'

'I suppose that might be necessary, sir.'

'So. I come to my point. Security. You recall what happened to the little comic Dick Emrey? What a pickle! Over he goes, and what happens? Mistresses coming out of the woodwork contesting the will. The big showgirl Fay and the matter of the undies. You saw the shots? *Sunday Times*, I think. Wife had fallen down *re* the undies, do you see? So often the case. Fay filed *re* the undies. Statement of claim. Full and better particulars. A tort established *re* the undies. Hard to credit that a will can rest upon the matter of the undies, but there you are. We don't want that. And there's the blackmail to consider. Normally not bothered. One way with a blackmailer. Straight into the cement-mixer. But I'm a public man. We'll be in the limelight, you and I. What I'm coming to is this: might it not be prudent to carry out the bulk of these investigations under an alias – after the manner of your friend Herbert Herbert – just in case a wheel comes off? We could find ourselves in some danger spots, you and I.'

I didn't like the sound of this at all. My shakes got worse, and the *Cosmo* Stress Guide wasn't working. 'We could?'

'We could. Now. I had this notion earlier, do you see? As I was ejaculating your pal Herbert Herbert, the fellow who left his mistress's knickers on a bus, I had this concept: "Herbert Herbert – that's a sensible name," I thought. "I'll trade myself as Norman Norman." When at risk, you understand. When blackmail could be an aspect. What do you say? Got a ring to it, Norman Norman, don't you think? A name with bottom?'

'It certainly has, sir. A splendid idea.' I'd have agreed to anything. I was concentrating fully on trying to quell my shakes. Any minute they could turn into a full-scale anxiety attack.

'Glad you like it,' said Root. 'That's settled, then. Two other precautions, however, might be of the essence. Things might happen here, might they not?'

'Yes sir? What sort of things?'

'Goings-on, lad. Research on the premises. Artistic pursuits. Girls here. Troilism in the home. Bondage might be attempted. We must have the place adequately bugged. No come back from the participants, do you see? We'd have a record on tape in the event of a court case. No chance of blackmail, do you see?'

'A sensible precaution, sir.'

'And another thing. This touches on the matter of security. We should apprise certain people in authority as to our literary intentions. We don't want to fall foul of Sir Kenneth Newman's *agents provocateurs*, do we, lad? Imagine the scenario: you and I, out in the field, up at the sharp end, dressed for research, touched up in a cubicle by one of Sir Kenneth's Gay Squad. The mind recoils. Three-quarters of the Met's on surveillance now, I'm told. Pulled off their normal duties – burglary, street crimes, fraud – instead they're up and down the Earl's Court Road in cocktail frocks or sipping Red Barrel with their zips undone. "Evening all!" We'll need to watch our backs, lad.'

'You're right, of course, sir.'

'That's decided, then. When at risk, when out researching, so to say, Norman Norman will be the name. Now – we must get the ball rolling. First we must inform those in authority of our intentions. A letter! Norman Norman to the Police Commissioner at New Scotland Yard.'

Root got up from his desk and went into the dictating mode, striding importantly round the room, occasionally jabbing at the air with his cigar to emphasise key points.

'Tricky one, this', he said. 'Important man, the Commissioner. Got to get the tone exactly right. Respectful, but to the point. Let's see. Let's see. Right! I have it! Here goes.'

139 Elm Park Mansions,
Park Walk,
London, S.W.10.

The Commissioner of the Metropolitan Police,
New Scotland Yard,
London, S.W.1.

22nd June 1984.

Dear Sir Kenneth,

You'll be up to your bollocks in it, so I'll come straight to the point. It's women and sex here on behalf of Lord Weidenfeld of Nicolson, back to back with Anna Ford on men. In the course of my researches, I shall be in the field myself, wired for sound and incognito, putting myself about in a literary mode in various red light districts, investigating contemporary mores and practices and availing myself to this end of professional services and perversions as advertised on noticeboards in family tobacconists and in What's On In London. Naturally, since this is a serious, though necessarily undercover operation, I don't want to fall foul of your lads researching on their own behalf. Kindly send a memo pronto to your district commanders informing them that Mr Norman Norman could be on their patch, and that notwithstanding his appearance (disguise will be of the essence) and unorthodox behaviour, he should be afforded every assistance (advice as to who's paying off etc most welcome) rather than be hauled in for questioning round the groin and kidneys. I am particularly concerned that your local Gay Squads should be informed as to my movements since I shall sometimes be comporting myself unusually for easy access to cubicles, certain clubs in the Earl's Court area and the ladies' quarters of municipal swimming baths where your lads man underwater observation posts for the entrapment of Tory MPs and old actors going for the touch-up below the surface.

I enclose a recent likeness of my head for easy identification purposes. Kindly return this after copying prior to circulation at divisional level.

I would point out that I have the support of Mr Leon Brittan in this matter and will be visiting him in chambers on Wednesday 11th July to discuss video nasties and intimate body probes as recommended by Mr Eldon Griffiths MP. It would be of relevance to our discussions if I could have your present views on these matters plus entrapment of MPs at gay clubs before I meet him. Might I also say that I am forming 'The Friends of Leon Brittan Fighting Fund' to answer in court allegations made against him in Private Eye. I would point out that you don't, to contribute, really have to be a friend, so perhaps you'd like to spring a quid or two in a worthy cause.

I look forward to hearing from you, Commissioner.

Here's to policing by confession!

Yours sincerely,

Norman Norman

Norman Norman (aka Henry Root)

P.S. Here's a tenner for yourself.

'Good. It's the Yellow Pages, then. We need a firm of snoops experienced in all forms of surveillance. We'll need this place wired and bugged against all eventualities.'

He found the book and scrabbled excitedly through the pages.

'What have we here? "A1 Assorted Detectives"? Sound a bit rum. Some of Sir Kenneth's lads moonlighting, if you ask me. "Euro-Tecs"? Don't want foreigners. Playing into their hands should the vice anglais be attempted here. Bad for our image in Europe, do you see? "Carratu International"? What sort of name's that? "Offices in Hong Kong and Taiwan." I'm not surprised. "Ian D. Withers. International & Consultant Investigator. 24 hours." Can't get much sleep, Mr Withers. Trades under his own name at least. Point in his favour. Ah, what's this?

"Argen Ltd. Corporative Investigative and Research Services. Industrial Counter-espionage. Personnel Screening. Evasive Driving Courses. VIP and Executive Protection Service." That's us, lad. "Technical Services and Equipment." This is it. "Electronic Counter-measures. Specialised Intruder and Perimeter Defence Systems. Sweeps." They're our men, lad. A letter!'

139 Elm Park Mansions,
Park Walk,
London, S.W.10.

Argen Ltd.
P.O. Box 136,
London, SWIH ORL.

25th June 1984.

Dear Sir,

In a nutshell, I'm a writer currently commissioned to cover all aspects, both straight up and down and with a spin to it, of female behaviour in contemporary Britain. It occurs to me that you can be of some assistance in two regards: (a) bugging and (b) security.

(a) Bugging. My investigations re current practices will involve research at close quarters with women on my premises and a record of their talk and actions will be necessary, I judge, in case of later denials and refutations as to their voluntary participation. I shall need two-way mirrors here, hidden cameras with zoom lens (fully effective in low lighting) and audio equipment sensitive enough to pick up asides, grunts and sudden demurrings (M and S will be attempted.) From time to time I shall have to take to the field myself, incognito and wired for sound, introducing myself into the working quarters of professional women. Please advise as to cameras and microphones that can be hidden about the person. I gather that the Thames Valley Police have in use a radio transmitter to fit the anus of an officer. Such a piece of equipment could be what I need for close contact with my man Kimbersley back in the incident room.

(b) Security. Operating as I shall be up at the sharp end of literary research, it seems to me that, as a public figure in the limelight, I could be vulnerable to threats, violence to the person and blackmail. In the course of researches into certain habits (the vice anglais, bondage, troilism, cross-dressing etc - rubber will not be attempted) I shall be going into unsalubrious parts, where, I'm told, black pimps jump on mugs from the tops of wardrobes and indulge in knife fights. Should I go two-handed, perhaps, with one of your operatives on the alert outside with a receiver up his anus so that we can communicate anus to anus in the event of a rough-house (my man Kimbersley's got a glass chin and his father's gay, so he'll be damn all use).

In the first instance, perhaps you could send me the literature re your services and the latest technology on the market, plus your prices. You mention sweeps in your advert. What are these? Should I have some?

About your address. Frankly it troubles me. A PO Box no? You're not a hole-in-the-wall operation, I trust. If you are, kindly ignore this letter. I cannot entrust security to bucket-shop types.

Yours faithfully,

Henry Root

Henry Root (aka Norman Norman)

'That's it, lad', said Root. 'That's me for the day. We're doing well.'

Frankly, I was a little surprised. Undoubtedly these security precautions are important, but we'd done no work at all on the actual book. At this rate the project will take much longer than Root supposes, the bright side of any delay being, of course, that I shall make more money. With this in mind I went a little mad in the King's Road on the way home and bought not only the Charlie Allen suit I've had my eye on but also a Bo Bo Kaminsky long silk jacket for £189. Both suit me brilliantly, but brooding at home about Mrs Root and my decision that she should, if possible, see me in a more dominating role – she is, after all, of that generation brainwashed into seeing men as the stronger sex – I reluctantly came to the conclusion that neither was suitable, if I wished to impress her with my masculinity, for wearing to work. By a happy coincidence there was a very interesting article in *The Observer* yesterday about a new fashion known as the 'Young Fogey Look'. This seems to involve your wearing one of your grand-father's suits and crumpled flannel shirt a size and a half too big for you. As luck would have it, Gay has left a couple of really dire old tweed suits here in the wardrobe. I shall wear one of them tomorrow and go to work as a young fogey. This new look might well impress Mrs Root, should she happen to be summoned to the ops-room, and if she is, I must see to it that I am on my feet, rather than at the wrong end of a duffing up from Root. There will be plenty of other opportunities to wear the Charlie Allen suit and the Bo Bo Kaminsky silk jacket.

TUESDAY 26 JUNE

Got to work a little late, having gone out early to buy an old-time shirt to go with Gay's thick tweed suit. Found just what I wanted in a second-hand shop at World's End, where I also bought a pair of old brown brogues. In this ensemble, with my hair parted in the middle and wearing my Old Etonian tie, I looked really great.

I arrived in the ops-room to find Root about to dictate a letter to Foyle's, the bookshop. He held up a hand, forbidding me to interrupt the flow.

139 Elm Park Mansions,
Park Walk,
London, S.W.10.

Ms Christina Foyle,
W & G Foyle Ltd,
113-119 The Charing Cross Road,
London, W.C.2.

26th June, 1984.

Dear Christina,

I'm of a mind to buy some books by the yard as per Jeffrey Archer in last week's Mail. They should be glossy, but of no particular quality. They are for the celebrity lunches merely and to impress the likes of Lawrie McMenemy, Frank Delaney, Ernie Wise, Dickie Davis, Michael Parkinson, Lulu and Barry Norman. Nothing too demanding, that's the gist of it, Christina. I suggest anything by Robert Lacey, Percy Allis, the philosopher of the golf course, Jilly Cooper plus cookery and keep-fit. Leave out the Cape. The memoirs of Streatham madames are not what's wanted at lunchtime.

I'd come to the shop myself but I'm flat to the boards on women here and I have a back to boot. Send your list and I'll order by return. I enclose a tenner on account.

The measurements of my coffee-table are eight feet by six. I'll leave the calculation as to the cubic necessity of books to you. You'll have done this kind of sum before.

I look forward to hearing from you, Christina.

Yours sincerely,

Norman Norman

Norman Norman

P.S. Available for literary lunches at 48 hours notice. Not with Robert Morley.

'You have a bad back, Mr Root?' I asked when he had finished. Had he been indulging in *le vice anglais*? He was certainly looking very calm.

'Of course not, lad. Threw that in so that I wouldn't be summoned for the browsing. Too busy here to go tramping round Foyle's what? It's women here.' He looked me up and down. 'A word in your ear, lad. I hope you haven't paid your tailor. Never mind. At least you don't look like a girl. You look like a pansy in a suit. Here's progress. Well done. Now. I've been thinking about the literary lunches. Drawn up a guest-list and sent out the invites to our opening do. Here. What do you think?'

He handed me a printed invitation card.

'Henry Root and Kim Kimbersley request the pleasure of your company on Friday 13 July at 12 p.m. Krug and vol-au-vents. Subject for discussion: women. Questionnaires will be promulgated. Bring a bottle.'

'Hits the nail on the head, would you say?'

I was impressed. The wording wasn't exactly as I would have chosen, but I was pleased that he had included my name. 'These have already gone out?'

'Indeed!' Root beamed. 'Printed by my man yesterday afternoon in time for the last post. Invites have gone to the usual crowd – Lady Antonia Fraser, John Motson, Frank Muir, Robin Ray, Fred Housego, Malcolm Muggeridge, Steve Davis the Plumpstead Potting Machine, Joan Bakewell, Sabrina Guinness, Kenny Lynch, Richard Baker, Joanna Lumley, Arthur Marshall, Lennie Bennett's Punchline Pals – plus Hickey, Dempster, Rook and Lee-Potter. Fleet Street must be alerted to our first do. What's your feeling?'

'An excellent start, sir.'

'As I thought. We need to work on the questionnaire, of course. It can save us a lot of work, the questionnaire. No need to pound round London with a tape-recorder like Anna Ford, asking impertinent questions. We'll do it by post. Salient questions through the letter-box. "Dear Madam.

Kindly complete the following and return. How often? Where? When? Why? With Whom? Was M and S attempted?" A confidential questionnaire affording us a profile of the modern woman. All those you mentioned under the letter "A" – friend who goes like a rocket, Lady Annunziata Asquith and so forth – will be receiving the confidential questionnaire. You have the picture, lad?'

I admit I had certain doubts. 'But how can we publish the results of a *confidential* questionnaire, sir?'

'Easy. Send it to the printers, lad.'

'But it's confidential, sir. The respondents might feel aggrieved.'

Was I being pompous? Obviously I was. Root dismissed my fears with a wave of the hand.

'That's their problem, lad. Now. Yesterday evening I had an idea while watching Wimbledon on television. Women tennis players. What do you think? Should we include them? A bit goes on off the ball, I gather. The grand prix. The ladies' plate. The love doubles. "New balls please." I'm of a mind to write to Wade. She's seen it all before, they say, and I want to bring up a matter concerning her between games commentary. I'll do it now while running hot. Root to Wade. Here goes.'

139 Elm Park Mansions,
Park Walk,
London, S.W.10.

Ms Virginia Wade,
The All England Tennis Club,
Wimbledon, S.W.19.

26th June 1984.

Dear Virginia,

Offering the between-games assessment on TV last week with Jo Durie 2 - 5 down to Miss Steffi Graf you said: "Well, we can all see what's happening here: the big English girl is getting stuffed by the little German."

Should you - a British heroine, according to Harry Carpenter and others - have worded it thus? Kindly advise.

It so happens that you can help me with another matter, Virginia. I am commissioned by Lord Weidenfeld to write on women, the book to appear next spring back to back with Anna Ford on men. I should like to talk to you about life on the circuit, living out of a suitcase, the pressures on court and off and other matters relevant to my theme, best not spelt out through the post. You'll take my drift.

You'll be busy this week, but how about a meeting next week after you've been dumped from the tournament yourself, albeit after a British struggle? I'll hop down to the All England Club with questionnaire on Thursday 12th July at 12.45. We'll have lunch in the members' dining-room and you can fill me in. You won't have to draw pictures, Virginia. Like you, I've knocked around the world.

Could you meanwhile send a photograph of Miss Bettina Bunge? She's certainly a looker. I'd write to her myself but, having been put out of the tournament herself by the above Miss Graf, she may, I fear, have returned to Germany already.

Yours sincerely,

Henry Root

Henry Root

'Spotted Bunge as a pretty lass', said Root, when that was done. 'A picture of her on second serve would cheer things up, what? I'm talking about the book now, do you see? Illustrations will be of the essence, that's my view. Draw the browsers in the shops. The zoom lens. The gusset shot. Most women tennis players look like men in my assessment, and ugly men at that. But Bunge's a pretty lass. Makes a change. Take the big Czech. Navratiwhatsit.'

'Navratilova, sir?'

'That's the fellow. Formidable, what? South paw. Big left arm. Is Navratilova good enough to beat a man? That's the question they're all asking. I say no. Spotted a weakness in her defence. Saw how she could be taken. Here. I'll demonstrate.'

He motioned me off my chair and lined me up on an imaginary tennis court.

'Right. You're Navratilova, the big Czech. Now – cock your left.'

I swung my left arm back, as though for the cross-court pass, and held it. Root, rather to my surprise, came in close and stood heavily on my feet.

'You pinned, lad?'

'I certainly am.' Had it not been for the sensible brogues I'd bought that morning the pain would have been unbearable.

'Can't move in any direction?'

'No. I'm held fast.'

'That's it, do you see? That's the secret.'

Surely this wasn't in the rules? One had heard of players crowding the opposition, dominating the net and so on, but this was over-doing it.

'Are you a tennis player, Mr Root?'

'I'm not talking about tennis, lad. I'm talking about a bar-room brawl. How to take the big Czech in a bar-room brawl. I say it's possible. Now – make your shot.'

I led with my left, he parried with his right and, standing suddenly on tiptoe, he butted me full on the nose. Over I went.

'My God, he's down again!' cried Root.

I was dimly aware, through a cloud of concussion, that he picked me up and spread me on the desk. He loosened my tie and dabbed at my nose, which was streaming blood. Suddenly the intercom buzzed loudly near my ear. Root swore. 'What does the woman want now?' I was vaguely conscious of the pass-door being opened by Root and of Mrs Root coming into the ops-room with two men. I was also conscious that yet again she was seeing me not at my best. Would she ever catch me on my feet and *compos mentis*?

'It's the law, Mr Root', she said. She sounded immensely pleased. 'Sergeant – er – I'm sorry, what was your name, dear?'

This was the moment I'd been dreading. The police had come at last to pick us up for racism, corruption and GBH. Dazed though I was, I started preparing my defence.

'Sergeant Pyle', said one of the policemen. 'And this is my colleague, Sergeant Pulley.'

'Sergeant Pyle and Sergeant Pulley, Mr Root,' said Mrs Root. 'They – my God!' She'd noticed me at last, spread out on the desk. She ran to my side. She rounded angrily on Root. 'Whatever have you done to the lad now?' She produced a handkerchief and dabbed at my streaming nose.

'It was nothing,' said Root impatiently. 'The lad walked into a door.' He turned to Sergeant Pyle. 'Happens all the time down at the nick, what? Crack. Bang. Oh dear. Another prisoner's walked into a wall. Ha! Ha! You'll understand.' He nudged Sergeant Pyle heavily in the ribs.

Sergeant Pyle wasn't amused. He cleared his throat and said he was here at the request of his boss at 'B' Division, Superintendant Ryan. There was a question concerning the holding of a black man in a broom-cupboard. There was too the more serious matter of attempted bribery. Mention was made of wasting police time.

Root, standing facetiously to attention, heard him out. Then, to my surprise, he fingered me.

'There's your man, sergeant', he said. 'Sit up, lad. Looks like you're for the high-jump here. Couple of officers from Chelsea to feel your collar. Doesn't look like a criminal, does he, sergeant? Just shows you. Tried to bribe your Superintendent, did he? Whatever next!' He roared with laughter. He slapped his thigh and doubled over.

Sergeant Pyle remained stony-faced. He questioned me. He asked me about the black man in the cupboard. He returned the ten pound bribe and made me sign for it. He warned me as to my future conduct.

Root, at last, came to my assistance. 'Right!' he said. 'Leave this to me. I'll handle this. Seems to have been some misundertanding here. We're working closely with the Home Secretary, do you see? You've heard the allegations, Sergeant?'

Pyle was confused. He said he hadn't heard the allegations. Root explained them, at length. Pyle shifted uneasily from foot to foot and then, to get back on to firmer ground, repeated his warning about capturing black men and attempted bribery. Root was amazed.

'Come now, sergeant!' he cried. 'A fine day indeed when the lads of "B" Division won't take a sweetener. Next you'll be telling me you're all straight down there! That's good! That's rich! Have you heard this one, sergeant? You'll like this one. One detective turns to another in the squad-room at Chelsea. "Lend us a packet of cigarettes, Ron. Just till the shops shut." Eh? Oh – you've heard it. Here's one. Woman rings up Chelsea Police Station. "Have you got a robbery squad, sergeant?" "Certainly, madam. Who do you want robbed?"' Root barked with laughter. 'Oh yes. Best way of getting your over-insured valuables burglarised. Tell "B" Division you're off on holiday.'

Sergeant Pyle was tremendously unamused. Suddenly Root lost interest.

'Can't piss about with the police all day', he said. 'There's work to be done. We're on women here. The whole shooting match from A to Z. The vice anglais could be attempted here. Oh yes. On the letter "A" at the moment, do you see? Lady Annunziata Asquith and so forth. She goes like a rocket, if our criminal friend here is to be believed. What's your view, sergeant?'

Sergeant Pyle had no view. He narrowed his eyes and took a cautious step backwards, squinting suspicously at Root as if he might have been a parcel bomb left outside a Wimpey Bar in Oxford Street.

'Here', said Mrs Root, who was still dabbing solicitously at my nose. 'Have you said something nasty about Susan Hampshire yet?' She turned to the sergeant. 'I can't be doing with Susan Hampshire', she explained. 'Can't be doing with her at all. Can you be doing with her, sergeant?'

Pyle's official 'move along please' expression was rapidly fragmenting into one of utter bewilderment. Nothing in his training, clearly, had prepared him for this. The glance he now exchanged with his colleague Pulley verged on the panic-striken.

'The woman's obsessed', explained Root. 'Pay no attention to the woman.' Suddenly he'd had enough. He banged his fist so hard on the top of the desk that I shot upright with alarm, cracking my nose against Mrs Root's head. My nose started to bleed again. 'Right!' bellowed Root. 'Everyone out! That includes you, woman. There's work to be done.'

He ushered the police and Mrs Root towards the family quarters, deftly stuffing the returned ten pound note into Sergeant Pyle's top pocket as he did so.

'Keep our hands off that boy', said Mrs Root, as she closed the door behind them.

I began to feel a little better. Properly exploited, the bang on the nose could be worth a couple of royalty points at least. I gave a little groan and made a brave attempt to sit up.

'Take it easy, lad. No need to rush things.'

'I'll be all right. What happened to our prisoner, Mr Root?'

'Had to release him, lad. The statutory ninety-six hours was up, do you see? A shame, a crying shame.'

He was immensely cast down, and so was I. With no prisoner in the cupboard, I would bear the full brunt of my employer's frustrations. Suddenly I had an inspiration.

'Never mind, sir! We can capture another!'

Root was immediately cheered. 'You're right, lad! I'll send a squad out tonight. Well done indeed!' He slapped me heartily on the back, sending me sprawling on my face. I'd have rolled off the desk had he not gathered me up as I was about to tip over the edge. 'Sorry, lad. Now. To work! How did you like my bit on women tennis players? Pretty much to the point, eh? You agree we should include a picture of the Bunge lass? The gusset shot on second serve?'

She might well be a pretty lass, but her name, unfortunately, didn't begin with 'A'. We must be systematic, we must have order, and, backed by the moral authority vested in me as a consequence of my bleeding and possibly broken nose, I said as much to Root.

'You're right, of course, lad. We must have order. It was my understanding, though, that we completed the letter "A" last week. Must crack on, you know.'

I was amazed. How could he think we'd finished? It seemed to me we'd hardly started. I had to point this out. Root looked troubled.

'Is that so? Hardly started, you say? Bearing in mind the questionnaire? The questionnaire will polish off a lot.'

I shook my head. I dabbed at my nose to underline my temporary ascendency.

'I have it!' cried Root. 'Athletes! Begins with "A", if I'm not mistaken. There's scope there. The ready-steady-go. "On your marks, ladies!" The buttocks straining at the starting-line. Up in the air. Hard against the satin trunks. The little gymnasts. The synchronised swimmers. The high hurdlers. They'd give you a chase, what?' He was becoming excited. He strode up and down the room. He punched the air. His breathing was heavy. 'We'll include them all under "Athletes", lad. Shirley Strong, the blonde hurdler. Sharron Davies, the big swimmer. She'd have learned a move or two during her time with Adams, what? She'd have you on the mat.' He mimed a judo throw. 'And what of Fatima Whitbread? Have you seen the thighs on the Whitbread girl? Thighs like an Aberdeen Angus. I tell you what, lad. If the Whitbread girl had you in a head-scissors you'd know about it. And what of her pal, the other big javelin thrower? Tessa Sanderson, that's the one. According to Marea Hartman – the Queen of the Track, if the *News Of The World* is to be believed, which I don't suppose it is – she walks around in the nude all day. "Oh Brother! Nude Tessa Stuns Monks!" That was the headline. Or was that in *The Sunday Times*?'

Root was back at the weights now, breathing heavily and muttering patriotic slogans. 'Gotcha!' 'I counted them all out and I counted them all in.' 'Hop off Tam!' 'Who speaks for Britain?' Thoughts of these big, raw-boned girls had disturbed him badly. Weights sailed to the ceiling with the speed of clay pigeons from an ejector. I had better steer him away from this dangerous area. We must press on. We weren't here to please ourselves.

'The Duchess of Argyll', I said, I'm not sure why.

'The vice anglais', retorted Root. He climbed on to his cycling machine. The pedals were a blur to the eye.

'The Duchess of Argyll', I repeated sternly.

'What's that you said? The Duchess of Argyll and the vice anglais? That's a notion.' He pedalled furiously. 'She'd be a practitioner, is that it? Upper-class. It all falls into place. We'll visit her. You have her whereabouts, lad? Scotland, is it? The family seat? The castle battlements? The lone piper? The vice anglais in kilts? She'd sit you on a thistle, I wouldn't wonder.' His squat little legs pumped like pistons.

I could have bitten my tongue out for mentioning the Duchess of Argyll while Root was in this mood, while he was in the thrall of his obsession. Apart from any other considerations, she is a close friend of my grandmother's, under whose will I have considerable expectations. Were Root to call on her, suggesting the vice anglais in kilts, I'd be disinherited for certain. I tried to head him off.

'In fact the Duchess of Argyll is by no means upper-class, sir. She's the daughter of a self-made man. She lives alone at the Grosvenor House Hotel with a poodle called Alphonse.'

That should have put him off. Alas, it didn't.

'Not upper-class, eh? Lives alone with a poodle called Alphonse, is that it? I know the type. We'll visit her. Suggest a whacking. "Good evening, your Grace: over you go".'

He climbed off his bicycle, sent some weights swinging angrily to the ceiling at the prospect, and then returned to his desk.

'Where were we, lad?'

'Still on the letter "A", Mr Root.'

'Is that so?' He thought for a while and then banged the desk with a triumphant crack, causing the blood to pour from my nose again. 'I have it, lad! Arts, The Martial! What do you say to that?'

He simply couldn't keep away from violence. This would be the most unbalanced book on women ever to reach the shops.

'Nothing to do with women, surely, Mr Root?'

'That's where you're wrong, lad. Ask my friend Sir David English. He's been running a campaign in *The Daily Mail*, trying to persuade women to train in self-defence. They must learn to protect themselves against black muggers, that's his point. Fine man, Sir David. The only editor in Fleet Street courageous enough to identify the Toxteth rioters as black, even though they were white. That's by the way. His initiative *re* housewives and the martial arts, that's our point. Imagine the scene. An agreeable English village. An idyllic day at Worpleston. A sleepy game of cricket unfolds lazily upon the green. Dick West, the village idiot, ambles slowly homewards to tap out a felicitous *Spectator* essay on his antique portable. Is that Mary Kenny sitting on a cowpat? A local housewife comes down the village street to buy a loaf. Rasta has at her. But she's a *Daily Mail* reader. She's taken the course in self-defence. Chummy doesn't know this. Splat! He's all over the pavement. Ear-phones. Woolly hat. He won't try that again. You read *The Spectator*, lad? Geoffrey Wheatcroft. His column last week. "The isle is full of noise." What an opening! Not given to many to write like that. Story of being harassed musically on the underground by coloured youths. Transistors at full blast. Didn't like to remonstrate. Sat there with his knees together, wetting himself. Couldn't have happened to Sarah Kennedy.'

'Not a woman, Mr Root.'

'Sarah Kennedy? You astound me.'

'No. Geoffrey Wheatcroft, sir.'

'So I've heard. But Sarah Kennedy – she's taken the course, do you see? Demonstrated it on television. Black johnny harasses her on the underground – biff! splat! crunch! Over in seconds. I tell you! Pop her down. Mrs Root's done the course, as it happens. We'll have a demonstration. You'll be impressed.' He spoke into the intercom. 'Mrs Root to the ops-room. Mrs Root to the ops-room.'

I sat up hastily and clambered off the desk. This time she must see me on my feet. Alas, the trousers of my father's tweeds – a foot at least too long – tripped me and brought me down, so that I banged my head quite nastily against the desk. Root just had time to pick me up and spread me out again before Mrs Root appeared.

'That blasted washing-machine, Mr Root. We'll have to get a another. Here! The lad's nose is still bleeding. Have you hit him again?'

'It's nothing', I said bravely.

'That's right', said Root. 'The boy will live.' Suddenly he went into a kind of boxing crouch. 'Come at me, Mrs Root', he cried, 'come at me!'

'Whatever do you mean, Mr Root?'

'Attack woman!'

Mrs Root sighed. She looked resigned. She assumed a 'boys will be boys' expression. She cautiously circled Mr Root. She looked quite menacing in her rubber gloves. Perhaps she'd knock him cold. I watched fascinated. It was like the slowed-down action in a Kung Fu film. Suddenly Root grabbed a copy of *The Daily Mail* and rolled it tightly. He smacked it hard against his thigh. It made a crack like a rifle shot. He chuckled wickedly.

'Good as a sword-stick in the right hands!' he crowed.

Mrs Root reached for a paper-weight sitting on the desk.

'No weapons, woman!' cried Root.

'But you've got a weapon, Mr Root!'

Root was indignant. 'Of course I've got a weapon! I'm a cheery coloured folk in Worpleston high street, aren't I?'

'But I never go to Worpleston', protested Mrs Root. 'This is silly.'

'It'll get a whole lot sillier if you don't lay aside your weapon, woman! Now! At once! Over there.' He pointed to the desk. She turned in that direction and as she did so, while her back was turned, he caught her a tremendous wallop on the neck with his rolled up paper. She went down with a bump that shook the room. She measured her length on the floor. There was a cry of triumph from Root.

'A clean knock-out!' He turned to me. 'Did you spot her mistake, lad? Took her eyes off my hands. Never take your eyes off the other fellow's hands. I tell you, lad, that course was money down the drain. Trained by Brian Jacks, the little judo man, and look at her now. Flat out. Good mind to ask for my money back.'

Mrs Root pulled herself slowly to her feet. For a while she staggered about in little circles, like a stage drunk, but even now, in this extremity, having received a blow that would have broken the neck of most people, she could think only of me.

'I'm going to see to the lad's nose and try to get some of the blood off his shirt, Mr Root, and then he's going home. That's final. There'll be no ifs and buts about it.'

To my surprise, Root agreed.

'As you say, woman. I've things to do.' He turned to me. 'What was the name of the hotel, lad? Where the Duchess of Argyll is staying?'

'The Grosvenor House', I said. Why did I tell him? Why didn't I say I'd forgotten, or given him the name of another one? He was up to something. He had a cunning look in his little eyes as he casually wrote the name on a piece of paper.

'Thank you, lad', he said. 'Right! Away with you both. There's work to be done!'

'Just a minute', said Mrs Root. 'What's that on your shirt?'

'She's obsessed with cleanliness', snorted Root impatiently 'Where, woman?'

Mrs Root stepped closer. 'There,' she said, touching the front of his shirt.

Root looked down and as he did so Mrs Root brought her knee up sickeningly into his groin. I felt the excruciating pain myself. Root looked amazed. He stood and stared at her, eyes bulging with surprise, mouth agape.

'Never take your eyes off the other fellow's knee, Mr Root', she said. 'I don't know how many times I've told you that.'

Root was delighted. He must have been delirious with pain, but he chortled happily.

'That's more like it, woman, that's more like it! What a move! Well done indeed!' Suddenly delayed shock caught up with him. His knees locked together. He went into a standing squat. He croaked. He hopped about. But he was beaming happily.

We left him still hopping about the ops-room, still repeating 'What a move!' Mrs Root led me through to the family quarters. She took me into her bedroom – a riot of pink, an explosion of candy-floss, with a fluffy pig on the bed. She told me to take my shirt off and to lie down. I did as I was told.

'My goodness!' she said, as my shirt came off, 'you're all skin and bone, you poor boy. We'll have to feed you up.'

I could imagine nothing more delightful than lying naked on her bed while she peeled grapes and popped them in my mouth.

'I'll see what I can do with this', she said, taking my shirt into the bathroom. 'I won't be a jiffy.'

All over the room, in every available space and corner, were little pots, cups and vases of the sort that tourists bring back from Spain as souvenirs. She obviously collected them and when she returned from the bathroom I said how nice I thought they were, though in truth I found them rather vulgar.

'Pottery class', she said.

'You go to pottery class?'

'Mr Root *thinks* I do. Every Monday and Friday evening.' She winked. 'In fact my friend Mrs Spong brings them back from Majorca. She says it's very nice, Majorca. She goes there every year with Mr Spong.' Mrs Root sighed and looked regretful. 'We don't get abroad very much. In fact we don't get abroad at all.'

I was outraged on her behalf. 'Why do you put up with it?'

She seemed puzzled. 'With what, love?'

'Well, with – er . . .' I nodded in the vague direction of the ops-room.

'Oh, bless your heart! With Mr Root, you mean?' She patted my knee and let her hand lie there for seconds longer than was strictly necessary. I was powerfully attracted, and aware that she was powerfully attracted too. 'He's not so bad! He's dependable, you know. He has broad shoulders. I feel – what? – safe, I suppose. That must be it. I want for nothing. It wasn't much of a future for me when I met him. Not at The Coq Sportif. The other girls – well, I hate to think what may have become of them. It was the road to nowhere, The Coq Sportif. Mr Root swept me off my feet, I suppose – literally, as it happens. He was only in eels at the time, but he had a way with him. "May I have this dance, madam?" he said. I was off the bar-stool and round the floor with my feet not touching the ground. Up in the air, I was, his head somewhere in my bosom. I was impressed. Well, I was only young. We got married the same week. And then there's the children. Doreen and Henry Jr. And – well – he sees nothing.' She winked again. What could this mean?

I lay back on the pillow and spread my arms languorously behind my head. I smiled mysteriously. It worked. She looked down at me. She wanted me.

'I think I'll slip into something a little more comfortable', she said. She walked towards the bathroom, pausing at the door to flash me a brilliant smile. 'And there's something you can do for me', she said.

This was it. She could take me now. I stretched out luxuriously on the bed. I purred a little, like a cat. I unzipped my trousers teasingly. I'd have taken them off, but I knew she'd want to do that herself. 'What's that?' I said. I knew, but I wanted to hear her say it.

'What's what?' she called from the bathroom.

'What can I do for you?'

She came back into the bedroom. She was carrying my shirt. 'You can say something nasty about Susan Hampshire,' she said, 'that's what you can do for me. Here's your shirt. I've got most of the blood off. And now we'd better call you a taxi. Can't have you using public transport in your condition.'

I went home in a daze. What does it all mean? I am attracted to her and she, quite obviously, is attracted to me. And yet she made no move. What's holding her back? I was at her mercy, after all, lying there on the bed with my shirt off. She is a mature woman, a woman who pretends to go to pottery class. And what *does* she do on Mondays and Fridays? Strange creatures, women. Perhaps I'm still not being dominant enough.

Charlotte phoned! I was very cold. I said I didn't wish to see her.

'Suit yourself', she said. 'Why?'

'Because', I said, 'I gather you're a pervert.' My voice was icy.

'A *pervert*? What *can* you mean?'

'I understand it's your habit to stand around in a suspender-belt,' I said.

'Oh *that*. Doesn't everyone?'

'No,' I said stonily, 'they don't.'

I rang off, no doubt leaving her feeling very silly at the other end.

WEDNESDAY 27 JUNE

I arrived at work to find Root in a more than usually triumphant mood. He'd definitely been up to something. His eyes twinkled wickedly above his fat cigar. He was agog to tell me his news.

'Didn't let the grass grow under my feet last night, lad. It was out in the field for me, do you see? Up at the sharp end. Oh yes. I visited the Duchess of Argyll! For the vice anglais, you understand. What do you say to that?'

My heart sank. I'd be disinherited if he'd mentioned my name. It was best to know the worst.

'What happened?'

'A triumphant episode', said Root. 'There were minor setbacks, but I prevailed. Went to the Grosvenor, as you suggested, armed with a ping-pong bat.' He mimed a short, decisive rally. 'Johnny at the counter refused to give me the Duchess's room number. Many would have been confounded. Not me. Sat in the lobby with my ping-pong bat, practising my strokes. Staked the place out, do you see? In she came with the poodle Alphonse. Spotted her at once. Tailed her up to her suite, gave her a moment or two to settle down, then knocked on her door. "Evening your Grace", I said. "Norman Norman's the name. It's the vice anglais." Seemed best to use the alias, even when dealing with the aristocracy. She hollered and took refuge behind the sofa. Part of the act, I supposed. Is that right?'

I couldn't answer. My mouth was dry. It was the end of my trust funds. I was in danger of bringing up my 'Stars' Crunch by Crunch Breakfast Diet'.

'I handed her the ping-pong bat and bared myself, as per your instructions, in a neutral corner. "Lay it on, you minx!" I cried. "I gather you know my collaborator, young Kim Kimbersley. He's told me about your sort. Tally ho!" It was an exciting moment, I can tell you. You were right on this. Well, bless my soul, she drew back and whacked me! It was a surprise, lad. I'd been expecting it, but it was a surprise for all that. I rounded on her, bellowing. Conditioned reflex, I suppose. Where I come from, down by the docks, one is not used to being whacked from behind. A docker considers his buttocks his own business, do you see? In this respect, unlike your Etonian. Down by the docks, only one way with someone who whacks you from behind. Head-first into the nearest bollard. A chase ensued in which I trod on the poodle Alphonse. May have squashed it. Then a man appeared who must have been *en suite* throughout. The butler, is that your guess? You recall the unfortunate publicity *re* the butler? Cabinet ministers involved, if I'm not mistaken. I chaffed her as to this. The butler tried to join in. You hadn't warned me about this. He went for the restraining hold. I threw him off. What a do! He called security. Johnny from the counter appeared. He wanted to join in too. You'd said nothing about it being communal, lad. I caught him a couple of strokes with the ping-pong paddle, but he didn't seem to take to it. Not from the top-drawer, I suppose. Not conversant with the mores. I got in some punches, recovered my trousers and, before taking off, left a copy of the questionnaire.'

'The questionnaire?'

'That's right, lad. Told you about it yesterday. It'll save a lot of time, the questionnaire. When? Where? How? Why? In what positions? Are share certificates involved?'

'*Share* certificates, Mr Root?'

'That's right, lad. My understanding some types only do it to improve their stock portfolios. Told her to fill it in and return to us. "Any time at your convenience, your Grace." And then I'm off. What do you think?'

I was finding it rather difficult to think. My brain ached. Thoughts scraped against it like wire wool on an old saucepan, setting my teeth on edge. I'd have to write to the Duchess, apologising on Root's behalf before she got in touch with my grandmother. Loyalty and teamwork were of the essence, but not when trust funds were involved.

'You're gaping, lad. Impressed, eh? I thought you would be. Enough of that, however. Must crack on. Did well yesterday. The letter "A", if I'm not mistaken. So – it's "B" today. What have we to say under "B", lad?'

Root looked at me expectantly, but I was too busy composing a letter to the Duchess to help him out.

'Down to me, is it?' said Root. 'Here goes, then. Henry Root on "B". I have it! Big Blondes who get the writing bug. Pat Booth in this category. She's done well. Knew her father, a fair-ground boxer. Also photographs herself in the nude and puts results on sale. Poses solo. Thighs spread in her own back-yard. The synchronised time-control. Must feel a fool, but there you are. We'll send her the questionnaire. Beach girls. The Germans a hazard on the beach, as I recall from my trip abroad. They throw frisbees, form human pyramids and sit on your towel. It's the knuckles under the nose. "Move over, fräulein. We haven't forgotten Dresden even if you have." French girls, on the other hand, merely urinate against rocks and undress without discretion, displaying boastful pubic bushes, reeking of garlic. Lindy Benson – the kiss-and-tell type. Recently blew the whistle on Robert Mitchum. "My Hot Nights with Big Bob Mitchum." *The Sunday Times*, I fancy. Silly old fool. Probably didn't know what was happening. Hard day on the set. Up to his hotel room. Half asleep. Girl comes to his room. He thinks it's room-service. Good publicity for him, though. Might try it myself. Good for the image, eh? "My Hot Night With Henry Root" by Lindy Benson. A letter! "Dear Miss Benson.

I gather that you expose others at a price. Depending on negotiations *re* vetting the manuscript I'm prepared to have you blow the whistle on me in the Sunday press. Profit participation by agreement. No actual intercourse, if you please." That sort of thing. What do you think? You're stunned, lad. We'll bear it in mind. File it under "Image, Henry Root's". Might write to various top agents seeking a full list of their kiss-and-tell types. Laraine Ashton. "Dear Miss Ashton, kindly furnish by return a list of girls available at forty-eight hours' notice to spend the night at Blake's Hotel and subsequently spill the beans in the Murdoch press." Boxers, Topless. Barristers. My friend Alan Williams – *The Mail On Sunday's* Voice Of Reason, The Man Who Writes What Others Scarcely Dare To Think – tells me that lady barristers wear mail-order knickers under their gowns and after a day in court like to be peeled roughly out of these by married men in furnished service flats. He should know. Brothels, French. According, once more, to my friend Alan Williams – The Man They Can't Gag – all the girls in French brothels are Algerian seamen, except the black girls, who go off like fire-crackers at the first touch. We'll not try Paris, lad. Tina Brown. She's in the fast lane. Angie Bowie, the multi-sexed chanteuse. Met her once at a showbiz do. It was the two-fingers up the nostrils. "Don't mess with Mrs Root, baby!" She got the picture. Bardot, Brigitte. A consummate professional, but did she ever master her most important role, her life? This piercing aperçu is due to Barry Norman, unless I'm much mistaken. Bergman, Ingrid. Throughout a long career, her only real love affair was with the camera. Another of Barry's, I fancy. Bogarde, Dirk. The British film industry, alas, scarcely knew how to handle such beauty and sensitivity. Too good an actor, paradoxically, ever to make a good film. Yet another of Barry's penetrating insights. Could make a stocking filler out of Barry Norman's insights. A letter! To Chatto and Windus. Here goes.'

139 Elm Park Mansions,
Park Walk,
London, S.W.10.

27th June 1984.

Miss Carmen Callil,
Chatto & Windus Ltd,
40-42 William 1V Street,
London, WC2N.

Dear Carmen,

Here's a stocking-filler for your Christmas list. The Apercus Of Barry Norman. E.G.:

Monroe, Marilyn: She represented freedom to others but she wasn't free herself.

Garland, Judy: She was sacrificed on the altar of our fantasies. We're all guilty.

Loren, Sophia: She's at the crossroads.

Cass, Mama: Like so many people with a full address book she found there were times when no one was in.

Queen, Her Majesty The: Though she lives in a gold-fish bowl it's important to remember that to many people she's as real as Elsie Tanner.

Rantzen, Esther: Yet on screen you couldn't meet a nicer person.

Spungen, Nancy: Her life lacked a third act.

Tushingham, Rita: Inside she's beautiful.

Piaf, Edith: The Little Sparrow. She did it her way.

McLaine, Shirley: She no longer needs a man to ratify her existence.

Dietrich, Marlene: The Dietrich eyes said it all.

Windsor, Barbara: She's been to hell and back.

Newton-John, Olivia: Livvy's looking more relaxed now that she's discovered who she really is.

Evans, Edith: She was no beauty, but she became beautiful the moment she stepped onto a stage.

I have one in the pipe-line, Carmen, which may prove too hot for Weidenfeld. Henry Root's A - Z of Women. I know what you're thinking - you're thinking: what's there to say on women? The bedroom and the kitchen. The duvet and the food blender. The corset and the rubber-glove. Normally you'd be right, of course, but Root on Women, that's marketable, Carmen. Don't concern your pretty little head with the promotional details; leave all that to me.

Kindly telex your offer for both these projects by return.

Here's to the weaker sex, God bless 'em!

Yours till the bed breaks, Carmen.

Henry Root

Henry Root.

'Birbank, Hottie. Once with Hunt the Shunt, now with Daley Thompson, the big decathlete. Runs a masseuse and keep-fit parlour in the King's Road. Bodys. We might enrol in dance class there. Pass round the questionnaire. "Good morning madam. It's ballet, is it? The *pas de deux*? Fill this in when you have a moment. Pardon my tights." Will tights be necessary, lad? I've not worn tights. We'll buy some later. What do you think? Covered a few there, eh? Under the letter "B". What's your feeling, lad?'

I'd been impressed, but I felt it was my duty to point out that we hadn't finished 'A'. Root was astounded.

'Not finished "A", lad? You're pulling my leg. This will take forever, and I've other matters to attend to. Had a concept *re* Henry Jr, do you see? Thought I'd persuade him to join the Moonies. Once in, you never see them again. Discovered this from Denning. Made a speech in the Lords. He was anti-them, I don't know why. Sound like sensible people to me. Didn't give Mr Moon's address and there's nothing in the phone book. Otherwise we'd write to him. "Dear Moon, kindly take my lad." That sort of thing. Might be able to get the address from *The Daily Telegraph* information service. And there's Doreen. Keen that she could become a researcher at the House of Commons. Quick way to a settlement. The Keays woman – she's laughing, what? Thought I might write to Fatty Dickens MP, the tea-time Romeo. He could advise. There's letters to go off, do you see?'

I was firm. I explained that the work we'd done on 'A' covered two pages at the most. At this rate the book would be only fifty-two pages long. Root was shocked.

'So, it's back to "A", is it, lad?'

'It's essential, Mr Root. We made a start – all those names, but they were only covered sketchily. We said nothing about them, if you remember. Jenny Agutter, Peggy Ashcroft, Leslie Ash, Maria Aitken . . .'

'Actresses, isn't that right?'

'That's right, Mr Root.'

'Leave this to me. Know a bit about actresses. Met a few in my time, do you see?' He got up from his desk and went into his composing mode, striding up and down the ops-room. 'Here goes. Root on actresses. Queer cattle for the most part. Egos the size of diseased livers. Shouldn't be indulged. If indulged, they stamp their feet and chew the carpet. Dirk Bogarde, on hearing that Julie Christie had landed the leading role in *Billy Liar*, ate three-quarters of his mother's Axminster. Point out there's nothing to it. Shirley Temple could do it at the age of four, isn't that so? They respond well to the firm approach. Here's the way of it. Present yourself backstage – not at half-time, unless your schedule demands – and compliment them as to the show and nudity, if any. This is important. If you'd been making a fool of yourself for two and a half hours in public a kind word would be of the essence. Then take firmly by the elbow. "I have a table for two at the nearest Steak House, madam." Accustomed to a less masculine type, do you see? Don't offer money, but let them see the credit cards. On arrival at the Steak House order for two and don't talk shop. Tell them about yourself. Acquaint her with your golf handicap and the July sales figures. Pass on a nugget of little known information. "Do you realise that if someone invented pantyhose that didn't ladder stocking manufacturers would be in Queer Street?" They divide, in my experience, into two categories, actresses: (1) those who appear decoratively but for the most part speechless in *The Professionals* and *The Sweeney*; and (2) the intellectuals, the new breed of thinking actresses who review books for *The Sunday Times* and display minds of their own on *Any Questions*. Your chances when you leave the Steak House depend on which category you've drawn. If (1) forget it. Your walk-on actress from *The Sweeney* will wish to be complimented as to her mind and will in any case be keeping an out-of-work pop *artiste* on the side. If (2) you could be on to something. They tend to have outside interests, though, as often as not literary. Diana Rigg is of this type. What was the name of her book?'

'*No Turn Unstoned*, I think.'

'That's right. A scissors and paste job, but no harm in letting her think you've read it. Diana! "*No Turn Unstoned*, eh? You rascal!" Then drive in hard while she's on the back foot. They like it head-on, the intellectuals. Take Joanna Lumley. Another thinking type. More "O" levels than Trevor Brooking, so they say, yet she raffled her knickers on the *Terry Wogan* Show. What does that tell you about intellectuals? No sense of humour either. Take the Aitken woman. You've seen her show? *Poor Little Rich Girls?* A debacle. It's the big blondes who have the sense of humour, often "zany", sometimes "bubbling". Met Goldie Hawn once, holidaying in Marbella. My trip abroad. Presented myself in a thong by the hotel piscine. Some could, some couldn't. I can. Upper body of a wrestler, do you see? "Sock it to me, baby!" I cried. I had her in a hold and pulled her knickers down. She had to laugh. Pushed her into the piscine and sat on her boyfriend's head when he tried to intervene. She was bowled over, I can tell you that. Gave me a very wide berth thereafter. Next!'

I was impressed. When Root concentrates on the matter in hand we really motor. 'That was brilliant', I said. 'I wonder, though, if we shouldn't actually talk to an actress, get it first-hand.' I imagined Root and I backstage, talking intimately to leading ladies, and then escorting them to dinner.

'Talk to one, eh?' It was Root's turn to be impressed. 'Straight from the horse's mouth, is that it? The Anna Ford approach? That's not a bad idea, lad. And I like this field-work. My experience with the Duchess gave me a taste for the field-work. I'll wine and dine an actress. Better draw an intellectual, though. Glenda Jackson, say. She's my type. Let's see if she's currently on show.'

Root consulted the classified ads in *The Daily Mail* and discovered that she is appearing at The Duke of York's.

'That's it,' he said. 'I'll go tonight. Park the Rolls and straight into her dressing-room with a bunch of flowers. A table booked in advance at the smart end of the market. She's a thinking type, do you see? A coruscating intelligence, according to Michael Parkinson and others. No good diving a coruscating intelligence into a fast-food bar in a kiss-me-quick hat. It will be Mario's in Putney High Street for her. An area for dancing. "Pepe and his guitar will entertain at 12." I see it all.'

I seemed to have been left out. I was bitterly disappointed, but I judged it best not to say so. There would be other opportunities to accompany Root into the field.

He looked at his watch. 'Hm. Only twelve o'clock. It's hard to settle down with such an evening ahead. Hard to concentrate, that's the truth of it. I tell you what. We'll buy some tights. For the dance class, you understand. For when we visit Bodys. We'll be visiting Bodys, you and I.

When we get to the letter "B", of course,' he added hastily. 'Must have order here. Must finish "A". It's tights meanwhile. To Harrods, lad!'

We drove to Knightsbridge in the Rolls, where Root parked in a bus lane under a policeman's nose. He jumped out and handed the car keys to the officer.

'Keep an eye on the Rolls, my good man. It's Government business here. Hand in glove with the Home Secretary, do you see? You've heard the allegations? Root's the name.'

While the policeman was trying to unpack this, Root ran into Harrods and button-holed the Marquess of Tavistock, easily recognisable, I'd have thought, from a TV appearance the night before in connection with the stolen Woburn treasures.

'It's tights', said Root. 'I'm a friend of Tiny Rowland's do you see? Where's the dance department, my good man?'

'Actually I'm a customer', said Tavistock politely. 'I'm afraid I can't help you.'

'A customer?' Root stepped back for a clearer view of Tavistock. 'You could have fooled me', he said. 'Had you down as a floor-walker.'

'It's the Marquess of Tavistock', I explained.

'Is it really?' said Root. 'Sorry about the heirlooms, your grace. Going for the insurance, were you? Two idiots find them in a ditch. Annoying for you.' He winked and nudged Tavistock heavily in the ribs, cannoning him off the Marchioness, who was approaching with some parcels and a peke. Root raised his hat, a pork-pie a size and a half too small for his enormous head. 'Pardon me, your grace. Took your husband for a floor-walker. We're after tights. Good day to you both.'

Leaving the Tavistocks to pick up their scattered parcels, we made our way to the dance department on the third floor. Here Root chose a leotard in canary yellow and, intending to try it on, started to remove his trousers. An alarmed assistant, who may I think have been my head of house at Eton, motioned him agitatedly towards the fitting cubicles. Root passed swiftly down the line, impatiently swishing open curtains and thus suddenly exposing a variety of surprised keep-fit enthusiasts adjusting themselves intimately in front of mirrors. Having discovered, to his annoyance, that all the cubicles were occupied, Root addressed himself briskly to an overweight, self-important looking man who was last in line and trouserless.

'You won't mind my joining you', said Root. 'A friend of Tiny Rowland's, do you see?'

He entered the cubicle and drew the curtain. There followed a series of grunts and bumps and indignant protestations as Root and the rightful occupant heaved and strained in the confined space. Suddenly the fat man shot out of the cubicle like a human canon-ball.

'I say!' he said, trying to pull his tights up.

'Never mind the "I say" ', said Root, who was also half-way into his tights. 'It's women here for Lord Weidenfeld of Nicolson. There's deadlines to be met.' He drew the curtain shut.

'Excuse me', said the fat man, still straining to pull his tights up. 'Game for a laugh? Is that it?'

I stared at him icily. 'We're writers', I explained. 'Currently back to back with Anna Ford.'

At that moment another cubicle became free, which the fat man, his tights still half-way up his thighs, hastily occupied.

'What do you think?' said Root, emerging from his cubicle with his tights in place.

He was an impressive sight. With his short, heavily muscled legs and waxed moustache he looked like an old-time acrobat or escapologist – Harry Houdini himself, perhaps – an effect by no means entirely dissipated by the pork-pie hat and traditional jacket.

'A little tight in the gusset, to tell the truth,' he said, 'but on the whole there's ease of movement.'

He proceeded to demonstrate the fact with a heavy jump and short series of ballet moves, causing the other customers to close their eyes and run for cover. A little tight in the gusset had been an understatement. He looked as though he'd stuffed an award-winning marrow down his front, his enviable endowment in this department not going unrecognised by our assistant, whose popping eyes followed every heavy swing of that enormous bulge. It *must* have been my head of house. He'd always been a boggler.

'If sir would like . . .' he said.

Root silenced him with a wave of the hand. 'A moment, lad. We'll need to check the arabesque.'

Leaning slightly forward from the waist, Root suddenly kicked out behind him like a mule, his heavy walking shoe catching the fat man in the stomach and driving him back into the cubicle from which he'd just emerged. He collapsed, winded, in a corner, dragging the curtain down on top of him.

'Yes', said Root. 'They're adequate for the *arabesque*. I'll take them.' He turned to me. 'What about you, lad? You've made your choice?'

'In fact I have a pair', I said.

'I might have known it. So. It's just the one pair.' He produced a bulging wallet and peeled some notes off an enormous bank-roll. 'Perhaps you'd be so good as to parcel up my trousers.'

'Sir is going to wear the leotard?'

'Indeed I am. Get the feel of it, do you see?'

The next few minutes, as we made our slow exit from Harrods, were among the most interesting of my life. People are very strange. You'd have thought they'd never seen two writers out in the field before. As Root strutted boastfully towards the lifts, occasionally performing little ballet kicks to left and right, pausing after each small variation to adjust the straining material round his crotch, strong men turned white and backed away, while women dropped their parcels and tried to cover their children's eyes. It was really quite pathetic. Only a Mr Humphreys type in Ladies Underwear behaved with any degree of sophistication. 'Ooooh I say!' he cried. 'What a big lunch! Is it all yours?' He went headfirst into the outsize corsets drawer. A moment of near panic occurred in the lift, where Root, suffering a sudden constriction between the legs, reasonably drew the other passengers' attention to his problem.

'It's the tights, do you see?' he beamingly informed the lady next to him. 'A trifle tight round the orchestra stalls. Pardon me, madam. If you could shift slightly to your left. Need to make a slight adjustment here.' After a tremendous struggle his swinging parts were satisfactory re-aligned. 'Phew! That's better', he cried. 'Root's the name. You may have read my work. It's women now. For Lord Weidenfeld of Nicolson. All aspects, do you see? The whole shooting-match from A to Z.'

We got outside to find the constable standing guard, as instructed, over the Rolls. Root tapped him on the shoulder.

'My keys, if you'd be so good.'

The constable spun round, ready to read the riot act.

'Now look here, this won't ... my God!' He'd seen the tights. He blanched and backed away. He threw Root the keys from a safe distance. 'on your way, sir, if you please.' Muttering distractedly to himself, he hid behind a news-stand, peeping out from time to time to see how we were doing.

Root now suggested that we take lunch at the Hyde Park Hotel, where, he said, the à la carte was much admired. I wasn't very hungry, as it happened, so I said I'd better get home and catch up with some typing. I was behind with the transcribing, I said.

Root was impressed by my professionalism, as I'd meant him to be. 'Well done, lad!' he said. 'That's the attitude. See you tomorrow, then. It will be on with the letter "A". Must be systematic. Must have order, do you see? And it's dinner tonight with the Jackson woman. We're doing well.'

Leaving the Rolls in the bus-lane, he marched in yellow tights and pork-pie hat down Knightsbridge, doing little ballet spins from time to time. The policeman who'd been guarding the Rolls now left the safety of the news-stand and approached me warily.

'Excuse me, sir. Would you be circus folk? Is that it?'

'Certainly not,' I said. I explained that we were on Government business and told him to keep an eye on the Rolls until Root returned. 'Taking lunch with the Home Secretary', I said. 'They're hand in glove, do you see? You've heard the allegations?' I'm learning fast. The constable saluted politely, and I went home, where I spent most of the afternoon writing a letter of apology to the Duchess of Argyll. There was still a slim chance that I wouldn't be disinherited if I could get the tone exactly right. After a great deal of thought, I finally typed and posted the following:

Dear Duchess,

You and I have never met, but you know my grandmother well and have stayed more than once, I think, at my father's house in Lambourne.

I am greatly distressed to learn that a colleague of mine, Mr Henry Root, came to your suite last night with a ping-pong bat and, having removed his trousers, suggested a session of *le vice anglais*. He was, in fact, representing Lord Weidenfeld of Nicolson in this, being himself a man of some literary distinction, currently researching all aspects of female behaviour for his lordship. I must stress that I myself was against the visit, arguing that there was no good reason to suppose that you would favour this particular habit, but he is a strong-willed man whom little can deter. He laid about him with a ping-pong bat, I understand, at one time hitting the butler and at another treading on your poodle Alphonse. I trust neither was badly injured.

Please accept my most sincere apologies for what was at best an ill-judged, but purely literary, invasion of your privacy.

Yours sincerely,
Kim Kindersley

THURSDAY 28 JUNE

I arrived at work to find Root strutting gleefully about the ops-room, punching the air triumphantly like a footballer who's scored a goal. His evening with Glenda Jackson, clearly, had been a great success. I felt a twinge of envy.

'You took her out?'

'I certainly did, lad. Didn't see the show, of course. Parked the Rolls and proceeded through the stage-door. Door-keeper tried to head me off but it was the knuckles under the nose and straight down the passage to Miss Jackson's dressing-room. Usual theatrical crowd, perverts for the most part, whinnying in self-regarding groups. I announced myself. "Norman Norman", I said. "I'm here to escort Miss Jackson to Mario's in Putney High Street." That silenced them. They were impressed. No sign of Miss Jackson at the moment. Some old boiler in a tea-towel seemed to be doing the honours, handing round drinks and so forth. The maid, no doubt. Didn't offer me one, so I helped myself. Found myself talking to one of the pansies. Flippers and a velvet jacket, you know the sort. Mentioned eels, how to salt and bottle them. He was interested. Then he happened to mention that *he* was taking Miss Jackson to dinner. Her walker, no doubt. You've heard of walkers, lad? Middle-aged back-door men available by the hour for escort work. They all have them. "Look, Dorothy", I said. "You *were* taking Miss Jackson to dinner. The privilege is now mine. On your bike, you savvy?" The seat of the pants and into the passage. Then the maid says: "Where's Gerald?" "Gerald who?" I said. "Gerald Harper", she said. "You were talking to him just now." Miss Jackson's dinner-date, do you see? "Sent him packing", I said. The maid seemed worried, and then Miss Jackson appeared. I'd had enough of theatricals by this time, so I took her by the elbow and steered her down the passage. Gerald was loitering at the entrance, so I showed him my fist. "On your way, Dorothy", I said. Miss Jackson was impressed. It was into the Rolls and straight to Mario's.'

I was impressed too. 'Terrific', I said.

'Nothing to it, lad. The firm approach. I told you. They like the firm approach, actresses. Not used to it, do you see?'

'And the dinner? The dinner was a success?'

Root seemed surprised that I should need to ask. 'A success? I'll say it was a success, lad. It was the prawn cocktail and escalope de veau with choice of wines. I ordered for both, of course, addressing the maitre d' in Italian. That always impresses. "Dos escalopes, por favor, captain, un bottle of Soave and chop chop with the finger-bowls." Didn't talk shop. Told her about myself. The drive to the top. The upward thrust. The eels. "I used to weigh fifteen stone," I said, "but with work on the heavy weights I've got it up to sixteen and a half." Displayed my pectoral development. Caused comment, I can tell you. Then I gave her the info *re* pantyhose. This always interests women, "Surprisingly", I said, "stocking manufacturers now have the technology to produce pantyhose that never ladders – but they don't make use of it because if they did their turnover would decline." She was all ears, I can tell you.'

'She must have been.' I was jolly envious that I'd not been there myself, but I had to admit that Root had done extraordinarily well. This would make an enthralling episode in the book and, since it had been I who had first suggested that we should get out into the field, some of the credit would be due to me.

'Then at midnight,' continued Root, 'it was on the dance-floor while Pepe played and others watched. Pepe was slightly restricted as to his repertoire so I taught him the Lambeth Walk and Hokey Cokey. He followed as I whistled. Then I instructed a party of Germans in the conga.'

'You wore your tights?'

'Of course not, lad. It was the black tie and boiled shirt. The tights are for when we visit Bodys. By now the Germans had joined our table. I told them about the vice anglais. Offered it to Miss Jackson, but she declined. She filled in the questionnaire, though. Here. What do you think? Not bad, eh?'

Root handed me the questionnaire, which Miss Jackson had indeed filled in. Here was a coup and no mistake. There was no time to read it carefully now, but a hurried inspection of its six closely printed pages proved Miss Jackson to be a woman of unusually vigorous appetites; a woman who claimed, among other things, that her preferred number of sexual connections per calendar month was 63 (actual, a mere 2), that she expected men to show consideration for 43 minutes, that she had no less than 70 hobbies (flower arranging and soixante-neuf) and that among modes and positions the Daisy-Chain, the Wheelbarrow and the Boston Crab had been attempted, though the Pile-Driver, 'up a chimney' and Nigel Dempster hadn't.

'Not bad, eh?' said Root. He was beaming proudly, as he had every right to do. 'A complete profile of the modern woman, would you say? After dinner I dropped Miss Jackson back at her place. A modest block of flats at the wrong end of the Fulham Road. I admit I was quite surprised.'

'I'm not sure that you should have been, Mr Root. She's famous for her unpretentious life-style.'

'That's true, lad. Anyway, she asked me in. I declined.' Root looked troubled. He examined the backs of his hands, always a sign that he wanted to get something off his chest. 'Fact is she's keen, lad. She had that look in her eye.' Root shuddered. 'I've seen that look in a squid's eye just before it gobbles up a prawn. Nasty. Not sure I'd ... well, she's not too good off, that's the truth of it, lad, that's the size of it. I'm not sure I could actually ... well, you get the picture. We have another date tomorrow night, but I'm not sure ...' He broke off. He looked most unhappy.

'You must go through with it', I said. 'For the sake of the enterprise.'

'That's right', said Root miserably. 'For the sake of the enterprise. Don't I know it. But I was wondering, lad, if you'd come with me? Would you accompany me to dinner? Just in case she ...' He shuddered again. The squid's eyes had come to mind.

'I'd be delighted to', I said. What an opportunity! I'd always been an ardent admirer of Miss Jackson, both for her excellent work on camera and for her no-nonsense personality off. Nor was I going to take Root's word for it that she didn't look so good in real life. He was merely making excuses for his own inadequacy – if that wasn't too harsh a word to use about a collaborator who had performed brilliantly so far. But the plain fact was that when it got past the talking stage he couldn't handle it. This was my chance to take over, to handle the practical, as opposed to the theoretical, side of things. Even if Miss Jackson had found Root attractive – and stranger things than that have happened – she'd obviously prefer me. This was a priceless opportunity to explore my new-found interest in older women. And what an older woman! Judging by her answers to the questionnaire, it would be hard to find another so broad-minded and adventurous. I began immediately to plan my wardrobe. Just because Glenda didn't give a fig for her own appearance it didn't follow that she liked her young men to be scruffy too. I'd definitely wear my new Charlie Allen suit, but I wasn't certain yet about my accessories. I was so excited that I hardly paid attention to the rest of the morning's discussion, not that it really mattered since it would all be on the tape.

When I got home my excitement was immediately doused by a telephone call from Gay. He was absolutely furious. He wanted to know why I had written a pornographic letter to the Duchess of Argyll. She'd rung him up early that morning to complain. I was astonished. How could my graceful letter of apology for someone else's behaviour be judged pornographic? And how could I explain the background circumstances without getting my collaborator into even worse trouble with Gay than he was already? I quickly decided that my trust funds took precedence over literary loyalty. I explained that I had merely been apologising for my partner's rather over-enthusiastic behaviour the night before. He had become slightly carried away, I said, while carrying out legitimate research on our book.

'Who did?' said Gay. 'That dreadful Root fellow?'

I explained that he wasn't a dreadful fellow, merely an artist who preferred to 'live at the dangerous edge of things'. Gay snorted with contempt.

'She didn't say anything about that to me', he said. 'She simply said she'd got this letter from you this morning saying you'd like to go over to her place and smack her with a ping-pong bat.'

This was so absurd that I could only laugh. 'It was Root', I said. 'I wrote to apologise for *him*. He visited her the night before last and made certain purely *literary* suggestions. In fact I tried to stop him . . .'

'You were there?'

'*No*!' Gay was being extraordinarily obtuse. 'He *told* me about it. That's why I wrote to her. Just in case he'd gone too far. I'm sure he didn't, of course. He left the questionnaire and . . .'

'What questionnaire?'

'The questionnaire for our book. We're asking women salient questions about their sex lives. Which of the following have been attempted? S and M, rubber, bondage, troilism . . .'

Gay groaned. 'He asked the Duchess that? My God, she said nothing about a questionnaire to me. This is worse than I thought.'

He said he was going to speak to the Duchess again and that I should stay where I was until he rang me back. Obviously there had been a silly misunderstanding which would now be cleared up. No doubt the Duchess had telephoned my father before he was properly awake and he, only semi-conscious, had picked up the wrong end of the stick. He's hopeless before lunch at the best of times. Everything would be all right once he'd spoken to her again. The telephone rang. It was Gay, sounding even angrier than before.

'What on earth are you up to?' he said. 'She denies that anyone came to her hotel last night, with or without a questionnaire, least of all that frightful Root man. She had dinner with some friends and then retired to bed. What's going on? Are you ill?'

I hadn't a clue what was going on, and said as much. I carefully explained the whole thing again, and my innocent part in it, but Gay clearly didn't believe me. He thinks I've become a pervert, sending pornographic letters through the post to my grandmother's friends. I told him that I was having dinner tomorrow night with Glenda Jackson.

'Rather you than me', said Gay. 'And I don't want her ringing me up first thing in the morning complaining about your behaviour.'

'That's hardly likely,' I said coldly. 'She's already filled in the questionnaire.'

'I'm not surprised', said Gay. He rang off.

What can the explanation be? Did Root simply invent the episode with the Duchess, and if so why? His account of it *seemed* completely genuine. Can he be such an accomplished fantasist? All artists embroider the truth, of course, but this would have been overdoing it. Anyway, I'll find out tomorrow.

Later this evening I summed up my first ten days at work. Although I have been beaten up twice, once badly, informed on to the police and accused of writing pornographic letters, I think I can say that things are going really well. The book, at last, is shaping up brilliantly, and I'm playing my part to the full. In fact we make an excellent team: Root, as was to be expected, is superb out in the field, where he shows an audacity which I, at the moment, could never equal, but I am learning fast and meanwhile I am bringing to the enterprise, I like to think, an ordering, restraining influence. There seems no reason to suppose that the book won't be a colossal best-seller like Root's others, and I'm on 50 per cent of the royalties. I shall be rich and famous. I shall be back to back with Anna Ford. I shall be interviewed, and possibly insulted, by Kenneth Robinson. There is my growing interest in Mrs Root. And tomorrow I meet Glenda Jackson! It's all very exciting. Minor setbacks are inevitable when a work of art is struggling to be born. Gay wouldn't understand, but he, alas, has not been blessed with an ability to appreciate such things.

FRIDAY 29 JUNE

In the ops-room, I confronted Root immediately in the matter of the Duchess of Argyll. I told him about the angry telephone call from Gay. Root was astonished. He assured me that the episode with the Duchess had taken place exactly as he'd described it. I believed him. I was nonplussed. Then, by carefully going over every detail, I discovered that he'd visited the wrong hotel – The Grosvenor at Victoria Station rather than the Grosvenor House in Park Lane. At first I was greatly relieved. Then Root beamingly pointed out that my position was somewhat worse than before.

'Could come on top for you, lad', he said cheerfully. 'Your name on the questionnaire, do you see? Me, I used my alias. I advised you to use an alias, lad. Now look at the mess you're in. Some old trout, in town to see the changing of the guard and, in the evening, *No Sex Please We're British*, receives a late night visit from a fellow with a ping-pong paddle. Not being the Duchess of Argyll, there's no reason to suppose she goes in for this sort of thing. What's she going to do? Report the matter to the police, that's what she's going to do, lad. And it's your name on the questionnaire. Oh dear, oh dear.' Root sucked his teeth and shook his head. 'It could be the slammer for you, lad. Never mind. At least we now know where the Duchess is. I'll visit her tomorrow night.'

What with that prospect, together with my certainty that at any moment Mrs Root would come through the pass-door with a squad from 'B' Division, I found that for the second morning running I couldn't concentrate on the work in progress. I was dimly aware that Root seemed more concerned with his children's future than with our A to Z of Women, and I think he wrote letters to the Moonies (having obtained their address from *The Daily Telegraph*'s excellent information service) and to Geoffrey Dickens MP, asking the former to accept his son as a disciple and seeking from the latter a list of MPs looking for a nubile research assistant.

By lunchtime I'd begun to feel more optimistic. I'd not yet been arrested for distributing pornographic questionnaires among old trouts in town on British Rail Senior Citizens' Package tours; and I was excited again at the prospect of dinner with Glenda Jackson. Root dismissed me at one o'clock, instructing me to be back in the family quarters at nine thirty, in plenty of time to get to the Duke of York's theatre by the final curtain.

'And don't let me down *re* your appearance, lad.'

I didn't need to be told. This was my chance, I realised, to impress not only Miss Jackson, but also Mrs Root, who was bound to be at home when I returned to collect her husband. I'd be looking really good, making her forget all those occasions when she'd seen me at the wrong end of a duffing up, off my feet and with blood pouring from my nose.

On the way home I went a little crazy in Beauchamp Place, buying a terrific black crêpe and pink spot chiffon blouse by Jacques Azaguty, to wear with my Charlie Allen suit, and a pair of Manolo Blahnik satin shoes. Both items were rather expensive, but they suit me brilliantly, and what's money when you're out to impress two older women in one evening? At home I carefully followed *Cosmo*'s 'Pamper Yourself Before That Special Date' programme, published last month. I washed my hair and then applied Henara treatment wax, which, though well worth it in the end, is a bit of a performance because you have to sit around for ages with a plastic bag over your head. It was a bit unfortunate that while I was wearing the plastic bag and nothing else I answered a ring at the front-door (thinking it might be Charlotte – I've decided I'm prepared to see her again, notwithstanding her appalling behaviour with Henry Jr) to find myself face to face with old Brigadier Wordsworth, a flog 'em all JP and shooting friend of my father's, standing on the door-step with a couple of dead birds.

'Brace of pheasants for your father ... Good God!' He dropped the pheasants and high-tailed it down the street on spindly legs as if he'd seen a ghost.

I then had a long, hot bath, during which I did the Jan Leeming thigh-stretch exercise, followed by an Aapri facial scrub and two applications of Fougère hand and body lotion. By the time I'd made up (just a little foundation moisturiser and a touch of eye-liner), the Jan Leeming Mirror Test told me that I was looking really good.

All this made me a little late for Root, and I was disappointed, having been let in by the quaking Filipino, to discover that Mrs Root was nowhere to be seen.

'Pottery class', explained Root. Why hadn't I remembered that? Still, there'd be other opportunities for her to see me at my best. 'Pardon me for mentioning it, lad, but you've got a plug of nasal phlegm sticking out of your nose.'

'That's a stud,' I said.

'Good God! Whatever next?' Then he said that we were running late and must therefore hit the road at once. On the way to the Duke of York's I asked him why he wasn't wearing his dinner-jacket.

'Decided to leave you and the Jackson woman alone together,' he said. 'For the sake of the project. Done my stuff, do you see? Time to get the younger man's perspective.' He looked me up and down doubtfully, as if "man" might not have been the correct word. 'Good grief! Never mind.

Booked you a table for two at Mario's in Putney High Street. The Jackson woman liked it. I'll drive you there and then depart.'

This suited me brilliantly. The only cloud hanging over the evening had been the fear that Root would utterly dominate the proceedings, monopolising Miss Jackson and reducing me to awkward silence. Now I would have her all to myself. I would really impress her, demonstrate that I was an example of Betty Friedan's Second-stage Man, as defined by her in a recent article in *Cosmo*, the new type of evolved man who really likes women, who is not confused by his new and as yet not clearly defined role in society/love/bed, etc., and is able to empathise with women's special problems, not least the problem of being a woman, as illustrated by Irma, Anna, Bel and so forth.

Root parked the Rolls on the pavement and, with a bunch of daffodils in one hand and his brief-case in the other, marched us past the stagedoor-keeper, who cowered in his cubby-hole when he saw who it was. Then it was down a long passage and straight into Miss Jackson's dressing-room without knocking. There were a dozen or so people in the room, sipping drinks and laughing theatrically, but there was no sign of Glenda herself. I did notice Kenneth Williams standing in a corner, listening with an expression of pained forbearance to a common-looking, stone bald little American, who was excitedly informing the room that he was the world's foremost authority on Freud and a great stage-director to boot, though his genius in this department, he said, had gone largely unrecognised by the theatrical establishment in London. But for his collaborative talents, he insisted, the works of J. P. Donleavy would be gathering dust in a sock-drawer and Mr Donleavy himself would be pulling up potatoes in an Irish bog.

'Silence, Hymie!' bellowed Root. The little American's mouth snapped shut. The whole room stared. Root raised his pork-pie hat. 'Norman Norman', he said. 'Plus research assistant, Kim Kimbersley. That is not, as you might suppose, a plug of nasal phlegm in his nose, but a stud. Young people. Step forward, lad.' I smiled politely. 'Right,' said Root. 'Where is she, the minx?'

At this moment Glenda appeared from an adjoining room. She was looking absolutely magnificent in a flowered silk kimono.

'Christ!' she said. 'Bernard Manning's back.'

Root took me to one side. 'A word in your ear, lad. It's the maid. She was here last night. I think I mentioned her. She hands round the drinks.' He turned to Glenda. 'Mine's a gin and tonic and the lad will have an orange juice. Big night ahead of him, do you see?' He chuckled fruitily. 'Chop chop woman! And put these in water before they die. Cost me £3.99.' He handed the daffodils to Glenda. 'Tell the minx we're here.'

I bent down to whisper in Root's ear. 'That's not the maid,' I said. 'That's Miss Jackson.'

Root recoiled with surprise, stepping on the excitable little American's toes.

'Watch it!' screeched the little American. 'I'll sue! Litigation will take place. You'll hear from Rubinstein! I have projects to set up – back-to-back, world-wide, revolving credit – and you've trodden on my foot! I'll sue! You'll get a writ! I'll take you for millions! I'll be rich!' He was beside himself, purple with fury, hopping about the room.

'You fucking little monkey!' cried Root, catching him in mid-hop and taking him by the throat. With his spare hand he raised his pork-pie hat. 'Pardon my French, ladies,' he said, 'but this little monkey got my goat.' He opened the door and threw the little American into the passage. 'On your way, Hymie!' he snarled. He closed the door and wiped his hands on Glenda's curtains as though contact with Hymie might have soiled them. 'Sorry about that', he said. He turned to Glenda. 'Is that right, madam? Is the lad correct? Are you in fact Miss Jackson? I confess I can scarcely credit it.'

'I most certainly am', said Miss Jackson icily.

Root looked her up and down. 'You've been in a fight, is that it?'

Glenda lost her temper. She appealed to the room. 'Who *is* this frightful man who keeps barging into my dressing-room? Can just *anyone* get in? Am I to be at the mercy of any fat lunatic wandering in off the street? That dreadful little American was bad enough.' She rounded on Root. 'Who *are* you?'

'Norman Norman, madam', said Root. 'And may I say what a remarkable thing stage make-up is? Whoever does yours should win an Oscar. Perhaps he has. That's by the way, however. We represent Lord Weidenfeld of Nicolson on this occasion and . . .'

Glenda was amazed. '*George*?' she gasped.

'If you must,' said Root, 'but I haven't got all night. It's women, do you see? Every aspect of the matter.' He addressed himself to the room. 'I'd be obliged if you'd fill these in.' He opened up his brief-case and produced a pile of questionnaires, which he handed to the assembled women. 'You'll find it quite straightforward. Who? Where? Why? What? Has M and S been attempted?' He handed one to Kenneth Williams. 'You look as if you'd like a trussing, madam. Ah! Here's your date, lad.'

A middle-aged woman, who looked a little like Virginia Woolf but worse, had just come in. She wore beads and a long dress the colour of a cowpat, her greying whispy hair was gathered in a bun, she had watery, pale blue eyes and large, yellowing, horse-like teeth. She looked like a woman who might play the cello in a string quartet. She was pretty rough. There was no obvious reason, as far as I could see, why Root should have confused her with Glenda Jackson – which was clearly what had happened. Both were tall and somewhat angular, but there the similarity ended. Who she was remained a mystery for the moment, though she clearly wasn't the maid. She was probably some mad old theatrical groupie who had been hanging around Glenda's dressing-room the night before and had now returned to keep her date with me and Root. I was a little disappointed, I must say. She greeted Root enthusiastically, bearing her yellow teeth and planting a wet kiss on either cheek. Root flinched and pushed her off, batting at the air between them with ham-like fists.

'You're late, my good woman', he said. 'We can't waste any more time here.' He doffed his pork-pie hat and bowed to the room. 'Don't forget to return the questionnaire. I'll bid you all goodnight. Come along, lad.'

He bundled us out of the dressing-room and down the passage. The demented little American was crouched in a dark corner, seething and chattering distractedly to himself. 'I'll sue them all! Then they'll notice me! And when I'm dead the masterpieces will come to light. My genius will then be recognised. They'll all look very silly when I'm dead. In the morning I'll see Rubinstein. Rubinstein will issue writs!' Root stamped heavily on his bad foot as we passed, causing him to yelp and hop about. His demented gibbering – 'I'll sue! I'll sue them all!' – followed us out of the stage-door and all the way to the Rolls. I might have felt sorry for someone so obviously crazed by failure had I not been worrying about my own predicament. Research was research, but dinner alone with this fairly barmy-looking woman was a depressing prospect. After the introductions – I didn't catch her name, but I think it was something pretty silly like Myrtle or Christobel – I fell into rather a boorish silence, I'm afraid, which I maintained all the way to Putney. Root came into the restaurant with us, which rather cheered me – perhaps he'd decided to join us after all – but my hopes were dashed as soon as we got to our table.

'Safely delivered,' said Root, 'so I'll leave you to it. I've ordered for two. It's the prawn cocktail, escalope de veau and choice of wines. Enjoy yourselves.' He winked, causing my companion to giggle archly. 'I'll be off, then.'

'Oh dear', said Myrtle, if that was her name. 'Are you leaving me all alone with this young man? Will I be safe?'

'Other matters to attend to', said Root. He winked again. What was he up to? The uncomfortable thought crossed my mind that he was off to visit the Duchess of Argyll. While duty to the project held me here, he was off to endanger my trust funds.

'Where are you going?' I said.

Root smiled mysteriously. He twirled his moustache importantly, like an old-time trapeze artist about to perform a triple somersault. 'Never you mind, lad.'

He *was* off to see the Duchess. Only my sense of obligation to the book kept me in my seat.

'Don't be frightened, dear', said Myrtle. She patted my hand with be-ringed, spindly fingers and lasciviously bared her enormous yellow teeth and glistening gums. 'I'll look after you.'

I didn't much like the sound of that. Root winked again and left.

'Tell me about yourself', said Myrtle.

She was gazing at me in an understanding way, which was pretty daunting. Her lips curled back over her wet gums, like a horse expecting a lump of sugar. I told myself that this was research, that I was up at the sharp end on my own and that I mustn't let Root down. Myrtle wasn't Glenda Jackson, but she was a woman. And I might learn more from her than I would have done from Glenda. With Glenda, personal feelings and desires might have obtruded, most unprofessionally, to the disadvantage of the work in progress. I began to enjoy myself, to revel in the confidence placed in me by Root. I took out my reporter's pad, ready to take notes. Judging by Myrtle's answers on the questionnaire she was a pretty remarkable woman. She'd have a tale to tell and no mistake. I wrote 'mad old theatrical groupies' at the top of a clean page.

'Let's talk about *you*', I said. There might be a whole chapter in this. 'There seems to have been a mix-up.'

'A mix-up? I don't understand. What mix-up, dear?'

'Last night. My collaborator seemed to think you were Glenda Jackson.'

Myrtle trilled delightedly. 'I *know*. Wasn't that amusing? I didn't mind, even though she must be *years* older than me. I tried to tell him countless times, but he simply didn't listen. He never stopped talking himself. He is a character, though.'

'Yes, isn't he?'

Suddenly Myrtle took my hand in a crab-like claw and gave me a fairly sickening 'you can tell me anything' smile.

'So', she said. 'You're the naughty boy who wants to have his bottom smacked!'

I was a bit surprised. 'Who told you that?'

'Why Mr Norman, of course. He said he was quite worried about you. He said you kept bringing up the subject of something called *le vice anglais*.' She gave my hand a reassuring squeeze. 'Don't worry, my dear. It's nothing to be ashamed of.' She laughed flirtatiously, spitting quite heavily as she did so into my prawn cocktail, a limp-looking concoction that had just been put in front of me. 'Who knows? Perhaps if you're a good boy ...'

Why had Root done this? He must have had his reasons. Whatever they'd been, I mustn't let him down. It was clearly my duty to play along with this, to draw her out. By pretending to an enthusiasm I didn't have I might gather telling information, about Myrtle and, by extension, about all women. I quickly wrote 'naughty boy', 'bottom smacked', 'le vice anglais' and 'spat at – see prawn cocktail' in my notebook.

'Well', I said, 'I've always thought that I might ...'

I was distracted at that moment by a loud, whinnying voice behind me. 'Full as a boot I was', it said. 'Had a skinful, do you see? Went smack into a bollard. What a prang! Wrote the car bloody well orf! Third this year. Plus some bloody gendarme tried to nick me. I arsk you!'

It was my friend Ned, accompanied by another blank-faced Henry and a very pretty girl whom I'd not seen before. And coming round the corner into view was a second, even prettier girl, who looked amazingly like Charlotte. Which wasn't so amazing really because it was Charlotte. I quickly turned away and tried to hide my head in my prawn cocktail, but it was too late. Ned had spotted me.

'Kim lad!' he bellowed. 'Long time no see! What brings you to this God-forsaken neck of the woods? Just telling Camilla here about . . . my Good God Almighty!' He'd seen my companion.

'Research', I said quickly.

'*Research*?' said Charlotte, coming up to the table.

I tried to withdraw my hand from Myrtle's grip and in the struggle knocked my reporter's note-book onto the floor. Myrtle laughed girlishly. 'He's shy, the dear boy. Isn't that adorable?' She tut-tutted scoldingly. 'Why don't you tell your young friends the truth?'

Charlotte picked up my reporter's note-book. '"Mad old theatrical groupies"?' she said. '"Naughty boy"? "*Bottom* smacked"? "Spat in prawn cocktail"? "*Le vice anglais*"? *That*', she said chillingly, 'is something I definitely don't want to know about.' She drew herself up to her full five foot nine inches of inherited *hauteur* (at West Heath the Princess of Wales had pipped her by the merest fraction for the best kept hamster award) and handed back my reporter's note-book. Her large, dark eyes blazed with contempt. At any other time I would have found her joltingly lovely. 'Come along, Ned.'

The other very pretty girl shot me an appalled, disgusted look, and then they made their way to a table in the corner. Suddenly I felt rather sick, whether from this unpleasant episode or from the prawn cocktail I couldn't tell. Without giving Myrtle any sort of explanation I got up from the table and stumbled across the room towards the gents, passing Charlotte's table on the way.

'Bottom's up!' cried Ned, cackling like a jackass. At least Charlotte didn't laugh. She just stared at me pityingly, and then looked quickly away.

Once in the gents I found I no longer wanted to be sick, but I was suddenly very depressed at the thought of rejoining Myrtle and continuing with my researches. It was very unprofessional of me, and Root would be entitled to be furious, but I'd had enough. A small window above my head offered an escape route. By scrabbling up the urinal (twice slipping splashily into it and ruining my Manolo Blahnik shoes) I found I was able to get my head and shoulders through the window, but at that point I got stuck, with my trunk in Putney High Street and my legs in Mario's gents. And there I might have stayed all night had not Mrs Root walked past at that moment, accompanied by a toy-boy (and, I must admit, a very pretty one at that) who was wearing a Charlie Allen suit like mine, though his accessories, I was glad to see, were less effectively assembled.

'Hullo, love', said Mrs Root, in a perfectly matter-of-fact way, as if finding her husband's research assistant stuck half-way out of a lavatory window in Putney High Street was the most natural thing in the world. 'Are you coming or going? This is Kevin, by the way. Can we help?'

What a perfectly splendid woman she is. No startled demand for an explanation; just that cheerful introduction to her toy-boy and offer of assistance. With her hair lacquered into a glossy beehive and her ripe curves spilling invitingly out of a tight trouser-suit made of some shiny, fluorescent material, she looked every bit as striking as her companion. I desired her strongly, and realised how fortunate I was that she had come across me like this rather than sitting cosily with Myrtle. If she'd seen me with Myrtle, that would have been the end of all my hopes.

'I'm stuck,' I said.

'Never mind, love', she said. 'We'll have you out in two shakes.'

She reached up and, taking my hands in hers, pulled mightily. I shot out of the lavatory window, falling on top of Kevin and, I'm happy to say, knocking him backwards into the gutter.

'Here!' he cried. 'Me new suit!'

'Never mind the new suit, dear', said Mrs Root. 'We've got the lad out and that's the main thing. Oh I say! You're wearing the same suit. That's nice. So, what happened, love?'

'I suddenly felt sick', I said.

'Of course you did, you poor boy. The food *is* rich here.' Anyone else would not have thought feeling sick a sufficient reason for exiting through a window in the gents. What a truly remarkable woman she is. 'So you won't want to come back inside with us? You'd be very welcome, love. Wouldn't he, Kevin?' Kevin growled and whimpered at the same time. Suddenly Mrs Root winked theatrically. 'It's my pottery night class', she said. 'Not a word to Mr Root.' I felt a stab of jealousy. Discovering that she *did* like toy-boys was more than cancelled out by the discovery that she already had one – and a very pretty one at that.

'Your secret's safe with me', I said, in a lemony tone of voice that must have been rather more self-revealing in its frostiness than I'd intended because Mrs Root looked at me quickly and then gave a little understanding smile. I tried to hit a lighter note. 'I'd have loved to join you both,' I said, 'but actually there's someone in there I'm trying to avoid.' That was certainly true. If Mrs Root saw me with Myrtle I'd never be able to look her in the face again.

'You've got a girl in there, haven't you?' said Mrs Root. She smiled approvingly. 'She'll be lovely, I bet.'

'Well actually she is, yes, very lovely, but . . .' I smiled modestly, suggesting, I hoped, that to a man of the world like myself one beautiful girl was much like another and that even now I had a dozen in different restaurants all over London, whom I could only accommodate by climbing suavely in and out of lavatory windows. I shrugged and spread my hands. At that moment Myrtle came out of the restaurant and, spotting me, gave a little cry of triumph and ran towards us.

'You *naughty* boy!' she trilled. 'You're going to get your bottom smacked, just the way you like it!'

'Oh dear', said Mrs Root. 'Oh dear, oh dear. I'd never have expected it.' There was an expression of infinite disappointment on her lovely face.

I could have explained. I could have said it was research for our book, but suddenly I'd had enough. I took off, not caring if this looked like skittishness on my part, and sprinted down the street. I wanted only to get home, to climb into bed and to pull the sheet over my head. The buses seemed to have stopped running and I couldn't find a taxi, so I stumbled all the way from Putney High Street to the Fulham Road, falling over from time to time and finding myself the butt of much late-night ribaldry from jerks in sports cars. Arriving home utterly spent, I was too exhausted to undress or take my make-up off. I climbed straight into bed in my Charlie Allen suit and turned my face to the wall. Perhaps things would seem better in the morning. Perhaps I would have forgotten how appallingly I'd let my partner down – and that look of disappointment on Mrs Root's face.

SATURDAY 30 JUNE

I woke up feeling as if I'd been hit on the head with a hammer. I felt sick and I had a huge boil on my nose, probably the result of going to bed without taking my make-up off. I felt really depressed. Worse than the memory of Charlotte's look of icy contempt and Mrs Root's expression of infinite disappointment was the realisation that I'd let Root down, left my post without completing the research. I sulked indoors all day behind drawn curtains. I neither shaved nor took a bath. I noticed that the trousers of my Charlie Allen suit were torn. The phone rang from time to time but I didn't answer it. I'd said I'd go home for the weekend, so it was probably Gay wondering where I was. I was reminded of Brigadier Wordsworth's pheasants. Perhaps, later in the day, I'd feel strong enough to eat them. I tried to pluck them. I'd never plucked a pheasant before. It was harder than I'd expected. I ripped and tore at them until they looked as if they'd lost a street fight with a mad cat. By the time I'd finished they were fit only for the garbage bin and I had blood, guts and feathers all over my Charlie Allen suit.

Twice there was a ring at the front door. I ignored them both. It could have been the police, here to arrest me for a variety of grave offences, including kidnapping, racism, GBH, attempted bribery, leaving pornographic questionnaires with away-day ladies from the north, writing smutty letters to the Duchess of Argyll and a new one: exiting from Mario's in Putney High Street through a window in the gents, leaving an unpaid bill.

An utterly unhelpful letter arrived from Jan Leeming's secretary. Apart from mistaking me for a girl, she gave me a lot of information I already had.

BBC TELEVISION NEWS
Television Centre · Wood Lane · London W12 7RJ · Telephone 01-743 8000

24th August 1984

Dear Ms. Kindersley,

Thank you for your letter to Jan Leeming who has asked me to reply.

As Miss Leeming gives some of her clothes to Charity Auctions, and keeps the classics and the ones she specially likes wearing - she cannot help you apart from telling you the designer names of the clothes she wears, then you could possibly look for the names yourself.

Tricoville and Parigi she has most of her clothes from them. Other names she wears are Gina Fratini, Christyne Forte and Gino Ferrare. Incidentally she is a size 10.

Yours sincerely,

Lydia Rider.

(Lydia Rider)
Secretary, Newsreaders' TV News

By the evening I had begun to think I should resign from my job. Of what use to Root was a research assistant who abandoned his duties uncompleted, exiting buffoonishly through windows and then, instead of explaining the circumstances, lit off like a startled rabbit? I'd let him down badly.

SUNDAY 1 JULY

Felt pretty low for most of the day – too depressed to go out for the Sunday papers – but by the evening, thanks to reading a chapter or two of Anna Raeburn's inspirational *Talking To Myself*, I began to feel a little better. It is absolutely superb, as was to be expected, moving, viable and extraordinarily caring. 'This book isn't for me', she writes in her introduction. 'It's for the boys who lined up for an autograph and a kiss at the only disco I've ever attended. It's for the girl who saw me walking down a street, recognised me and squeezed my hand as she went past, without a word. It's for the couple who stopped me on 5th Avenue to say: "We think you are the most beautiful girl we've ever seen". It's for the girl who wrote to me at *Cosmopolitan* saying: "I shall feel less safe as a woman when you stop speaking up for me".' What a marvellous person she must be. Her account of her feelings after her abortion is one of the most tactful, moving pieces of writing I've ever come across. 'Whenever I think about it,' writes Anna, 'I think of a song Edith Piaf made famous called *Je Ne Regrette Rien* and I think what a proud boast that is. I have prayed and I do regret, I do, I do indeed.'

Suddenly my own small troubles seemed absurdly trivial compared to the colossal burdens uncomplainingly borne on our behalf by Anna. I was strong enough now to make a decision. Would I spend the rest of my life hiding in a dark room, or would I go back to work tomorrow to face Root's anger and Mrs Root's contempt? There was no doubt which option Anna would have chosen. Having spent many years redefining her validity and discovering who she really was, she would have performed the self-assertiveness test, gazing sternly at her reflection in the mirror and crying: '*I AM ME!*' Then she would have marched off bravely to face the worst that life could offer. I would do the same. Tomorrow I'd go back to work, resolved never to let Root down again. Thank goodness for Anna Raeburn.

MONDAY 2 JULY

Horrors! I couldn't go to work after all. The boil was back, and twice as big as before. In spite of my Anna-inspired resolve of the night before, I realised I couldn't possibly risk Mrs Root seeing me like this. I rang up Root. I told him that I had got food poisoning at Mario's and was still too weak to come to work. To my surprise, Root was most sympathetic. 'Don't worry, lad,' he said. 'Get your health and strength back. Fact is I need you at my side.'

I found this immensely reassuring. We were still a team in spite of my failure on Friday night. And nothing, I now saw, had happened which was so appalling that I couldn't explain it, if I got the chance, to Mrs Root. Tomorrow I'd dress with special care. I would astonish her. I would replace Kevin in her affections. Kevin, in my assessment, had the appearance and address of a hairdresser. His suit had been okay, but his accessories had been utterly uncoordinated. If I couldn't win the inside track from a hairdresser who couldn't even coordinate his accessories something was seriously wrong.

I put a piece of plaster on my nose and went to the Pan Bookshop, where I bought Stephen Vizinczey's famous novel *In Praise Of Older Women*. Passing Bolton's Wine Bar on the way home I bumped into Charlotte and Ned. Ned stared rudely at my nose. 'I thought it was your bottom you wanted to be smacked', he said. I ignored them and walked on. They are sadly immature, and more than welcome to each other.

TUESDAY 3 JULY

I woke up feeling totally refreshed. Even the boil on my nose seemed to have receded, as though by magic. I dressed with special care. If Mrs Root came into the ops-room today I'd dazzle her. By the time I left for work I was looking and feeling really good. How strange life is. Two days ago the world seemed dark and arbitrary. I was a victim. A punch-bag in fate's gymnasium. Now the sun was shining, there was a spring in my step and, with my creative batteries recharged, I viewed the world and my chances in it with unquenchable optimism. I suppose these swings of mood, these switchback ups and downs, are the price one pays for having the artistic temperament.

In the ops-room, Root greeted me solicitously.

'You better, lad?' he asked. He looked really concerned. 'I was worried, I don't mind admitting it. You're sure you're up to it?'

I was touched. My resolve never to let him down again was doubly strengthened. I assured him that my recovery was complete.

'Good night out, was it?' He winked. 'Friday night?'

I said that apart from the food poisoning it had been fine. How much did he know? Mrs Root could hardly have said anything without incriminating herself. It gave me a small, pleasurable twitch in the stomach to realise that we shared this secret, Mrs Root and I, that each of us had something on the other, so to speak.

'Got back in the small hours myself', said Root. 'Long time since I'd been up West. Did a tour of the old haunts. All gone. Percival Murray's Cabaret Club a garage. Jack Spot's *La Dolce Vita* a wholesale fruit-shop. And The Coq Sportif? It's become an old-time delicatessen, lad, run by an Italian character in an apron, helped by his cheery wife. Can you beat it? They're trying to turn Soho into an agreeable little village, fit only for family shopping. Disgraceful. When I got home, I happened to pass Mrs Root's bedroom. She was talking in her sleep. Calling out a name, she was. "Oh Kevin, Oh Kevin," she kept saying. Over and over again. Must have been having a nightmare. Poor woman.'

I froze. The toy-boy had been back! He'd stayed the night! His name was like a knife between my ribs. I mustn't show the pain, but it hurt intensely.

'Thought of going in and waking her', continued Root. 'Decided not to in the end. In her sleep she might have got me in a wrestling hold. In the old days her arms would suddenly ...' He broke off. He shuddered. 'Nasty, I can tell you. Anyway, I thought it best to proceed to my room.'

What did he know? Mrs Root said he noticed nothing, but he was squinting at me cunningly now, he seemed to be testing me in some way. I should warn her. But if I did, she might think I was jealous, that I was trying to put her off her toy-boy.

'Anyway', said Root. 'That's neither here nor there, eh lad? Better press on. It's the letter "B", if I'm not mistaken. Budd, Zola. Paying off for *The Daily Mail*, wouldn't you say? The Zola Budd experiment? Had this concept while you were off. Thought I might write to my pal the Lord Matthews. Suggest *The Daily Express* sign up some Canadian canoeists and have them paddle for England at the next Olympics. Have you seen the Canadians paddle, lad? I tell you! Three Canadians in a bucket could win the America's Cup.'

'That's a brilliant concept, sir, but we really haven't finished the letter "A" yet.'

Root was aghast. 'Can that be so? The questionnaire's gone out, lad. That, surely, will polish off all those friends of yours – the one that goes like a rocket, Lady Annunziata Whatsit and so forth. What's still to do?'

'Well, sir, there's Abroad. American women, African ...'

'*Abroad*!' Root was horrified. 'I've never got on too well with abroad, lad. Not since being over-charged in Llandeilo. Only been abroad on one other occasion. Marbella. Eight years ago. Think I mentioned it. Surely we don't have to go abroad, lad?'

'I think we should, Mr Root.' Abroad was outside our brief, no doubt, but I was keen to string the project out – I was on a retainer, after all – and I might be able to get Root out of the country for a time, leaving Mrs Root behind. 'Australian women, Asian women, African women, American women. They all begin with "A", Mr Root.'

'That's true.' He thought about it for a while. He tugged at his moustache. 'Hm. Australian women. Know something about Australian women, as it happens. The men ride side-saddle and wear lace body-stockings under their business suits. Gay capital of the world, do you see? Sorry. Your father. Been there, has he? Anyway, the women as a consequence are the most frustrated on earth. At a beach barbecue they'll wrestle you upside down and stick a chop-bone up your arse. Trouble is they all look like Kerry Packer.'

'Come sir! Germaine Greer?'

Root winced. 'That's right, lad. They all look like Germaine Greer, the big doughnut. Imagine this. You're alone with Germaine. She's of a mind to read you extracts from her work. She has you down and takes you in a head-scissors. I'd box her off, but things would go badly for the average man.'

I tried again. 'Olivia Newton-John?'

'Right again, lad. You're getting the picture. All the men look like Olivia Newton-John. We'll not be flying Qantas to Australia, I tell you that. Next!'

'American women?'

'Mad, that's my guess. Skins like leather and veins like ships' hawsers, due to aerobics. Because of facelifts, few can smile without hitching their knickers up. Take Nancy Reagan. Plus there's the Women's Movement. Due to IRA influence the women of California pack their sexual organs with industrial dynamite and incite rape attacks in crowded supermarkets. We'll not go to America, lad. Next!'

'Asian women, sir.'

'No need to go to Asia, lad. We can farm this out to my young friend Waugh. He speaks most highly of the massage parlours of Bangkok. Fat literary men from England are especially welcome at the massage parlour of Bangkok, being happy to recline like Wallies on the slab having oils rubbed into their little pot-bellies. Makes a pleasant change for the girls, do you see? Your Asian male is more demanding. He's an active little monkey, your Asian male. Don't be fooled by the absence of body-hair. He'll hop around the room, your Asian male, and then drive in from an unexpected angle. Next!'

I was determined to get him somewhere. 'What about Europe?'

Root pulled a disapproving face. 'Not too keen on Europe, lad. Did I mention the Major's experience of Europe? He was eager to get away, do you see? Brain shot out at the Upland Goose. Needed a break. Saved up all year. Not a rich man, the Major, and this was to be something of a last fling. Always been interested in women. Bit of a womaniser, to tell the truth. Odd that. Sensible man in other respects. Anyway, he intended to have an experience to last him the rest of his life, do you see? This would be it. His last stand, as it were. He studied the brochures and finally made his choice. A Greek Island. Then he spent money on a summer wardrobe. A range of Lacoste T-shirts and accessories by Ardidarse. Spent six months getting into shape. In here every evening working on the weights. Taking it seriously, do you see? This was his last chance. Make or break. The big day came. Gatwick at some unearthly hour and by lunchtime he's outside a little Taverna sipping whatever. It's everything he could have wished for. The sun. The wine. The orange trees. The agreeable unspoilt local folk. And, best of all, an abundance of pretty, available girls – American students for the most part, yomping earnestly through Europe. "This is it. I've cracked it here", the Major thinks. That night he's enjoying a drink outside the taverna with a group of laughing young folk when he notices bright lights across the bay and the sound of girlish laughter wafting over the water from a nearby island. He decides to check on this with the taverna owner. "What's over there?" he asks. "Paradise", says the taverna owner. "Even better than this?" asks the Major. The Taverna owner winks. "So they say." He mimes someone getting out of their clothes. "They're nudists?" asks the Major. "Nudists, that's right", says the taverna owner. "Run around all day without their clothes, making love." That was enough for the Major. That was the place for him. The boat only went there once a fortnight, but as luck would have it tomorrow was the day. The next morning the Major's on the jetty with his suitcase. The boat arrives, the Major jumps aboard. As they approach the island he hears the sound of laughter and can see naked bodies gambolling on the beach. This indeed would be an experience to last a lifetime. It's off with the Ardidarse accessories and he hops ashore as naked as a plucked chicken. A nude man approaches, bollocks swinging. He touches the Major. "Your nipples, sir", he says, "are like the first primroses of spring." The Major gazes around him. He is surrounded by naked men. There's not a woman in sight. It suddenly dawns on him. He's on an island reserved for gay naturists. He clutches his suitcase and high-tails it down the jetty. But the boat has already left. And there won't be another for a fortnight. He was stuck there for two weeks, lad, cheek by jowl with international benders. Been saving up for six months, do you see? His last holiday. I tell you, lad, by the time he got home his hair had turned white. Couldn't speak for a week. Had to go to bed. Still a bit odd. Don't mention Greece if you should meet him, lad. No – I'm not too keen on Europe, that's the truth of it.'

I wasn't going to give up yet. A terrible experience indeed, I said, but an isolated incident surely, one easily avoided with a little care. The Major, it must be said, had been a trifle hasty. I extolled the advantages of other parts of Europe, particularly Spain. Spain provided a priceless opportunity, I said, for Root to study the effects on female behaviour of the democratic process. He could do a grand tour of Europe comparing the women of the old democracies with those of the new. Anna Ford would have nothing as relevant as this. Root was impressed.

'A grand tour, eh? You might be on to something, lad. How long would that take? Six days? Into the Rolls and through France on the autopiste, avoiding Belgium. Across the border into Spain, distributing questionnaires. "Buenos dias, senorita. I gather that since the death of Franco you girls go a bit. Gracias." I like it, lad. But first we must satisfy ourselves as to a couple of points. A letter! Root to the Spanish Ambassador.'

139 Elm Park Mansions,
Park Walk,
London, S.W.10.

His Excellency, The Spanish Ambassador,
The Spanish Embassy,
24 Belgrave Square,
London, SW1.

3rd July 1984.

Your Excellency,

Adios! Your local dish, I'm told, is rice and gubbins. Please advise.

For literary reasons I shall shortly be travelling through Europe (not Greece) and plan to visit your once great country. I should be grateful for some information prior to departure as to:

1. Language. Staying in '74 with the Sinclairs in Marbella I had occasion to visit the local supermarket with Mrs Sinclair (Who'd lived in Spain, I may say, for twenty years). She wanted eggs. She flapped her arms and went "cluck! cluck!" but they still gave her toilet rolls. "Funny people, the Spanish," she said at the time, "but you get used to it." Have things improved?

2. Law and Order. I'm told that this is at sixes and sevens since the tragic death of Franco and that on the Costa del Crook English bank robbers now outnumber the locals.

3. Please advise as to local hotspots and redlight districts where young folk can be studied unobserved. I'm told that the senoritas go like rockets these days and that there are floor shows featuring acts as explicit as anything to be seen in France, with the wives of the Government officials dancing on tables and, with encouragement, picking up beer mats with their sexual organs. A mixed blessing democracy, and no mistake.

If you are unable to deal with these questions yourself, perhaps you'd instruct a dogsbody to send me the relevant brochures (illustrated please) and down-town numbers. No tourist junk or traps, you understand. I shall be covering Spain in three days flat so I can't waste time looking round a lot of old cathedrals.

Hands off Gibraltar, your Excellency, unless you want a dumping like the Argies!

Yours sincerely,

Henry Root

Henry Root.

'That should do the trick,' said Root. 'So – what does that leave us with? Remember, we're still on "A", lad. We must be systematic. We must have order.'

'Air hostesses', I said. 'Appliances, Charlie's Angels, Acrobats, Adolescents . . .'

'Adolescents, eh? That's good. That's relevant, wouldn't you say? Where do we find them? Adolescents. The discos, is it?'

'That's right.' This was a brilliant idea. We'd go to a discotheque. I could really help him in a discotheque.

'Tramp, is it?' Jackie Collins? She'd still look good, shot through a sock. Remember that when we get to "C", lad. We'll write to her. Ask for a photoshot through a sock.'

'Not really the place to find adolescents, sir. Tramp is for the older single. Lance Perceval and so forth.'

'Say no more. I have the picture, lad. The older single sniffing coke. "Pardon me, my nose has fallen off." Where, then? The Lone Star, is it? Terence Blacker and The Old Fools? "Tie a yellow ribbon . . ." We'd do the barn-dance, lad.'

'Still not exactly right, sir. Stringfellows, that's the place. Or the Hippodrome.'

'Excellent! We'll go to Stringfellows, you and I. There'll be dancing, is that it? Dancing a bit rusty, as it happens. The foxtrot. The Palais Glide. The Military Two-step. Not quite the thing, eh?'

'Not really, Mr Root.'

'I have it! We'll practise, lad. You teach me the new moves here, and then it's off to Bodys for advanced instruction. At Bodys we'll polish up our steps and quiz the ladies at the same time. Two birds with one stone. First it's the tights. Pardon me, lad, while I put my tights on.'

Root retired to the bathroom, emerging minutes later in his yellow tights and walking shoes. The award-winning marrow between his legs was, if anything, more excessive than I'd remembered. He strutted proudly to the centre of the room and clapped his hands.

'Right, lad! It's the Viennese Waltz. I'll lead.'

Humming an old-fashioned tune from before my time, he took me beefily in his arms and swung me round, actually lifting me off my feet at the fullest point of the twirl.

'We're getting it, lad!' he cried. 'We'll be all right. *One* two three, *one* two three. "Wuuuuuun-de baaaar! Wuuuundebaaaar! We're alo . . . o . . . onnn and hand in glo . . . o . . ove!" '

'Dancing, is it? That's nice. The law are back, Mr Root.'

Mrs Root had come into the ops-room with Sergeant Pyle and Mr Pulley just as Root, with a final flourish, bent me backwards over his knee, holding me tightly in place with my head inches off the floor.

'It's the reverse turn, do you see?' said Root. 'We're off to Shoestrings, the lad and I. Yes, sergeant? What's the lad done now?'

Pyle was thunderstruck, mesmerised by Root's tights and the great pendulum between his legs. At last he found his voice.

'If you could suspend your dancing for a moment, sir.'

'If we must.' Root let go of me so suddenly that I fell in a heap on the floor, cracking my head.

I got to my feet and turned away. Yet again Mrs Root had found me off my feet. It was such a downer I couldn't look her in the face. I went to the desk and pretended to be studying some papers. Pyle read the riot act. He was returning the ten pounds, he said, that Root had stuffed so adroitly into his pocket in the course of his last visit. He was not amused. Nor, apparently, was his superior, Superintendent Ryan. There was talk of wasting police time. Superintendent Ryan, he said, would like Root to call on him at Chelsea Police Station on Friday at 2.30.

'Strange chap, your Superintendent', said Root. 'Doesn't seem to appreciate a sweetener. Not like Sir Kenneth Newman. We sent him money on ... when was it, lad? When did you try to straighten the Commissioner? Never mind. Must have been two weeks ago. He simply trousered it. Not so much as a "thank you very much, that'll come in handy". I tell you what, sergeant. You tell your Superintendent that I'm a busy man. Far too busy to piss about with him down at the Station. If he really wants to see me, he can come here. Not this Friday, I'm off for the long weekend. The Cunard Hotel, Hammersmith, do you see? Have my own suite and credit arrangements there. In cabaret this Saturday, Gladys and the Pimps. A top turn from the late Sixties. The Lord Matthews a personal friend of mine, do you see? If your Superintendent would like to come here the following Friday at about 12.30 I could give him a few minutes. All right?'

Pyle said he would pass on this message.

'Here', said Mrs Root. 'Have you said something nasty about Susan Hampshire yet?'

'We are still on the letter "A", Mrs Root,' said Root. 'And there we are likely to remain unless our friends here stop interrupting literary men in mid-composition and, instead, return to more conventional duties such as clearing the streets of dangerous criminals.' He turned to Pyle. 'You could start with my boy. The lad's a desperate type. Lives with dissident elements in a squat in Deptford. My lad's Mr Big. Don't let appearances fool you, sergeant.'

Pyle made a note of Henry Jr's address. He looked Root up and down, his eyes resting, awestruck, on the tights. 'My God', he said. He shook his head in wonderment. Then he and Mr Pulley withdrew, and Mrs Root departed for the family quarters. I'd not been able to look her in the face. When they'd gone I tackled Root about having grassed up Henry Jr. Although I'd not spoken to him since he double-crossed me with Charlotte, I did think informing on him to the police was going a little too far.

'I know what I'm doing', said Root. 'You read the papers today? This fellow Geoffrey Mycock? Released yesterday by the Lord Chief Justice after doing ten years for a crime he didn't commit. A bit over the odds, what? According to the latest Home Office statistics, five or six years is considered reasonable for something you didn't do. In Chile it's only three or four. No wonder Chile has a law and order problem. Not our concern, however. Point is there's talk that this Mycock fellow will get £100,000 by the way of compensation. That's £10,000 for each year he was banged up wrongfully, you understand. Gave me this concept, do you see? We cause Henry Jr to be arrested for something he didn't do – quite a minor offence, perhaps, carrying two years maximum, say. He does his porridge and then you come forward with an alibi. Night in question you and Henry Jr at needle-class. They'll believe that. Apologies all round and Henry Jr cops £20,000, shared with us because we had the concept. *And* he's been out of our hair for two years. What do you say? A letter! We'll check the details with the Lord Chief Justice. Want his ruling in another matter too. Root to the Lord Chief Justice.'

139 Elm Park Mansions,
Park Walk,
London, S.W.10.

Baron Lane of St Ippollits,
The Royal Courts of Justice,
The Strand,
London, W.C.2.

3rd July 1984.

Your Lordship,

The speculation re financial compensation due to one Geoffrey Mycock, recently freed by your good self after doing ten years in the slammer for a crime he didn't commit, makes me wonder whether there is a fixed scale for miscreants wrongfully gaoled. There is talk that Mycock could walk away with a cool £100,000. Does it follow that were my boy Henry Jr to be banged up for two years for something he hadn't done he would, on release, cop £20,000 plus subsidiary rights? There's no point in my fingering the lad without your assurance that this is money in the bank.

May I seek your advice in another matter? My problem centres on the Police and Criminal Evidence Bill and the powers vested therein (or not, as the case may be) for the private citizen, like Old Bill on the community beat, to stop and search and carry out anal probes on suspicious types, not least our cheery coloured friends. I assume that since the responsible citizen (by which I mean Tories plus those of the Sensible Left) had, prior to the bill, an obligation to effect a citizen's arrest whenever possible, he will, after the passing of the bill, have a similar obligation to stop and probe and hold ethnic minorities incommunicado for up to ninety-six hours. I have sought a ruling on this from the relevant authorities, but so far without success. Some old duffer at 'B' Division called Superintendent Ryan has asked me to go and see him, but the Police

Commissioner has failed to respond altogether, simply trousering the tenner I sent him! Perhaps I could get a ruling from you, your Lordship, before my flying vigilantes overstep the mark (perhaps, too, you could send the Commissioner a well-deserved rocket, pointing out that 'sweeteners' should either be acknowledged or returned.)

Congratulations on your recent initiative in the Lords re the scandal of our times - drugs. What we've got to do, as you have correctly twigged, is get our young folk on to alcohol as quickly as possible so that they no longer sit around in squats minding their own business but start instead to behave like grown men: driving their cars the wrong way up the M1, setting fire to cross-Channel ferries and fighting one another with broken bottles. There's nothing wrong with a little healthy horse-play, your honour, as you have understood.

One for the road, your lordship!

Here's to the Judiciary against the unions!

Yours sincerely

Norman Norman

Norman Norman (aka Henry Root.)

'It's Bodys then', said Root, when that was done. 'Come lad, we'll take the questionnaires. It's a lovely day, we'll stroll it.'

We set off down the King's Road, with Root, in tights, leading the way. He looked good, but you'd have thought, from the interest he aroused on all sides, that no one had ever seen a man in tights before. It was really quite pathetic. We were, after all, at the international headquarters of avant-garde fashion, yet punks with bolts through their noses shrieked and ran for cover and Sloanes, emerging from S and M boutiques selling barbed-wire bondage pants and Hitler T-shirts, yelped and dropped their shopping-bags. Root, quite unconcerned (and correctly so, in my opinion) beamed to left and right and practised his ballet moves.

At the entrance to Bodys, a beady-eyed woman in a white uniform tried to head us off. She had the intimidating aspect of a matron at a mental hospital, but her protests were brushed aside by Root.

'Friends of Hottie's', he explained. 'It's women for Lord Weidenfeld, do you see? The whole shooting-match from A to Z. It's "A" at the moment, madam, but don't worry, we'll get to Hottie under "B". Make a note of that, lad.' He put a beefy arm round Matron's waist and drew her fractionally to one side for discretion's sake. 'A word in your ear, madam. Between ourselves, I hear she goes a bit. Daley Thompson up a drain-pipe in the early hours? Isn't that the size of it? We'll get it under "B". On lad!'

As Matron reached for a telephone (I hoped she was calling Hottie; we could interview her now), Root marched us down a passage, opening and closing doors, until he found the room he wanted. A dozen or so overweight ladies were bending and stretching to a disco-tape.

'It's ballet, is it?' cried Root. 'The *pas de deux*? Don't mind us. Just brushing up. The lad and I are off to Shoestrings.'

He took off his jacket and joined in, still holding his briefcase, hopping and pirouetting round the room, occasionally lifting ladies off their feet in surprise adagio moves. Glad of this opportunity to demonstrate my prowess, I joined in too, my expertise not going unnoticed, I imagine, by the beginners in the class. Nor, more importantly, by Root. I was proving at last that in one skill at least I could excel him, demonstrating what an asset I'd be when we went up west on our disco-run. Suddenly he ran out of puff.

'I'm fucked!' he cried. 'A moment ladies! Stop the music!'

The class came to a halt. Root bent over, gasping for breath, his meaty hands resting on his knees. When he straightened up it was noticeable that his tights had torn between the legs.

'Phew!' said Root. 'It's close in here. You'll pardon me for saying so, but some of you ladies could do with a tubbing. Let's have some windows open.' Suddenly he became aware that the class was staring at him. He glanced down. 'Well well,' he said. 'Gone in the gusset, do you see? Thought there was a bit of a breeze.' He displayed himself to the lady standing next to him. 'Do you see what's happened, madam? Expensive tights, these. Got them at Harrods. Don't worry, I'll take them back.' He raised his pork-pie hat. 'Norman Norman's the name. And this is my research assistant, Kim Kimbersley. The questionnaire!'

As Root rummaged in his brief-case, Matron came bustling in, accompanied not as I'd expected by Hottie but by two policemen – our old friends Sergeant Pyle and Mr Pulley, as it happened.

Sergeant Pyle didn't seem pleased to see us. 'Oh dear,' he said, 'it's you two again, is it?'

Root straightened up and turned to confront Pyle. Matron gasped and Pyle took three paces back as if punched in the chest. Root greeted him cheerfully.

'Afternoon, sergeant. Just handing round the questionnaire. Here you are, ladies.' He looked them over critically. 'You'll be past it for the most part, that's my guess, but do your best. Cast your minds back. Who? Where? Why? When? Has trussing been attempted? We are empowered to ask such questions on behalf of Lord Weidenfeld of Nicolson, you understand.'

That established our credentials pretty clearly, I'd have thought, but while Root and I distributed the questionnaires, Pyle and Matron held an agitated conference. Then Pyle approached.

'Right, gentlemen', he said. 'On the understanding that you now leave quietly, the manageress has very reasonably agreed not to press charges on this occasion.'

Root protested, but at last allowed himself to be ushered from the room. He paused at the door to wave good-bye. 'See you tomorrow, ladies! I'll be back for the completed questionnaires.'

Outside, Pyle delivered a stern warning. Trying hard not to look Root between the legs, he gave us to understand that things would go badly for us should we have the misfortune to cross his path again. After he and his colleague had climbed into their car and driven off, Root suggested that we should take lunch at Stocks-in-Town. I declined, saying that I was behind with the transcribing – which was true.

'As you wish, lad', said Root. 'We're doing well. See you tomorrow, then.'

He swung off in the direction of Sloane Square, still practising his ballet steps from time to time and raising his pork-pie hat to passers-by. I returned home, reflecting that, notwithstanding our brushes with the law and despite the fact that Mrs Root had yet again seen me off my feet, this had been a most successful day. Some of the ladies in the dance class had still had a twinkle in their eyes, in my judgement, and their replies to the questionnaires would undoubtedly yield invaluable material for the book. To gather it, audacity had been required – but audacity was the essence of research and for once I hadn't let Root down. He would see me in future as a fit companion, as a staunch aide, up at the sharp end of literary research.

The telephone rang soon after I arrived home. It was Gay wanting to know why I had greeted Brigadier Wordsworth at the front-door wearing nothing but a plastic bag over my head. What new perversion was this? he asked. Since the experience, he said, the Brigadier had been in shock, handing down sentences of unusual savagery from the bench, witnesses as much as defendants bearing the consequences, Gay informed me, of my performance. So far, he said, two ambulance men, a psychiatrist, a probation officer, three social workers and the local vicar – the latter appearing as a character witness for the prosecution – had each received six months and a bollocking.

WEDNESDAY 4
THURSDAY 5 JULY

The boil on my nose is back. Remembering the article in the *Sunday Times Colour Supplement*, and fearing that it might have been caused by my nasal stud, I went to see Dr Butt, who put me on anti-biotics and told me to take a couple of days off work. I rang Root, who was very understanding. I said I'd use the time to catch up with the transcribing.

On the tapes I found three letters which Root must have dictated last week when I wasn't paying attention. One was to the Archbishop of York, one to Samantha Fox, the Page 3 lovely, and one to Victor Lownes. I typed and signed them on behalf of Root, and sent them off.

139 Elm Park Mansions,
Park Walk,
London, S.W.10.

The Archbishop of York,
York Minster,
York.

29th June 1984

Your Grace,

Paul Johnson, The Daily Mail's occasional guest thinker, pointed out in a recent article that faith is in rapid decline among senior clergy and gave as an example of this the fact that the new Bishop of Durham doesn't believe in God and as a consequence keeps pronouncing on ethical matters that are none of a Christian's business. Lambasting the current rise in phoney sects, Johnson wrote:

> 'I blame the established Churches for the growing success of these sects. They no longer offer the clarity of doctrine and the certitude of faith which simple people demand and have a right to expect.'

I'm with Johnson all the way on this one, Your Grace, and now demand from you certitude of faith by return. I enclose a stamped addressed envelope to facilitate you in this matter. Don't worry if you aren't a believer yourself. As Dr Scruton argues so forcefully, the important thing is to maintain the myth, even though educated people like him know it's a lot of horse feathers. The rank and file must be kept in order and how is this to be achieved without religious sanctions?

I enclose a pound towards the restoration of your roof after God's recent thunderbolt.

Yours sincerely,

J.J. Henry Root

Henry Root.

P.S. I read in a recent Spectator that the thunderbolt 'proves that God has an agreeable sense of humour'. Do you agree?

139 Elm Park Mansions,
Park Walk,
London, S.W.10.

Miss Samantha Fox,
c/o The Sunday Times,
P.O. Box 7
200 Gray's Inn Road
London WC1X 8EZ.

29th June, 1984

Dear Samantha,

In this week's soar-away Sunday Times, under the headline 'The Bedroom Secrets Of The Page 3 Lovelies', you revealed that the veteran heart-throb Tony Curtis has invited you and another busty lovely to share a sunshine holiday at his luxury American mansion.

Forget it, Sam! Do yourself a favour career-wise and accompany me on an investigative weekend (all expenses paid by Lord Weidenfeld of Nicolson) to Stocks, the luxury country home of my good friend Vic Lownes and his wife Marilyn, the big centre-fold.

I myself will be going for purely literary reasons and will not be indulging in the jacuzzi or elsewhere, but what you did would be your business. I can't take my wife, Mrs Norma Norman, on this one, Sam, for reasons that would be obvious to you if you saw her. Like my friend Jeffrey Archer, I have to think of my image. (When did you last see Mrs Archer at one of his celebrity lunches, Sam, and she, they tell me, writes books.)

On our return I would have no objection to your blowing the whistle on me in the Sunday press as per such kiss-and-tell types as Lindy Benson, Vickie Hodge, Mynah Bird, the big Ibo, and the little brunette from the Cadbury's advert who's just dropped John McEnroe in it. I'm writing on women at the moment, Sam, so having my name linked with a busty lovely like you couldn't do me any harm. Since I'm a married man, however, you'll have to sign an undertaking that you won't, in the event of my death, contest my will or otherwise commit a tort by appearing in The Sunday Times in your frillies, as per Fay the big showgirl after Dick Emery the little comic fell off the perch.

I'm writing to Vic today, telling him to expect the two of us next weekend or the weekend after, so look out your country undies, Sam, and get your skates on.

Yours sincerely,

p.p. Norman Norman

Norman Norman (aka Henry Root.)

139 Elm Park Mansions,
Park Walk,
London, S.W.10.

Vic Lownes Esq,
Stocks,
Nr Tring,
Herts.

29th June 1984

Hi there Vic!

How's the marriage working out, you rascal? You'll find the first few years the worst. No, I'm only joking.

It's women here, Vic, so for research purposes I shall be visiting you next weekend or the weekend after, accompanied by Samantha Fox, The Sunday Times's Page 3 Lovely of the Year.

I've not indulged communally before, Vic, so perhaps you'd give me a couple of tips ahead of time. Is it all-in and no-holds barred, or are we paired off on arrival with well-matched contestants as to body-weight and savvy on the mat? Are group activities signalled by you by a blast on the hunting horn or is it help-yourself at any time? Most importantly, how do we know - your circle being a mixed bunch to say the least - who are the guests and who merely the hired help? I'd hate Sam to up-end Nigel Dempster in the hall only to be told that he was serving the drinks on this occasion and doing the washing-up. It's hard enough to get staff these days without guests rummaging for their G-spots on arrival.

Is Marilyn'anybody's? Hands off Sam, you rascal. She's mine!

See you on 14th or 21st July.

Yours in a kaftan,

J.L. Henry

Henry.

FRIDAY 6 JULY

Thanks to the anti-biotics the boil had gone and I returned to work thoroughly refreshed and keen to proceed. Root, however, was in a black mood, brought about by two letters that had displeased him, one from Foyle's and one from the Home Secretary. He handed me the one from Foyle's.

STOCK OF FOUR MILLION VOLUMES

W. & G. FOYLE LTD.

The World's Greatest Bookshop

113-119 CHARING CROSS ROAD
LONDON WC2H 0EB

Directors:
CHRISTINA FOYLE
RONALD BATTY
Giro Account No:
519 1254

Telephone:
01-437 5660
Telegrams:
FOYLIBRA, LONDON, W.C.2.

Please reply to Dept. Post
Quote ref. TF/ROO

139 Elm Park Mansions
Park Walk
London
SW10

31st July 1984

Dear Mr. Norman

Thank you for your letter of 25th June 1984. We apologise for the delay in replying, but as we receive a vast number of enquiries every day there is inevitably a time lapse before they gain attention.

Enclosed is a list of suggestions of books you may be interested to purchase. Naturally, as our store has a stock of over 4000,000 volumes the list cannot claim to be exhaustive, but if you care to call and browse round the shop when you heve recovered from your bad back, our knowledgeable staff will be happy to help you further.

Yours sincerely

pp. Post Dept. (W&G Foyle Ltd.)

P.S. Your £10 will be credited to you.

Registered Office: 6 Long Lane, London, EC1A 9DP   Registered in England 945131

PLEASE REPLY TO DEPT
POST / TF R00

Giro account no: 519 1254

THE WORLD'S GREATEST BOOKSHOP

W & G FOYLE LTD

113-119 CHARING CROSS ROAD, LONDON, WC2 OEB

Date 31/7/84

~~Your~~ Ref. CMC

We thank you for your enquiry and can offer the following books. The details quoted have been taken from the publishers' latest catalogues and if (when your order is received) the books are temporarily out-of-stock, we shall order immediately and advise you accordingly.

W. & G. FOYLE, LTD.

PRO FORMA INVOICE

	£	p
Food From the sea by Nicolson (Cassell)	6	50
Stress and Fish by Pickering (Academic P.)	25	80
A Living From Lobsters by L. Stewart (FNB)	5	00
Treasures of the sea by Cribb (Oxford University Press)	21	00
Ireland Sea Fisheries by De Corcey (Glendale)	10	00
Marine Fisheries Ecosystem by Lavestan (FNB)	9	50
Advances in Aquaculture by Pillay & Dill (FNB)	52	00
Know Your Fish by Brown (Blackie)	2	95
Gareth Edwards on Fishing (Collins)	7	95
Itchen Memories by Skues (Deutsch)	5	95
The Good Cook Fish & Shellfish (Time-Life)	9	25
The FishLover's Cookbook (Rodale)	6	95
Lasalle Adventurous Fish Cookbook (Macmillan)	5	95
Red Sea Reef Fishes by Randall (Immel)	19	50
TFH Book of Goldfish by Neil Tetler (TFH)	2	50
European Inland Water Fish (Multilingual edition)(FNB)	13	00
Surface Mail Postage and Packing		
SUBTOTAL	203	80

TO ORDER - Please fill in the details below and return this COMPLETE Invoice to us **WITH YOUR REMITTANCE**

AMERICAN, FRENCH AND GERMAN CLIENTS

If you prefer to pay in your own currency, you need merely advise us and send your cheque (payable to W.&G.FOYLE LTD) to our bankers as under:-

U.S.A. Manufacturers Hanover Trust Co., 40 Wall Street, New York, 15. (Account No. 0140.0.10198).

FRANCE: Barclays Bank S.A. Cedex No. 24, Paris (Magenta). (Account No. 021445780171).

GERMANY: Deutsche Bank A.G., Filiale Frankfurt, (DM Account No. 72/1845).

Please supply the Books invoiced above, I enclose £

NAME Norman Norman

ADDRESS 139 Elm Park Mansions, Park Walk

LONDON, SW10

Date 31/7/84

Overseas customers (excepting those in Europe and U.S.A.) should add a further £1 for registration.

Foreign Currency
Conversion rates fluctuate very much and you are recommended to ask at your local bank for the current rate of conversion.

Airmail
Airmail charges vary greatly according to destination. Customers are therefore advised to remit a substantial sum to cover postage. Any excess will be credited (or refunded if required).

PLEASE REPLY TO DEPT POST / ...TF R00

Giro account no: 519 1254

THE WORLD'S GREATEST BOOKSHOP

W & G FOYLE LTD

113-119 CHARING CROSS ROAD, LONDON, WC2 OEB

Date 31/7/84

~~YOUR~~ Ref. CMC

We thank you for your enquiry and can offer the following books. The details quoted have been taken from the publishers' latest catalogues and if (when your order is received) the books are temporarily out-of-stock, we shall order immediately and advise you accordingly.

W. & G. FOYLE, LTD.

PRO FORMA INVOICE

	£	p
Your First Goldfish (TFH)	1	99
Complete Freshwater Fishes of the British Isles by Newdick (Black)	2	99
Eels by Whitlock (Wayland)	3	95
The Ocean World of Jacques Cousteau (Angus & Roberts)	7	95
The Salmon Handbook by Sedgewick (Andre Deutsch)	12	95
SUB TOTAL	29	83
Estimated *Surface Mail Postage and Packing*	15	00
TOTAL	248	63

TO ORDER - Please fill in the details below and return this COMPLETE Invoice to us **WITH YOUR REMITTANCE**

AMERICAN, FRENCH AND GERMAN CLIENTS

If you prefer to pay in your own currency, you need merely advise us and send your cheque (payable to W.&G.FOYLE LTD) to our bankers as under:-

U.S.A. Manufacturers Hanover Trust Co., 40 Wall Street, New York, 15. (Account No. 0140.0.10198).

FRANCE: Barclays Bank S.A. Cedex No. 24, Paris (Magenta). (Account No. 021445780171).

GERMANY: Deutsche Bank A.G., Filiale Frankfurt, (DM Account No. 72/1845).

Please supply the Books invoiced above, I enclose £

NAME Norman Norman

ADDRESS 139 Elm Park Mansions, Park Walk

LONDON, SW10

Date 31/7/84

Overseas customers (excepting those in Europe and U.S.A.) should add a further £1 for registration.

Foreign Currency
Conversion rates fluctuate very much and you are recommended to ask at your local bank for the current rate of conversion.

Airmail
Airmail charges vary greatly according to destination. Customers are therefore advised to remit a substantial sum to cover postage.
Any excess will be credited (or refunded if required).

'What do you make of that?' said Root. 'Damn silly, if you ask me. All about fish, do you see? Nothing wrong with fish, but literary types need variety on their coffee-tables. Their list includes nothing by Robert Lacey, you notice, nothing comical by Gyles Brandreth, no TV-tie-ins or illustrated stuff for movie buffs from Penguin, nothing by Paul Johnson *re* castles, nothing about our vanishing coast-line and nothing from our older, more respected houses, such as *The Philip Larkin Pop-Up Book Plus Bingo Offer* from Faber and Faber, or *The Art Of Intimate Body Massage* from Macmillan (Educational). In a nutshell, lad, we'll have nothing on the coffee-table in time for our first literary lunch on Friday 13th.'

I'd forgotten all about the literary lunch; that was certainly something to look forward to. The letter from the Home Secretary displeased him even more.

From: THE PRIVATE SECRETARY

HOME OFFICE
QUEEN ANNE'S GATE
LONDON SW1H 9AT

July 5 1984

Dear Mr Root,

Thank you for your letter of 21 June to the Home Secretary which was received yesterday.

The Home Secretary has asked me to send you his best wishes for the success of your new publication which he will look forward to reading, but to decline your offer of a meeting.

... I am returning the £5 which you enclosed with your letter.

Yours sincerely,

Sarah Charman

SARAH CHARMAN

Henry Root Esq

'Some people you just can't help', said Root. He fell into a gloomy silence. Luckily his black moods never last for very long. Suddenly he slapped his forehead. 'I have it!' he cried. 'We'll proceed without him. That's it. That's what he wants us to do.' Root winked and did an elaborate pantomime, conjuring up an impression of the Home Secretary giving us the go-ahead with a finger-to-lip 'what I don't know about can't hurt me' gesture. 'Can't be directly involved himself, do you see? Wouldn't look good. Wants us to crack on anyway. I see that now. We'll form the fighting fund. The Friends of Leon Brittan. Get some influential folk on our side. Lend it an air of respectability. We need to advertise, lad, listing eminent contributors to the fund. That's what he'd like us to do. It's clear from his letter. I should have caught on quicker.'

I had no doubt Root was right, but I was keen to get on with the book, instead of which we now wasted valuable time, as I saw it, discussing the best place to advertise the Fund and famous people likely to contribute to it. In the end we decided that *The Daily Telegraph* was the best medium for our campaign and that those who, as Root put it, had 'been in the shit themselves', were more likely than others to be sympathetic to the cause. He wrote first to *The Daily Telegraph*.

139 Elm Park Mansions,
Park Walk,
London, S.W.10.

The Classified Ads Dept.
The Daily Telegraph,
135 Fleet Street,
London, EC4.

6th July 1984.

Dear Sir or Madam,

Kindly insert the following advertisement in your personal column at the earliest convenient date:

'Announcing the formation of THE FRIENDS OF LEON BRITTAN FIGHTING FUND to answer in the courts allegations in Private Eye. Contributions should be forwarded to: Norman Norman Esq, 139 Elm Park Mansions, Park Walk, London, SW10. American Express not accepted'.

I note your charges as £5 per line or £4 per line for charities. I assume that this appeal has the status of a charity and therefore now enclose £20 to cover the cost of five lines. I intend to repeat this advertisement with some frequency, naming in the next contributing 'friends' of Mr Brittan's (real friends of Mr Brittan's will, of course, be a little thin on the ground) to encourage the mugs and give the impression that we're on the up-and-up here. I am writing to Cecil Parkinson MP, Lord Lambton and Profumo (pity to put him back to square one again, but there it is), Mr Algy Cluff, Mr Peter Cook and, to add an air of respectability, Mr John Selwyn Gummer. They are all men of the world and will see what's going on, so I expect the necessary permissions re the use of their names by return.

I look forward to receiving your confirmation that the first insertion will take place next week.

Yours faithfully,

Norman Norman

Norman Norman

139 Elm Park Mansions,
Park Walk,
London, S.W.10.

The Rt Hon Cecil Parkinson PC, MP,
The House of Commons,
London, S.W.1

6th July, 1984

Dear Mr Parkinson,

I should like to congratulate you on your recent showing on 'Face The Press' with Anthony Howard. You looked good (mind you, anyone would look good face to face with Anthony Howard) and you left the viewer in no doubt that you're still the man the party needs. You also managed to convey your contempt for that ass Gummer without actually spelling it out. Well done indeed.

I should now like to address you on two rather more sensitive matters.

1. You may have read in a recent *Private Eye* allegations of a characteristically unsubstantiated nature *re* our Home Secretary, Mr Brittan. These cannot go unanswered. The man's dangerously liberal, but the party cannot afford another scandal so soon after your cock-up, so, whatever he may have done, I am forming, with his knowledge and approval, 'The Friends of Leon Brittan Fighting Fund' to nail these allegations through the courts. It occurs to me that as someone who has been in the shit himself as a result of inferences in *Private Eye*, you may well wish to make a generous contribution to the Fund. Cheques should be made out to me and sent to the above address. I am also taking an advertisement in *The Daily Telegraph* announcing the formation of the fund and it is my intention to name therein the initial contributors. May I take it that you have no objection to my utilising your name? If I don't hear from you by return I will assume that you are happy for your name to be promulgated.

2. I am concerned about my daughter Doreen. She is currently a Scargill bully-boy and showing every sign of going the wrong way. I feel she could be straightened out if she were to meet others than Yorkshire miners and Greenham Common women, relieving themselves in the road and taunting Old Bill with their used sanitary towels. Is there a place for her on your research staff, such a position, I gather, being the quickest way to a settlement these days? The lass went to Essex University so is not without an education, having acquired a first class degree in philosophy, politics and sociology, for what that's worth. I, like you, Cecil, have a first from the University of Real Life. Could you at least see the girl? She's no looker, but then nor was Sarah Keays. I address you as a Tory and a father.

Yours sincerely,

Norman Norman

Norman Norman

cc. John Selwyn Gummer MP
Lord Lambton
Lord Jellicoe
Mr John Profumo
Sir John Junor
The Rt Hon Geoffrey Rippon
Mr Algy Cluff
Mr Peter Cook
The Rt Hon Leon Brittan PC, MP
Mr Jeffrey Archer
Mr John Stonehouse

'The book', I said, when these were done. 'I do think we should get on with the book.'

Root sighed and looked displeased. 'Still on "A", lad? Is that it?'

I said we were.

'Hm', said Root. 'I thought we might be.' He seemed momentarily, vis-à-vis the book, to be a pricked balloon. I wasn't too alarmed. All artists suffer these days of bleak disillusion with the work in progress. The thing is to stay loose and wait for inspiration to return. Wasn't it Alexander Chancellor who said: 'The art of writing is to be as relaxed as you would be at an agreeable dinner party or when sending a letter home'? Sure enough, Root suddenly brightened. He banged the desk.

'A concept!' he cried. 'I've had a concept!'

He was more excited than I'd ever seen him. This, I realised, could be the idea that would bring the whole project to life, powering us triumphantly to the top of the charts. I waited patiently while Root, humming to himself and drumming his fingers on the desk, spun the concept through the threshing-machine of his extraordinary mind.

At last he spoke. 'I have it, lad! It's water-tight. Listen to this. We take an advertisement in *The Daily Telegraph* announcing the formation of a "Blacks Go Home Voluntarily" charity. We point out in our advert that, welcome though they are here, many would take the first banana boat home had they the funds. The Government can't put the money up, of course, much though they'd like to. They'd have the race relations industry down on them like a sack of bricks. A thought occurs. Do you suppose there was a race relations industry in Nazi Germany? No doubt there was. Do-gooders at all times everywhere. German equivalent of my pal Alan Williams – the Man They Can't Gag – would have exposed them, of course. Wasn't it Josef Goebbels who pointed out that prejudice was merely inherited wisdom? Actually it was Richard West, but the point holds. That's by the way. The fact is *Telegraph* readers – old ladies, estate agents, prison officers – would fall over themselves to contribute to the fund. We'd raise millions, lad! What do you say?'

Frankly, I was a little shocked. I don't know which was greater: my disappointment that the concept had nothing to do with the work in progress or the damage done to my liberal conscience.

'But Mr Root', I said. 'Isn't that a little racist? No one would believe that all those black folk had gone home *voluntarily*.'

Root stared at me incredulously. 'Oh dear, oh dear', he said. 'I worry about you sometimes, lad. Who said anything about them going? Either involuntarily or of their own accord? We trouser the money *ourselves*, of course!'

I was hugely relieved. Making off with the funds ourselves would be all right. Was it W.H. Auden, the famous poet, or Alan Bennett, the north country playwright, who had it that artists and criminals were but two sides of the same coin?

There was no more work to be done on the book today, however. Root was already totally involved in the practical details of his concept, striding up and down the ops-room, composing the announcement in *The Telegraph*. Judging that the less I had to do with the scheme in its initial stages the better, I made my excuses and let myself out.

SATURDAY 7
SUNDAY 8 JULY

Rather a depressing weekend. The sun was shining, but I still didn't want to go home to the country to be quizzed by Gay. Instead, I sat around in airless rooms worrying about Root. We're making little progress on the book and he seems almost to be losing interest. If we stay in the ops-room his mind dwells on other matters. We have spent more time in the last few days writing letters to politicians than on the A to Z. It would be better, I think, to get him out and about. We need to gather more material from the field. On Monday I shall suggest that we move up to the sharp end, researching adolescents. I can help him here. We shall go dancing. Root had been looking forward to his night at Stringfellows. A night out gathering material will revive him.

MONDAY 9 JULY

I went to work full of literary resolve, and bounced cheerfully into the ops-room. Root, alas, was again cast down, the cause of his gloom being once more the morning post. This had included a letter from *The Daily Telegraph*, seeking further and better particulars concerning the Brittan ad.

The Daily Telegraph

CLASSIFIED ADVERTISEMENT DEPARTMENT
GOTCH HOUSE 30 ST BRIDE STREET LONDON EC4A 4DJ TELEPHONE: 01-583 3939 TELEGRAMS: TELENEWS LONDON PS4
TELEX: 22874 TELENEWS LONDON

Please Quote Our Ref:
BPSD/117 Ext. 204/209

11th July 1984

Mr. N. Norman,
139 Elm Park Mansions,
Park Walk,
London,
SW 10

Dear Sir,

re advertisement:
"Announcing the formation..."

Thank you for your letter of 5th July together with Treasury Notes £20.00.

Before we can insert your proposed advertisement we will require written confirmation from Mr. Brittan that he has no objection to its publication.

Yours faithfully,

L. McDermott

pp B. Padbury (Miss)
Classified Advertisement Department

THE DAILY TELEGRAPH LIMITED REGISTRATION No. 451593 ENGLAND REGISTERED OFFICE 135 FLEET STREET LONDON EC4P 4BL

We now wasted precious time while Root composed a letter to Brittan's PA, seeking the necessary permissions.

139 Elm Park Mansions,
Park Walk,
London, S.W.10.

Miss Sarah Charman,
The Home Office,
Queen Anne's Gate,
London, SW1H 9AT.

9th July 1984

Dear Miss Charman,

Thank you for your letter of 5th July. I am disappointed, of course, that the Home Secretary doesn't wish to see me at this time, but he will be a busy man. Please thank him for his kind thoughts re the book and tell him that it's progressing well. We're still on the letter 'A' at the moment (Lady Annunziata Asquith, the vice anglais, Abba, AC/DC etc - rubber will not be attempted) but should shortly be getting onto 'B' (bondage, Tatti Bourdillon, Dirk Bogarde etc).

Reading between the lines of your letter, I gathered that the Home Secretary would like us to take action on his behalf, the proviso being that he himself could not be seen to be involved. Fair enough. Nod's as good as a wink etc. He will be pleased to hear that I have taken it upon myself to go ahead with'the Leon Brittan Fighting Fund', inserting an advertisment in The Daily Telegraph announcing its formation. I now enclose a copy of the letter I sent them on 5th July together with their reply. As you can see, they want the Home Secretary's approval before inserting the ad, so I would be grateful if you could let me have this in writing as soon as possible. We want to get moving on this one, Sarah.

Can you tell me how you got your job? Frankly, I'm worried about my daughter Doreen and am keen that she should land a position under a member of parliament as being the quickest way to an out of court settlement. What is the first step on the ladder? What were your own experiences, before landing the job, on the, so to speak, parliamentary casting couch? How can I get Doreen an appointment?

I look forward to hearing from you shortly on both matters, Sarah. Don't be confused by the fact that in the correspondence with The Daily Telegraph I use the name Norman Norman. This is for security reasons and not something with which you need concern your pretty little head.

Yours sincerely,

Henry Root

Henry Root (aka Norman Norman)

Root then handed me the letter from Argen Ltd, the experts on security and bugging.

Argen
Limited

Midland House 5 Jubilee Place London SW3 3TD Telephone 01-352 8151 Telex 8811786

Henry Root Esq
139 Elm Park Mansions
Park Walk
London SW10

18 July 1984

Dear Mr Root

Thank you for your valued enquiry. Argen does not have extensive experience of assisting eminent hornithologists, such as yourself, with their pursuits. However, we would expect the quality of the pick-up to be important to success; and there are products on the market which will satisfy your requirements for discreet visual and audio surveillance of birds and their mating behaviour. (Incidentally, reputable enterprises in this industry generally avoid the word 'bugging', as we feel that the derived noun could lead to misconceptions).

The products we have in mind are sold as integral parts of chandeliers, to assist with the study of caged varieties. Portable versions for your field research would need to be specially manufactured to lend verisimilitude to your pretext approaches to the subjects (or objects) of your investigations.

Security, we agree, could be a problem. You might well find yourself the object (or subject) of surveillance, or indeed other forms of physical invasion. And then of course there could be health risks. What aids can firms in this industry offer you?

Clearly, you need to be fitted up for the tasks you will have in hand. How about a one-week course on personal survival in hostile or adverse environments? It will include counter measures, both active and passive, and an intensive programme of sweeping. The special forces will be with you throughout the week. They guarantee that anyone who completes the week will have the fitness and speed of response suited to purposes such as you have in mind. We have reserved a place for you. Please bring your own doctor and arrange insurance cover. We return your down-payment of £5 in anticipation of your cheque for £3,000.

Yours truly

John Fairer-Smith
Managing Director

Directors J Fairer-Smith FBIM CPP G Fairer-Smith

Registered in England number 936793
Registered office 91 Buckingham Palace Road, London SW1W 0RS

'What's your opinion, lad?' said Root when I had read it. 'A joke, do you think? Is that your guess?' He read it carefully for a second time, squinting suspiciously at the paper, holding it at some distance from his body, as if it might be booby-trapped, his lips moving as he read.

I said that I thought it might be.

Root scowled. 'Jokers, eh? In that case we'll not engage them. Don't want jokers to put the hard-ware in. We'll engage others.'

Then he asked me why he had received a letter from the Archbishop of York, agitatedly seeking to dissuade him from 'travelling north this weekend with your friend Miss Fox, since I won't myself be here', and another from Miss Fox herself informing him that 'there is nothing wrong with my roof, but I do agree whole-heartedly with Paul Johnson'.

I admitted that, due no doubt to the side-effects of the anti-biotics I'd been taking, I must have put the letters in the wrong envelopes. Root, to my relief, wasn't in the least annoyed.

'Easy mistake to make, lad', he said. 'Did it myself once. Grassed up Ladbrokes to Victor Lownes, and Lownes to Ladbrokes. Both, as a consequence, lost their gaming licences. Serve them right.'

The memory of this seemed to have put him in a better mood, so it was a good moment, I judged, to take the initiative, to remind him of our plan to study adolescents in the field.

Root was delighted by the suggestion. 'You're on, lad!' he cried. 'Tonight's the night. Tonight we'll go to Shoestrings. What time's curtain up?'

He was momentarily disconcerted when I told him that there was little point in getting there before midnight, but he wasn't cast down for long.

'Never mind', he said. 'We'll make a night of it. No point sitting around here in our disco pumps. We'll visit Soho, you and I. Saw a couple of things the other night we'd do well to research. The sex boutiques, the tableaux vivants, the live shows up alleys, the assisted showers. It's not all family sausage shops and agreeable, unspoilt pubs. Oh no, not by a long chalk. There's research material for the older man in Soho, lad. It'll be up alleys for you and me, a fish dinner and on to Shoestrings.'

He dismissed me then, telling me to pick him up at eight o'clock in the family quarters. This, I realised, might be my last chance to impress Mrs Root (she was bound to be there when I returned for Root), so on the way home I bought some rather interesting coordinated casuals and a pair of all-in-one trouser boots by Ralph Lauren. I washed my hair – not blow-drying it, because that causes split-ends – had a long relaxing bath, covered myself with Christian Dior *Eau Savage* (I had decided to go for a rather more butch image tonight, out of respect for Root, and to show Mrs Root that I was rather more of a man than Kevin the hairdresser), and then spent an agonising hour trying to decide which of my favourite T-shirts to wear: the one with a diamante spaceship flying over Stonehenge or the one with King Kong air-brushed on to it, which lights up by means of a hidden battery. In the end I opted for King Kong.

I was back in the family quarters soon after eight-thirty, which wasn't bad considering the trouble I'd taken with my appearance. Root recoiled with surprise as I entered his lounge-room.

'Good God, lad! Whatever do you look like? It's fancy-dress at Shoestrings, is it? Novelty night, is that it? You've got a monkey on your front.'

'It's King Kong actually.'

'Never mind. We'll smuggle you in somehow. We'll say you're my niece.'

I wasn't bothered. I knew I was looking good. Root, in an old-fashioned dinner-jacket a size and half too small and with his hair slicked down like a twenties crooner's, looked like a bouncer at a Mafia wedding. There was no sign of Mrs Root, so I casually asked where she was.

'Pottery class', said Root. 'Mondays and Fridays.'

Why do I keep forgetting? She was out on the town with Kevin the hairdresser. I felt a momentary stab of jealousy. Root offered me a drink. The cocktail cabinet played *Hallo Dolly* and then dispensed something brightly coloured and absolutely lethal. By the time Root announced that we should be on our way I was completely drunk. Not too drunk, however, not to notice that Root now had an expensive looking camera round his neck, complete with complicated flash equipment, nor that he was carrying a tape-recorder. I asked him what they were for.

'Research, lad. We must record the adolescents at it, do you see? Get the latest mores down on film.'

That seemed sensible.

He was a little drunk himself, I thought. His speech was slurred and it seemed unlikely that his high colour was entirely caused by the starched collar of his boiled shirt. He drove at speed up west, scattering pedestrians and other motorists, and then parked ostentatiously on the pavement in Old Compton Street. He left a note on the windscreen – 'Henry Root. Government Business' – and then marched us towards Brewer Street, where, he said, we would start our researches by investigating Dr Lovejoy's sex-boutique.

'Popped in the other night, lad. There's telling matter under "A". Must stick to the letter "A", do you see? Appliances, Accessories, Aphrodisiacs. Here we are.'

He announced us loudly at the door. 'Good evening all. Norman Norman.' He raised his hat. 'Don't mind us. It's research for Lord Weidenfeld of Nicolson.' He set up the tape-recorder and switched it on. Then he unslung his camera and took some photographs. 'Smile please.' Some of the customers – a cross-section of middle-aged lurkers – left at once and Dr Lovejoy, a large man in a vest, looked at us a little doubtfully, I thought. To reassure him that we were serious people here on business I took my reporter's note-book and started scribbling. Root, meanwhile, had moved to the sex-aids counter, where he rummaged among the appliances on offer, taking them out of their packets and holding them up for inspection.

'Will you look at these condoms, lad? "Tahiti contraceptive sheaths in five adventurous South Sea colours." Bless my soul. Clad in these three black men could link arms on a dark night and attend a fancy-dress party as the Italian flag at half-mast. Nothing like these in my day.'

He waved the condoms under the nose of the punter browsing next to him, a stout, perspiring man in nylon socks. A midlands property developer, I'd have said, or a provincial mayor.

'Anything like these in your day, sir?' asked Root. 'Speak into the microphone, if you'd be so good.'

The Mayor moved off shiftily to the back of the shop, where blue films were being shown in cubicles.

'Suit yourself', said Root. 'My God, what's this? This could spoil your chances, lad. "The Masculiner from the House of Pan, a masturbating device complete with vibrator, £8.99." You'd know all about it if you sat on this, lad. No wonder Clive James publishes with Pan. Nothing by Penguin or Futura, you'll note.'

'A letter, Mr Root? A letter to Futura?' I was on the ball, I had my note-book ready.

'Later, lad. Hullo, what's this?'

His eye had alighted on something called a Thruster. He took it from its box. It was the size of an elephant's trunk, but pink.

Dr Lovejoy approached. It was an inflatable rubber penis, he said, to be worn under the trousers. It occurred to me that it was the last accessory Root would need, but he was immensely taken by it. Dr Lovejoy explained how it worked. Attached to it, and to be carried in the pocket, was a small cylinder of compressed air. At the press of a button the Thruster would inflate instantly like a rubber dinghy. Root was impressed. He started to take his trousers off, explaining that he'd like to try it on. Dr Lovejoy persuaded him to go to the back of the shop, where Root mistook the viewing cubicles for changing-rooms. He banged up and down the line looking for an empty one, causing the doors to fly open on their occupants, many of whom had removed their trousers for ease of viewing. Last in line, crouching in the dark, was the provincial Mayor from the sex-aids counter. Root took him by the ear and hauled him out. 'Steady on', said the Mayor. 'Never mind "steady on"', said Root. 'We're here on behalf of Lord Weidenfeld of Nicolson.' He went into the Mayor's cubicle and closed the door behind him. The Mayor moved off to the discipline corner, where the latest S and M literature was displayed on racks.

After a few minutes, Root emerged from his cubicle, looking delighted. 'I tell you what, lad. They're showing blue films in the changing-rooms.

Not a bad idea, what? Might catch on at Harrods, do you think? I'll alert Tiny Rowland.'

'A letter, Mr Root? A letter to Tiny Rowland?'

'Later, lad. Right. Here goes. Stand back everyone.'

He activated the compressed air and the Thruster came dramatically to life, like a fireman's hose attached to a hydrant.

'Fuck me!' cried Root, recoiling with surprise and cannoning into the Mayor, knocking him and the discipline display to the floor. 'Pardon my French, gentlemen, but it was the Thruster. My word! Will you look at that?'

The Thruster, enormous in its inflated state, strained angrily against his flies. Would they hold? It seemed unlikely. Root helped the Mayor to his feet and brushed him down. Then he noticed the smacking magazines.

'Hullo! What's this? *Kane*? *Swish*? *Sadie Stern*? We're on to something here, lad!' He flipped excitedly through the magazines. He breathed heavily. He adjusted the lie of the Thruster. 'We'll have a selection of these, lad.' He bought half a dozen, and also a copy of Paul Raymond's *Club International*. Then he said it was time to leave. He gathered up his camera and tape-recorder and bowed to the other customers. 'I'll bid you all good-evening. The lad and I are off to Shoestrings.'

Outside in Walker's Court an ITN camera crew, led by Brian Hanrahan, had arrived meanwhile to film an item about Soho. I might have slipped quietly past, but Root doesn't miss a trick.

'Our chance to publicise the book, lad', he said

Brilliant!

'Since the passing of the Obscene Displays Act,' said Mr Hanrahan, 'Soho has changed out of all . . .'

'Never mind that', said Root, stepping in front of the camera and taking the microphone away from Mr Hanrahan. Mr Hanrahan muttered something about being live and tried, unsuccessfully, to wrestle it back. Root beamed into the camera.

'Root's the name, viewers.' He raised his hat. 'It's women for Lord Weidenfeld of Nicolson.' He realigned the Thruster. He gave a short résumé of the book. 'A simple A to Z. That seemed best. Back to back with Anna Ford next spring. Hers will be pornographic, that's our guess.' He turned to me. 'Isn't that our guess, lad? My research assistant, Kim Kimbersley.' I was delighted to be included. I stepped forward. I confirmed that that was indeed our guess. I hoped Charlotte was watching. She'd be impressed. Then Root appealed on behalf of the Home Secretary. He described the allegations. He reminded the viewers of the Parkinson scandal. 'Party can't afford another cock-up. Cheques should be sent to . . . well fuck me!'

The Thruster had exploded out of his trousers, knocking him backwards into Dr Lovejoy's sex-boutique, clutching his pork-pie hat.

He staggered out seconds later, trying unsuccessfully to stuff the Thruster into his trousers. He handed the microphone to Mr Hanrahan. 'Thank you', he said. 'We're off to Shoestrings now.'

We moved off in the direction of Old Compton Street, with Root as he walked, heaving and wrestling and going into sudden angry squats – like a man trying to stuff foam rubber into a cushion cover – as he struggled to get the Thruster back inside his trousers. At last he had it caged. That battle won he was able to turn his attention to the passing scene, researching with an audacity that I, on my own, could never have hoped to equal. Risks were taken and occasional mistakes were made, but that is in the nature of research. Cars were waved to a halt, and their occupants accused, if single men, of being kerb-crawlers, though some, I suppose, may have been innocently employed; and of the many single women buttonholed and invited to speak into the tape-recorder about life as a street-walker, some must have been theatre-goers whose husbands had temporarily abandoned them to park the car. One rather unfortunate altercation did take place outside L'Escargot in Greek Street with a nice-looking couple whom I recognised too late as Bryan Forbes and Nanette Newman.

'Been at it long, have you, madam?' said Root. 'Your secret's safe with us.' He thrust the microphone under Miss Newman's nose. 'A few words into this, if you'd be so good.' He turned to Mr Forbes. 'Just pulled her, have you, sir? Rather you than me, but good luck to you anyway.'

Miss Newman glanced at the bulge in Root's trousers and ran hurriedly into the restaurant, but Mr Forbes seemed ready to protest.

'Now look here ...'

'On your way, John', said Root. 'She'll have her meter running.'

As Mr Forbes followed his wife into the restaurant Root put his arm round my shoulder and began to walk us back down Greek Street. 'We'll write some letters about this, lad,' he said. 'Mary Kenny must be informed. "Soho, once one of London's most agreeable little villages, etc., etc." You take my drift?'

Suddenly he announced that he needed urgently to find a gents. We were outside a live peep-show. 'I won't be a jiffy, lad', he said. 'You do some research in there. I'll be back in a moment. Hang on to these.' He handed me the smacking magazines and then disappeared round a corner.

Here at last was my opportunity to do something useful on my own. Determined not to let Root down, I took out my reporter's note-book and went into the peep-show. I found an empty cubicle and put a fifty pence piece into the slot-machine. A flap shot up, allowing me to peer through a spy-hole into an enclosed, circular cage, with a door on one side. The eyes of fellow punters could be seen peeping lasciviously through other spy-holes placed at intervals round the cage. Seen from above we would have looked like a ring of crouching men peering into a *pissoir* from outside. I just had time to jot this agreeable image down in my note-book before the door of the cage swung open and a naked, scrawnily unattractive girl stepped into the small arena. She had thin, bruised legs and bright yellow hair that looked as if it would break if you touched it. She began to dance suggestively, in a bored, disheartened way. I felt ashamed and looked away. She was quite young, maybe not yet twenty, and already her life had come to this: performing lewd evolutions in a cage for invisible, hot-eyed punters and one beady-eyed researcher. And did the cover of 'research' absolve me of all responsibility for her plight? After the show Root and I should, by all means, present ourselves backstage and quiz her about her life – we had a responsibility towards the book and to our readers – but, as fellow human-beings, we had a responsibility towards her too. We should interview her, certainly, but we should also try to help her, point her, perhaps, towards a better life. I was jotting down 'No man is an island – not even a researcher' in my note-book when a hum of approval round the cage suggested that things were hotting up. I returned to my spy-hole to discover that Root had hurried into the arena, his Thruster rampant. The girl screamed. All round the cage, eyes gleamed expectantly in the spy-holes.

'Mixed, is it?' said Root. 'Never mind. Stand aside, madam.'

With a deep sigh of satisfaction, he relieved himself against the side of the cage, causing the dancer to gyrate more energetically as she tried to avoid a splashing. Root raised his hat and exited through the *artistes'* entrance. I left my cubicle and found myself caught up in a mass exodus of punters, muttering to themselves and shaking their heads in disbelief. Root was waiting for me in the street.

'That's better, lad', he said. 'Strange toilet arrangements round here. Found one in the end. Had to share it with a naked lady. Peep-show any good?'

'It was rather sad', I said. 'There was this girl. Young. Lost. Confused. Dancing naked for a lot of strange men.'

'Dreadful', said Root. 'Someone's daughter, do you see?' He shook his head. 'Tragic.'

'A man came on.'

'There to help, was he? From the council? Missing persons? "Let me take you away from all this." Was that it? Thank God.'

'He pissed all over her.'

Root was scandalised. He stopped dead in his tracks.

'Great heavens!' he cried. 'Whatever next! A man from welfare? Glad I missed that. Another letter to Mary Kenny, I think. Mary Kenny must be informed. Pissed all over her, you say. Well, well, well.'

I hoped it might be time for dinner now – all this research had given me quite an appetite – but walking back down Greek Street we were accosted outside *Les Amis Rendezvous Club* by a very pretty girl who huskily invited us inside. Root decided that we should accept the offer.

'There'll be topless dancing partners, lad. We can practise our steps before we go to Shoestrings.'

I was keen. If the topless dancers were as pretty as the tout, dinner could wait for a while. Ten pounds changed hands and we were sent down a passage into a dimly lit room with a bar and a small area for dancing. Three or four heavily made-up hostesses – none of them topless, alas – were perched on bar-stools, chatting to half a dozen men – one in jeans, the others in city suits. One of the hostesses climbed off her bar-stool and came over to talk to us. She was wearing a short, red-leather skirt, black fishnet stockings and black high-heels: a rather obvious ensemble, I thought, making her look like an extra in *Irma La Douce*, the film about Parisienne tarts starring that very fine actress, Shirley McLaine. Root, who must have been reminded of his nights at The Coq Sportif, was instantly captivated and, raising his pork-pie hat, he invited her to dance. They made an ill-assorted couple on the floor – she towering over him by a foot or more – and one of the city-suited customers, sensing some embarrassment on my part, perhaps, winked at me sympathetically. I returned his wink and smiled in a friendly fashion: gestures I rather regretted when he sidled over and, placing a soft white hand on my knee, invited me to dance. I was saved at this potentially tricky moment by the return of Root, beaming happily and clutching his partner in a beefy waist-hold. I was about to ask her for a dance myself – not so much because I wanted to but rather to mark the card of my city-suited friend – when Root, standing on tip-toe, whispered suggestively in her ear. She giggled flirtatiously and pretended to swat him with her handbag. Root drew me to one side.

'A word in your ear, lad. I think I've scored. It was the Thruster that did it.'

He stood on tiptoe to make another suggestion in her ear, but this time she swatted him rather more earnestly, catching him a tremendous blow, in fact, that knocked his hat off and brought him almost to his knees. Speculation as to how a mere girl had managed such a thing was quickly cut short when she identified herself as Detective Constable Brian Ashmole, adding that we were under arrest for soliciting.

'Do what!' roared Root. 'It's you that's under arrest, you monkey! Wearing a cocktail frock in a public place! Entrapping literary men engaged in research! You come with us, lad!'

Taking D/C Ashmole in an arm-cracking half-nelson, he frog-marched him out of the club and bounced him along Old Compton Street to where the Rolls was parked. He stretched him out on the front seat – 'No good asking you to hold on to him, lad!' – motioned me into the back, and then drove to West End Central sitting on Ashmole's head. On arrival there, Root bundled him out of the car and carried him, semi-conscious by this time, into the station, where he dumped him on the duty sergeant's desk. I kept my distance, rather, since I was still holding the discipline magazines. Root had acted with exemplary resourcefulness and it would be a shame if his entirely justified arrest of D/C Ashmole were to be compromised by *my* arrest as a dealer in porno mags.

'What's that?' said the sergeant.

'One of yours', said Root. 'An *agent provocateur*. Soliciting in *Les Amis Rendezvous*. I used the minimum amount of force necessary to effect a citizen's arrest. Pardon my Thruster.'

D/C Ashmole moaned and tried to sit up. Root took him by the neck and drove his head hard into the desk-top like an auctioneer bringing down his gavil. The desk sergeant peered into Ashmole's face.

'Not one of ours', he said. He hit Ashmole in the stomach. Then he called over to another sergeant who was typing a report. 'This isn't one of ours, is it, Nigel?'

Nigel got up and walked heavily over to the duty sergeant's desk. He was an enormous man. It would be curtains for Ashmole if he was hit by this one. 'No, Trevor', said Nigel. 'This isn't one of ours.' He hit Ashmole in the stomach.

'I'm not asking you to identify him', said Root. He picked Ashmole off the floor, where Nigel's punch had deposited him, and spread him on the desk. 'I'm asking you to take over. I've done my bit in arresting the pervert. Now it's up to you. I'm a busy man. Can't piss about doing your job for you. The lad and I are off to Shoestrings.' He gave Ashmole a parting shot to the stomach. 'I'll bid you good evening. Come along lad.'

We drove back to Old Compton Street, where Root, having parked the car, said that the tussle with D/C Ashmole had made him a little peckish. I'd been looking forward to the promised fish dinner, but Root, to my disappointment, took us into something called the Nosh Bar in Great Windmill Street, where he ate six salt-beef sandwiches, each at a mouthful.

'What a night!' he said, wiping his moustache. 'We've done sex-shops and peep-shows, we've raided a gay club and we've appeared on TV. We're doing well, lad.'

I had to agree. And the best was still to come. I'd played my part, I hadn't let Root down, but so far my contribution had been of a back-up nature. At Stringfellow's, I'd come into my own. Root was an incomparable researcher at street-level, but he'd be out of his depth at Stringfellows.

'Bit of luck his name being Ashmole, what?' said Root. 'I'm referring to the pervert. Begins with the letter "A", unless I'm much mistaken. We're still on "A", I take it?'

I said we were.

'Just as well', said Root. 'Must have order. Must be systematic, do you see?' He consulted his watch. 'It's time to go dancing, lad. It's Shoestrings for you and me. I'll take the magazines. You might get mugged. Can't afford to lose the magazines.'

We walked through Piccadilly Circus and along Coventry Street to Leicester Square, where Root paused outside The Hippodrome.

'Hullo! What's this? Used to be The Talk Of The Town in my day.'

I explained that it was now a discotheque, also owned, as it happened, by Peter Stringfellow.

'We'll give it a go', said Root. 'Used to come here in the old days. Sir Delfont a friend of mine. Saw the Bachelors here on Mrs Root's birthday, as I recall. Not with Mrs Root, of course. Came with the Major, unless I'm much mistaken. A good turn, the Bachelors. Remember the Bachelors, do you, lad?'

He sang two verses of *Charmaine*. A small crowd formed. The doorman, a large man in a uniform, approached.

'Don't worry, lad', said Root. 'We'll bluff you in somehow. I'll mention Sir Delfont. Say you're my niece. Leave this to me.'

The doorman looked at me. 'You can come in', he said. 'But he can't. He's too fat.'

Root's eyes bulged with rage. He clenched his fists. He stood on tiptoe and squinted menacingly into the doorman's face.

'Fetch an ambulance', he said.

'Who needs an ambulance?' said the doorman.

'You will in precisely thirty-three seconds', said Mr Root, 'unless you step aside.'

The doorman got the picture. He stood back and let us in. Once inside, Root was unimpressed, it must be said, by the changes made by Mr Shoestring. There'd been a band in his day, he explained – two, in fact, one straight, one rhumba – and there'd been tables by the dance-floor at which executive dinners had been served, wine included. Nor did the customers impress him.

'Wouldn't have let in types like this in the old days, I tell you that, lad. I must inform Sir Delfont. Still, we're not here to enjoy ourselves. We're here to study the young folk, isn't that it? The latest mores?' He looked around him. 'It's girls only, is it? I'm surprised they let us in.'

I said it was pretty much fifty-fifty as far as I could see. Root was astonished.

'You're telling met that some of these girls are men? Is that what you're saying? It's pot-luck what you get? Never mind. We'll risk it, lad. We'll dance.'

He cast his eye to left and right, finally coming to rest on a rather striking blonde who was chatting nearby to Charlie Althorp. The blonde was wearing a very nice Yves Saint Laurent trouser-suit, but Charlie as usual looked a mess.

'She'll do', said Root. 'Hold these, lad.' He handed me the tape-recorder and the smacking magazines, but held on to the camera and flash equipment. He approached the blonde and Charlie Althorp. I realised, seconds too late, that the blonde was Charlotte's brother, Jasper.

Root bowed to Jasper and raised his pork-pie hat. 'It's the gentleman's excuse me, madam', he said. Suddenly he jack-knifed over. 'Damn. It's the Thruster. I shouldn't have done the bow.' He squatted and wrestled with his private parts until he had the Thruster satisfactorily realigned. 'That's better.' He unslung his camera equipment and handed it to Althorp. 'Haven't I seen your face in the papers? A drugs charge, was it? Never mind. Hold on to these while I take your girlfriend for a spin on the dance-floor.'

Jasper, spotting me, called out for help. 'I say Kim! What's going on actually? What's doing here I say?'

He backed away but Root was on him. 'Aha! A chase, is it? You minx! I know what your sort likes!' He lifted Jasper on to the dance floor and spun him away into the crowd.

'Hullo, love', said Mrs Root. 'On your own, then?'

She was with Kevin the hairdresser, who was looking good, I must admit, in a panné velvet jacket by Janice Wainwright, which I happen to know must have cost nearly £300. Shocked as I was to see them I was yet able to register the awful thought that Mrs Root might have bought it for him.

'No', I said. 'I mean yes. I'm on my own.' I tried to hide the smacking magazines behind my back. I dropped a couple. Kevin picked them up.

'Hullo', he said. 'What's this, then? *Club International*? A bit tame, isn't it, a bit hum-drum for a man of your unusual tastes? What's this? *Sadie Stern*! That's more like it. Model for it, do you?' I tried to snatch it back. 'Hold on! Don't panic, John.' John! This hairdresser had called me John! I'd have punched him on the nose, but I deplore violence. He opened the magazine and sniggered crudely. 'I think we should confiscate this.' He turned to Mrs Root. 'What do you think, my love? Should we confiscate it?'

My love! The oaf had called me John and Mrs Root 'my love'. My chest tightened with fury and embarrassment. I couldn't let Mrs Root think I read such vile material.

'They . . .' I was about to say that they belonged to Root, but I realised just in time that I couldn't show such disloyalty to a partner who even now was dutifully researching on the dance-floor. 'They're research', I said.

Kevin cackled like a jackass. 'That's what they all say!'

'Don't mind him, love', said Mrs Root. 'Each to his own, that's what I always say.' She smiled understandingly, but in her eyes was the same expression of disappointment as I'd seen outside Mario's in Putney High Street. I'd had enough. Aware that I was once again letting Root down, I turned on my heel without a word and walked towards the exit.

It was raining when I got outside and I couldn't find a taxi. I got one eventually at Hyde Park Corner, but I was soaked to the skin by then. By the time I got home I had begun to sneeze.

TUESDAY 10 JULY

I woke with a streaming cold. I telephoned Root to say that I was too ill to come to work.

'Can't take the pace, eh, lad?'

He sounded immensely cheerful. That was a relief. He could have been furious with me for letting him down again. He said he'd been reading *Club International* and *Sadie Stern*. Here was a mystery. I'd left them at The Hippodrome. Had he bumped into Kevin and Mrs Root? I was pondering the implications of this possibility when he said he'd found the magazines on his desk. Mrs Root must have put them there, but it didn't seem to occur to Root to wonder how they'd found their way into the ops-room. Mrs Root is perfectly right about him. So involved is he in his own concerns that he notices nothing strange or irregular going on around him. No doubt he could have seen Mrs Root and Kevin dancing at the Hippodrome and yet not registered the fact. He hears only what he wants to hear and sees only what he wants to see. He has the tunnel vision of the true artist. Was it Clive James or Jorge Luis Borges, the famous Argentine poet, who pointed out that if we saw every leaf on a tree we would go mad?

'"Free Phone Sex", lad', said Root. 'That's the thing these days. Advertised in *Club International*. New one on me. You call a number and converse pornographically with the subscriber. Subscriber happens to be a single lady sitting by the telephone with her legs behind her ears. What do you think? Better investigate it, eh?'

I said I looked forward to doing so when I returned to work, which I hoped would be tomorrow.

‹WEDNESDAY 11 JULY›

Still feeling pretty rough, so took another day off.

THURSDAY 12 JULY

Still feeling a little weak, but on the whole I was strong enough to return to work. As soon as I arrived in the ops-room Root excitedly brought up the matter of free-phone sex. He showed me the advertisements in *Club International*, which were exactly as he'd described them. 'Baby, I've got the hots for you and I can prove it. Ring Natasha on 307 4017' was one, and 'Let's come together on the Telephone! Ring Abigail on 239 0668' another.

'What do you think?' said Root. 'On to something, are we? Give it a go, should we?'

'I think we should, Mr Root.' I was dead keen. Natasha and Abigail were exceptionally classy-looking girls, sitting by the telephone without their clothes, coolly awaiting our calls.

'Still on the letter "A", are we, lad?'

I said that we were.

'Better ring Abigail, then. Doesn't give her other name. Don't like to address a stranger by her Christian name, but in the circumstances there's no alternative. Right. Here goes!'

He dialled a number and waited, his expression registering gradual disappointment.

'No reply', he said. He replaced the receiver. 'She'll be doing the shopping, Miss Abigail. Fair enough. Life must go on. We'll try another.' He searched through the advertisements. 'No one else whose name begins with "A" We'll move on through the alphabet. Here's one. She sounds good. "Call now! Cum now! Stick it to Miss Hot-Pussy, lover boy. Call Deirdre on 473 7144." Sounds promising, eh? We'll give Miss Deirdre a call.'

He lifted the receiver and dialled again.

'Hullo! Hullo! Is that Miss Hot-Pussy? What! Miss Deirdre, that's who. Known to her friends as Miss Hot-Pussy. Oh, you've heard that, have you?' He covered the receiver and spoke to me. 'Must have got the maid. She seemed confused. Sounds as if there's a party going on. Hullo? Miss Deirdre? You rascal! I've got the magazine in front of me. I like the picture, Deirdre. Is that right? Always keen to get new readers, are you? I bet you are!' He covered the receiver and addressed himself to me. 'She sounds a trifle mad, Miss Deirdre. Pleasant enough, but a little excitable. We're doing well.'

'You ought to say something pornographic', I said. 'That's what she expects.'

'Pornographic, eh?'

'That's right.'

'Hm. Here goes.' He removed his hand from the mouth-piece. 'Bosoms!' he said. He held the receiver away from his ear. 'My word, that did the trick!' He waited for the hot talk at the other end to burn itself out, and then he spoke again. 'What do I want? I want to hop over there and pull your knickers down, that's what I want! Good-day to you, madam.' He rang off. 'Care for a go, lad? She's good.'

I was intrigued. I said I'd be glad to take my turn. I dialled the number.

'Hullo', said the maid. She sounded nice. Efficient, but welcoming.

'Miss Deirdre?'

'No. Who wants her?'

'Kim Kindersley.' I shouldn't have said that, really. When making pornographic phone-calls, even at an advertiser's invitation, one ought to use a pseudonym.

'Hang on', said the maid. 'I'll see if she's available.'

'Don't disturb her if she's tied up with a client!' I said.

'Hullo', said a crisp, commanding voice. No wonder Root had thought her good. 'This is Deirdre. What can I do for you?'

What I said next was totally out of character, but I was keen to impress Root. 'You can suck my cock', I said.

There was a gasp at the other end of the line. 'I *beg* your pardon?' said Miss Deirdre. She was good. She was putting on a show. 'This is the *second* dirty call I've had this morning.'

'Don't worry!' I said. 'It's early yet!'

'Do you know who I am?'

'Miss Hot-Pussy', I said.

'Look, young man', she said. 'I don't know what your game is, but this is *Cosmopolitan* and I'm Deirdre McSharry. If you think ...' She was struck by a thought. 'That's not Charles Wintour, is it?'

'Yes', I said. I rang off.

How had that happened? I looked again at the advertisement in *Club International*. 473 7144. We'd dialled the right number. Then I spotted our mistake. We'd bought the American edition of *Club International*. These were New York numbers.

'This is the American edition', I said. 'That was Deirdre McSharry we were speaking to. Sheer bad luck. Oh dear. I told her to suck my cock.'

'She'll have had that said to her before', said Root. 'Can't place advertisements like that and expect people to chat about the weather. Oh well. So much for the *Cosmo* girl.'

'But she *didn't* take the advertisement. These are New York numbers.'

'Nonsense, lad! We couldn't have phoned New York, not without dialling 0101 and the rest of it. She was asking for it, if you want my opinion. Perhaps you shouldn't have given your name, though. Could have been a mistake, that. Never invite a lady to fellate you under your own name.'

For such a brilliant man, he really can be a little slow. I tried to explain.

'We *didn't* dial New York. Deirdre in New York's number is the *same* as Deirdre's in London. Sheer coincidence.'

'I see, I see', said Root. 'Both at it, are they? In business together, do you suppose? Well, well, well.' Suddenly he lost interest in the matter. 'That's enough of that. Must get on. Might return to it when we get to the letter "C". The *Cosmo* girl. Second string to her bow. Could be an eye-opener. Not many people will know about the hot phone-calls. But we must have order here. We must be systematic. Must finish the letter "A", isn't that right, lad?'

'That's right', I said.

'Glad you're learning at last', said Root. 'So. What shall we do today? To be truthful, I'm keen on this field-work. Learn more than sitting here, what? I thought we might investigate the vice anglais. I fancy I'm ready for it. What do you say?'

This seemed a good idea. His desires were off the leash now, out in the open, no longer sublimated – with all the crushing harm that that can do to the personality. Already he seemed easier with himself. Talk of *le vice anglais* had caused him to breathe a trifle heavily, but he could now mention it without going to the weights and singing patriotic songs. We could satisfy his compulsion and at the same time unearth some invaluable material for the book.

'That's a good idea', I said.

'It's relevant, do you see?' said Root. He still needed to justify the craving, but that was reasonable enough. It was quite something for a man of Root's pulverising masculinity to come to terms with such desires. 'Been reading an article in *The Daily Mail*,' he said. 'Says the younger Royals indulge. Andrew and Edward particularly. Both spoke highly to *The Daily Mail* of the whackings they received at Gordonstoun. Charles less keen, it seems, but there you are. It's character-forming, says *The Daily Mail*. That's their summing-up. Certainly nothing wrong with the characters of the younger Royals – on the male side, at least.' He'd managed at last to justify to himself cravings that must have unsettled him for years. It was as if a drain had been unblocked, allowing the refuse of many years to flow at last to a safe, neutralising destination. I had reason, I felt, to congratulate myself. I had been the plumber in this enterprise. 'So', he said. 'Where do we research? Among your friends, is that it? Among the upper-classes?'

'Perhaps not.' I didn't think that was such a good idea. 'It would take too long to organise. What we need, I think, is a professional girl.'

'A professional girl, eh? Like Deirdre, is that it? You think the McSharry woman would cooperate?' He picked up one of the smacking mags – *Sadie Stern*, I think – and rifled excitedly through the pages. His breathing became heavier. 'These girls seem keen. Who's this? She's laying it on. My word! It's Roasie Swales, the round the world yachtsperson. Whatever next! Claire Francis at it, do you suppose? She could be haughty. Small but haughty. The Sealink adverts? A clue there, do you think?'

'It's the notice boards', I said. 'That's our best bet. That's where they all advertise. Particularly in the Earl's Court area.' I knew this from the time I had a flat in Nevern Square and bought my papers from a newsagent's in the Earl's Court Road.

Root was delighted. 'The yachtspersons advertise in the Earl's Court area? Come, lad! It's the Earl's Court Road for you and me! I'll need the Thruster.'

We were into the Rolls in no time, Root wearing the Thruster, which was dormant, and carrying his investigative equipment – the camera, flash-gun and tape-recorder. We parked in Earl's Court Square by dint of Root actually lifting a Mini sideways on to the pavement and then scanned the advertisements outside the newsagent's where I'd once bought my papers in the morning. There was a little crowd of men furtively writing down telephone numbers on the backs of envelopes, some of whom moved off as Root started his loud commentary on what was offered.

' "Miss Birch Gives Dancing Classes." We'll not need those, lad.' He turned to the man who was scanning next to him. 'The lad and I have been to Bodys', he explained. 'My word they put you through it there!' His new friend seemed interested. He asked for the number. 'Check with the lad', said Root. 'He carries the numbers. Mention my name and ask for Hottie. What's this? "German model gives riding lessons." A horse is involved, do you suppose? A horse in a basement in the Earl's Court Road? Could be one for the younger Royals. Make a note of that, lad. Here's one. "Kennelling. £5 a day." Cheap, but we don't want a kennelling. We won't be kennelled, lad. "Plumber. 24-hour service." The dyne-rod, is that it? Could be nasty. We'll have nothing to do with dyne-rods, lad. "Greek Massage." We know about the Greeks. It'll be a fellow on a suspended sentence, mark my words. Ah, this is more like it. "Miss Stern seeks new pupils. Fully equipped punishment room." She was featured in one of the magazines, Miss Stern, unless I'm much mistaken. Miss Sadie Stern. She's the one for us. To the telephone, lad!'

I rang from a nearby kiosk and was given an address in Cornwall Gardens. What a strange coincidence. Charlotte lives in Cornwall Gardens.

'We'll walk it', said Root.

I was quite excited now, not that I intended to indulge myself, of course. I'd never been to an establishment like this, and it would be interesting, to say the least. It would be interesting, too, to see how Root took to the experiment. Would his craving become a compulsion, needing weekly satisfaction, or would one traumatic experience exorcise the beast for good, leaving him calm and refreshed, able to channel all his abundant energy into the production of literary masterpieces? I didn't intend to be present myself, of course, while the punishment was being administered. Such intimate moments of self-discovery should take place in private.

We soon found ourselves outside a rather smart house in Cornwall Gardens, several doors, I was glad to see, away from Charlotte's. Root took a deep breath and squared his shoulders.

'Right, lad. This is it.'

He rang the front-door, which was opened after a while by an old crone in bedroom slippers.

'My God, madam!' cried Root. 'You're rough! You've seen better days. Never mind.' He raised his pork-pie hat. 'Norman Norman. We're here for the vice anglais. My card.' He put his hand into his pocket, inadvertently activating the Thruster, which exploded out of his trousers, knocking him backwards down the steps. 'Pardon me, madam. It's the Thruster.' He battled to subdue it, struggling to get it back inside his trousers, and eventually succeeding in this endeavour.

The crone looked doubtful. She removed a cigarette from her mouth and looked us up and down. At last she let us in, leading us down a passage and showing us into a small waiting-room where four dejected-looking customers were reading old copies of *Punch* and *Harpers & Queen*. Root sat down next to a little man whose black coat, pin-stripe trousers and brief-case suggested he might be a solicitor.

'Budge up', said Root. 'Here for a whacking, is that it? Eton, was it? Harrow? Gordonstoun?' He raised his hat. 'Norman Norman. And this is my research assistant Kim Kindersley.' He set up the tape-recorder and switched it on. He unslung his camera and took aim. 'Smile please!' The Thruster exploded out of his trousers. The solicitor shot to his feet and scuttled from the room, closely followed by the other punters.

'Oh, are you off?' said Root. 'Strange lot. Here, did you catch sight of Miss Stern, lad? She was no oil painting. Nothing like the photo in the magazine. Still, she must be good, must know her business. That was quite a queue she had in here. You don't build up a clientele like that unless you know your business.'

'That will have been the maid', I said. 'They always have a maid.'

'The maid, eh? Got you.'

The maid returned. She seemed surprised that everyone but us had gone. 'Here. Where is everyone?'

'Suddenly remembered previous appointments', said Root. 'Privy Council meetings, Question Time in the House, bump luncheons, conference in chambers, that sort of thing.'

'It better be you, then', said the maid. It was a cheerless invitation.

'Gloomy business this', said Root, as she led us back down the passage. 'No wonder your friend Ingrams looks so down in the mouth.'

We were shown into the punishment room. Root was impressed. He inspected the various racks, pulleys, stocks and bondage-bars, nodding and grunting with approval. 'There'll have been a few top Tories spread out after hours on these, lad', he said. His need to convince himself that he shared this taste with the highest and most reputable in the land was touchingly obvious. Nor was it far off the mark, if received opinion is any guide. Thank goodness I've not been brushed by the clammy, unlovely caress of this particular perversion. A beating was something I tried to avoid like the proverbial parrot. At school it was the ultimate deterrent. How strange that so many well-born men should have acquired a taste for it, the very same people who once a year at the Conservative Party Conference excitedly recommended it as the most suitable punishment for young offenders.

'Madam will be with you in a minute', said the maid. 'She's washing off.' She looked at us suspiciously. 'I don't know what she'll think about there being two of you.' She gave us a final contemptuous glance and then withdrew. Personally I found being treated so disdainfully quite a turn-off – or rather I would have done had I been turned on – but it was part and parcel, I supposed, of what most of the customers came for.

After a minute or two Miss Stern entered from the bathroom. 'Hullo, love, sorry to keep ... oh, there's two of you. I don't know about that.' She was a plump, good-natured-looking lady in her late forties, I'd have guessed, dressed in thigh-boots and a black bodice, laced in red.

'Good-day to you, madam', said Root. He raised his hat. 'Norman Norman and my assistant Kim Kimbersley.' He took me to one side and addressed me piercingly. 'You've drawn the short straw here, lad. She's rougher than the maid.'

I'd drawn the short straw? I didn't like the sound of that. I tried to edge backwards from the room, but Root caught me by the collar. He beamed at Miss Stern.

'It's the vice anglais, madam', he said.

Miss Stern looked bewildered. 'Do what?'

'A whacking, madam', said Root. 'That's the gist of it.'

'Oh, a *whacking*, that's all right, but why's there two of you?' Her round, good-natured face looked quite unhappy. It was hard to believe that this cosy, blousily reassuring little woman could give anyone a beating. She was more the sort to put the kettle on and say: 'You'll feel better after a cup of tea.' There seemed a danger that Root's first experience would be woefully inadequate, entailing further, time-consuming visits. I hoped, for the sake of the project, that Miss Stern would shortly brush up her act.

'It's for him', said Root. 'He went to Eton, do you see? I'm here for literary reasons merely and to see fair play.' He switched on his tape-recorder. 'Tell me, madam. In the strictest confidence, have you had many of the younger Royals here? We are commissioned to ask such questions I may say, by Lord Weidenfeld of Nicolson.'

It dawned on me, only slowly, I don't know why, that it was I, not Root, who was to receive the whacking. I wriggled in his grasp but he held me fast.

'Don't worry, lad', he said. 'I'll be on hand in case she goes too hard.' He addressed himself to Miss Stern. 'Don't worry, madam. He likes it really. It was Eton, do you see?'

I protested angrily and struggled in his grasp, but to no avail. When he threatened to remove my trousers himself, I decided it was time to strike a bargain. In the interests of research, I said, and for the sake of the work progress, I'd accept one stroke, on condition that I could keep my trousers on and that there'd be no photographs. Root was disposed to haggle, but I was adamant.

'Hm. Just one stroke, eh?'

'That's correct.'

'And there are to be no photographs? We need illustrations, lad.'

'No photographs', I said.

'That's right', said Miss Stern. 'I'm not having photos taken here.'

'And you remain trousered throughout?'

'Throughout,' I said.

'Come lad! Where's your spirit of adventure?'

'Where's yours?'

'Hm.' Root was disappointed, but he knew when he'd been out-debated. 'It's a deal, then. Over the vaulting-horse!'

For purely literary reasons, for the sake of the book, I spread myself over a piece of gymnastic equipment and closed my eyes. Was it the immortal Pepys or was it Boswell who said: 'I will go through almost anything with a degree of satisfaction if I am to put an account of it in writing'? One stroke, in any case, wouldn't be too bad, and I was confident that the kindly-looking Miss Stern would only simulate a whacking. There was the consideration too that after this I'd hold a moral advantage over Root, having shown myself willing, unlike him, to sacrifice myself in the interests of research. One stroke could mean extra royalty points for me, to say nothing of the good-will banked and, if properly exploited, accruing interest.

I sensed Miss Stern drawing back and seconds later I received a stroke that caused me to jerk upright, yelling with pain and surprise. Then, before I could remove myself from the line of fire, I received another! Root, to do him justice, was immediately scandalised at this departure from the contract.

'My God, madam!' he cried. 'You nearly killed the lad!'

He spun round and laid her cold with a short boxing shot to the chin. Then all hell broke loose. Miss Stern's maid, alerted by the noise of the fracas, ran into the room and, seeing her mistress stretched unconscious over the discipline bench, began to screech like an alley-cat. Then Miss Stern's pimp, an over-weight Maltese, appeared from nowhere and, putting his head down like a bull, charged across the room at Root. He would have done better to look where he was going. Root, timing his move quite brilliantly, stepped aside, chopping the pimp on the back of his meaty neck as he hurtled past. The pimp went head-first into the wall, knocking himself cold, and slithered to the floor. The maid withdrew. Root was exultant.

'What a work-out, lad!' Miss Stern should put her prices up. Do all ladies offer this as an extra, do you think? The fisticuffs? A fat man charging from left field? My guess they don't.' He hauled the pimp to his feet. 'What shall it be, then? The citizen's arrest? Back to the ops-room and into the broom-cupboard with him, is that it? We need a prisoner, lad.' He looked at me hopefully.

I managed to dissuade him. We were some way from where the car was parked, I said, and carrying the body that distance would arouse comment. The sooner we were out of here the better. In all probability the maid was already on the telephone to the police. We should move off quickly, I suggested, before Sergeant Pyle and his colleague Mr Pulley arrived on the scene.

Root at last agreed, with some reluctance. He gave the pimp a final, disappointed whack on the neck, before padlocking him back to back with Miss Stern and perching them on the bondage bench. Then he peeled some ten pound notes off the bank-roll in his wallet and put them in Miss Stern's handbag.

'Always pay my debts, lad,' he said, 'except when I don't. And that was good. Best work-out I've had in years.'

Outside the punishment room the maid was nowhere to be seen, so we walked quickly down the passage and let ourselves out. Now that the excitement was over, I realised that my bottom was extremely sore, and I wasn't at all amused when, a few yards down the street, Root goosed me painfully from behind.

'Watch out, for pity's sake!' I yelled. 'I've just had my bottom whacked!'

I turned round to discover that Root was still coming down Miss Stern's front-steps. It hadn't been Root who had playfully assaulted me from behind, but Charlotte. She was standing by her Mini with a Harvey Nichols shopping-bag looking absolutely great in that haughty way of hers, but with an expression of shock and disappointment on her face.

'Oh dear', she said. 'My mistake. I'd come to the conclusion that it was all a joke – your smacking thing – but I see I was wrong.'

She turned on her heel and started to walk briskly down the street.

I called after her. 'Charlotte! Wait! I can explain.'

She turned and, after a moment's hesitation, began to walk towards me. Then Root appeared at my side.

'Is this young lady annoying you, lad?' He turned to Charlotte. 'I'd thank you not to molest the lad, madam. He's had his whacking for the day. You'll have to take your turn with the others.' He chuckled fatly. 'It's bondage tomorrow. We'll be restrained in the a.m., mark my words. I say! Pardon me!' The Thruster had exploded out of his trousers, driving him backwards up Miss Stern's front-steps.

That did it. With a little alarmed gasp, Charlotte turned on her heel and ran towards the safety of her own front-door.

'Thank you very much', I said.

'Don't mention it, lad. A pretty lass. A friend of yours, is she?'

'She was.' It was the first time that I'd been angry with Root since the start of our collaboration.

'Upset her, did you?' Root tut-tutted disapprovingly. 'That was a mistake, lad. You shouldn't have done that. It's girls like her you should be mixing with, not with low-life types like her.' He jerked his head in the direction of Miss Stern's front-door.

'I'm going home', I said. I began to walk briskly towards the Gloucester Road.

'See you tomorrow, lad!' called Root. 'We're doing well. It'll be bondage tomorrow!'

FRIDAY 13 JULY

I woke up still a little cross with Root, but my annoyance was soon forgotten in the cauldron of the creative process. As I got out of the lift I noticed that there was something different about the ops-room. After a while I realised what it was: the hard-ware was in. There were strobe-lights everywhere and two expensive-looking video cameras were suspended from the ceiling in opposite corners of the room. Root was beaming.

'Installed yesterday afternoon', he said. 'Knightsbridge Video. Excellent people. It's research in the home now, lad. Bondage on the premises. What do you say? Trussed like gooses, you and I. We'll get a couple of ladies over: experts in the art of trussing executive types in the a.m. We'll have the initiative here, do you see? Out in the field things can become untidy. Contingencies. The unexpected. Turkish pimps lobbing from nowhere. We can be caught on the hop, lad. Laboratory conditions, that's what's needed. Here, in our own quarters, nothing can go wrong, we'll be in control at all times, with a record on video in case of trouble. No chance of being blackmailed, do you see? You're keen?'

I was keen, all right. I had no desire to be tied up, of course, but for our findings to be valid we must personally investigate every aspect of human sexuality. Was it Camus, or was it Taki Theodoracopulos, who said: 'A writer who discusses and exploits what he has never experienced is detestable.' And what Root had said made a lot of sense; in laboratory conditions we'd be the masters of our own research. However, I didn't intend to be the guinea-pig again.

'Let's get this straight', I said. 'You're suggesting that you and I should be tied up by two girls, is that it?'

'In a nutshell, lad. For purely literary reasons, you understand. For the sake of Lord Weidenfeld of Nicolson. For the sake of the book.'

'*Both* of us?' I insisted. 'You'll be tied up as well?'

'Absolutely, lad! Good heavens, we're collaborators, aren't we?'

I was reassured, and quite excited. It would be extremely interesting to meet the sort of girl prepared to tie you up before lunch, and, with the video on, nothing, as Root had said, could go wrong. The video would confirm that the experiment had been undertaken voluntarily, from the ladies' point of view, and, from ours, for purely literary reasons. I had one more condition, however. I'd insist that Root be tied up first. Once he'd been trussed, I might join in, or, on the other hand, I might not.

'Okay', I said. 'But on one condition. You're tied up first.'

'Of *course*, lad. By all means. Now – we're wasting time. Two ladies, that's what we need. Two ladies available to truss you on your own premises in the a.m. Where do we find such types? In wine bars, is it? Answering the phone at John D. Wood? In Parrots? In Cork Street art galleries? You've read about gallery girls, lad? According to *The Daily Mail* Prince Andrew forms 86 per cent of his sexual connections at gallery openings. "Good evening, your Highness. Gordonstoun, was it? Over you go!" It's Cork Street, is it, for you and me?'

'It might be quicker to look at *What's On In London*', I said.

'Is that right? It lists the gallery girls, does it. *What's On In London*?'

'I don't think so, no. But it does list the escort agencies.'

'The escort agencies, eh? They do bondage, do they, the escort girls?'

'They're call-girls, really. The escort agency bit is just a cover. They'll do anything for money. They're not cheap, though. They start at a hundred pounds.'

'Petty cash, lad! We'll charge it to Weidenfeld. Legitimate research. Two birds with one stone. Bondage and escort girls. Useful to have quizzed an escort girl by the time we get to "G". Girls, Escort, do you see?' He suddenly squinted at me cunningly. 'You're very well informed, lad.'

'An American friend told me about them', I said. This was so. 'First thing he does after he checks into the Hilton is to go through *What's On In London*. They're all in there, he says.'

'I believe you, lad,' said Root, looking, most annoyingly, as if he didn't believe me at all. '*What's On* it is. Now. Do we have a copy? Nuisance to have to go out for one.'

He scrabbled through a pile of magazines on his desk. A cry of triumph. 'We have it, lad!' He opened it up and began to search. 'Where are they, then, the call-girls? I see nothing *re* call-girls in the table of contents. Restaurants. Night-clubs. Theatres. Cinemas. Agreeable walks. This very Sunday, I see, old Godfrey Smith is to lead a stroll through Dickens's London, stopping at taverns once frequented by the creator of the immortal Mr Pickwick. That's one to miss. What else? Discotheques. Greyhound tracks. Church services. Richard Ingrams, I see, is to preach this Sunday in St Mary's-atte-Bow. His text – "God and 'Plum' Wodehouse". There's an outrage. The man's a saddle-sniffer. A common informer. Can't have a saddle sniffer in a pulpit. One way with common informers in my day. Head-first into a cement-mixer. Yet Ingrams will end up with a knighthood, mark my words. I tell you what, lad. I've a mind to do this bondage as Richard Ingrams. Double security, do you see? Have you noticed how rarely muggers stick up other muggers? It's the same with common informers? Don't read much about Ingrams in *Private Eye*, eh? Or about Dempster's after-hours cavortings in the Hickey column? Honour among grasses, that's the point. Last person to be grassed on is another grass. I'll do the bondage as Ingrams, lad, be trussed under an alias, do you see? Just in case a wheel comes off.

Your friends at *What's On* may not have an adequate security classification, do you see? Can't find the bondage girls, by the way. No mention of bondage girls among the church services and agreeable walks.'

'They're at the end', I said. 'Under Escort Agencies.'

'Is that so? You'd know, of course.' He winked. 'Ah, here we are. Great heavens! There must be fifty of them. Have you found – I beg your pardon, has your friend found – any of them to be markedly more obliging than the others? Have you – excuse me – has *he* a favourite?'

I replied with dignity. 'He has made favourable mention of someone called Jackie.'

'Jackie, eh?' Root scanned the page. 'Here we are! "For the friendliest girls in town call Jackie Escorts. 655 3333". Sounds promising. We'll give her a ring.' He reached for the telephone. 'Should I mention the trussing? What's the form here?'

'Better not', I advised. 'I don't think they like to discuss details over the telephone.'

'Quite right. Probably being tapped. Here goes, then.'

He dialled the number. He introduced himself as Richard Ingrams and asked for two of Jackie's top-drawer types. No, he said, they weren't both for him. One of them would be for his young friend Kim Kimbersley. (Only one of us, I noticed, was to have the privilege of pseudonymity. I'd change all that when the girls arrived.) They should present themselves at 12.30, said Root. Yes, it was rather early in the day, but that was the way of it. He gave our address. He emphasised that the girls must go to the basement garage and come straight up to the ops-room in the lift. 'Don't want them meeting Mrs Ingrams, what?' He mentioned Anna Ford and Lord Weidenfeld. Rather to my surprise he failed to appeal on behalf of the Home Secretary. He told Miss Jackie that it had been a pleasure doing business with her. He invited her to one of our literary lunches. Lynda Lee-Potter, he said, was to be guest of honour at the first. Yes, he quite agreed that she had a remarkably silly face, but her opinions, in his view, were always sound. Good gracious! He was quite surprised, he said, to hear Miss Jackie express herself so forcefully. We were all entitled to our own opinions, of course, but he'd never heard Miss Potter called *that* before. Then he rang off. Mention of literary lunches had stirred some uneasy memory, but I couldn't pin it down. Mention of Mrs Root had brought to the surface a more immediate fear.

'What happens if Mrs Root walks in?' I said. Parcelled up and helpless I'd hardly impress her as a likely replacement for Kevin the hairdresser.

'Not a chance, lad. Can't open the pass-door from the other side. Hasn't got a key. I told you. We're secure in here.'

I was reassured, and becoming more excited, I suddenly realised, at what lay ahead. While having no desire to be tied up, there was, I had to admit, something undeniably interesting about the prospect of two girls, neither of whom one had met before, offering themselves so intimately within minutes of being introduced. It was the certainty of their participation that made it so exciting, that and the *un*-certainty, paradoxically, as to what they'd be like. They might be unspeakably rough, of course, but on the other hand they might be absolutely stunning, they might be debutantes or air hostesses or Princess Diana look-alikes from Parrots making a little on the side. Quite a lot of that went on, or so I'd always been told. One of them might be Charlotte! My stomach turned a somersault and my feet went cold. It didn't occur to me for the moment that in such an event she, if anything, would have better grounds for embarrassment than I.

'Did Miss Jackie say what their names were?' I asked in a casual way.

'She did', said Root. 'Lindi and Charlotte. You've gone pale, lad. Don't pass out on me now. They'll be here in an hour. We must test the equipment.'

I spent the next hour in a daze. I was vaguely aware of Root playing with the lights and adjusting camera angles, but I was distracted by this strange possibility. *Could* it be Charlotte? No! The idea was too extraordinary. But more extraordinary things had happened, particularly in the last three weeks. And cooking a bass guitarist's dinner in a suspender-belt was but a short step, surely, from restraining executives before lunch. In Mrs Thatcher's Britain people had to keep their heads above water as best they could.

I was redoing my make-up in the bathroom when our guests arrived (Root's strobe lights were merciless and I had no intention of looking washed out on camera) and when I heard a commanding, unmistakably Sloane voice I decided, for a panicky moment, to stay where I was. Then, very gradually, I began to realise that if it was Charlotte her embarrassment, if she had any modesty at all, would be at least as great as mine, and should, in all conscience, be greater. I, after all, had the excuse of literary research, but what, conceivably, could hers be? Mrs Thatcher's devil-take-the-hindmost economics? It wouldn't wash. I began to hope that it might be Charlotte. The prospect of this cool haughty girl being revealed as a part-time trusser of strange men before lunch was joltingly exciting. Was I becoming weird? Had our research corrupted me already? I didn't care. I strolled casually into the ops-room.

Root was chatting to two very attractive, smartly dressed girls, one dark, one blonde, neither of whom, alas, was Charlotte – not my Charlotte, at least. Root introduced us. Lindi, the brunette, the less obviously pretty but more commandingly striking of the two, worked, he said, for the BBC.

'Only freelance,' she said. 'I make documentaries.'

I could well believe it. She looked capable and forthright. She could have posed for *Esquire* as an executive woman. She had slim legs. 'How interesting,' I said. 'On what subject?'

'Anthropology. I used to lecture at Norwich University. I gave that up to make documentaries. I like to travel.' Suddenly she seemed to notice the lights and cameras. She turned to Root. 'And what about you, Mr Ingrams? Do you make documentaries too?'

'You could say that', said Root. 'We're researching a book on women, my young friend and I. For Lord Weidenfeld of Nicolson, as it happens. We will shortly arrive at the letter "B". "B" for bondage, do you see?'

'Here', said Charlotte, speaking for the first time. 'I don't want to be tied up, me. No way. Jackie didn't say anything about being tied up.' She was very pretty, in a blue-eyed, doll-like way, but much less classy than Lindi. She had dimples and plump knees. She would go red in the sun and complain. She would wear pantyhose and novelty knickers. If there was to be something after the bondage I hoped I'd get Lindi. It might have been unprofessional of me, but I began to work out how I could lay claim to Lindi in advance. There was something extraordinarily exciting about a BBC producer who did this sort of thing on the side. And reassuring too. Such a classy girl would never rip us off. Had they both been like Charlotte, I'd have been a trifle nervous.

'Don't concern yourselves, ladies,' said Root. 'It's *we* who'll be tied up.'

Charlotte was relieved. 'Oh well,' she said. 'That's okay, I suppose.'

Lindi, however, seemed a little doubtful. 'What? On camera? You want to video it?'

Charlotte gave a little squeak of alarm. 'No way', she said. 'I'm not being filmed, me. No way. Not me.'

'You're worrying unduly, ladies', said Root. 'Where's the risk to you? It's *we* who'll be trussed. Men of some eminence, if I may say so. It's *we* who'll be at risk. We are hardly likely to show the tape to others. It will be merely for our records, and destroyed once the book is finished.'

It sounded like a good argument to me, but Lindi and Charlotte still looked doubtful. 'Excuse me a minute, Mr Ingrams', said Lindi. 'We'll be with you in a moment.'

She took Charlotte to a far corner of the room, where they held a whispered conference. Lindi seemed to be trying to convince Charlotte that everything would be all right. As a producer of documentaries herself, of course, she would see the logic of Root's position.

'Leave this to me, lad', said Root. 'If they refuse to do it on film the deal's off. Too risky without a record on our files. Could be open to blackmail, do you see?'

'Surely not with your doing it as Richard Ingrams', I said. I was immensely aroused now, and the last thing I wanted was for the experiment to be cancelled. 'You said yourself that no one would dare to inform on Ingrams. *And* she works for the BBC.'

'The worst sort', said Root. 'All Trots at the BBC. They'll do anything to raise party funds. Not worth the risk. Take my word for it, lad. I know what I'm doing.'

I agreed, reluctantly, that he might be right. Without the video to refute them they could claim we had forced them into things against their will. The video was our only guarantee against blackmail.

Lindi and Charlotte had finished their conference. 'Okay', said Lindi. 'We don't mind the video. But we want a bit more money. Two hundred each.'

Fair enough', said Root. He went to his desk and produced a bundle of notes, which he handed to Lindi. While she counted it, he switched the lights on and set the cameras working. Then he produced a selection of old ties and dressing-gown cords from a drawer in the desk. 'For the trussing', he said, handing them to Lindi. 'Right, lad! Off with your clothes. Let's roll!'

I wasn't going to be caught like that again. 'Oh no', I said. 'You first. You agreed.'

'By all means, lad.' Root turned to Lindi. 'The lad's shy. Probably doesn't shape up too well without his shirt. Some do, some don't. Myself, the upper-body of a wrestler. Here goes.'

He took everything off except his shoes, socks and suspenders, and piled his clothes neatly on a chair. The girls gasped when they saw him naked. The Thruster had indeed been an unnecessary appendage.

'My God!' cried Charlotte.

'Not bad, eh?' said Root. He performed a series of boastful poses, as though limbering up for the Mr Universe contest.

'Reminds me of a joke', said Lindi. Root looked displeased. 'No, no', said Lindi quickly. 'It's not disrespectful to you, Mr Ingrams. This girl, you see, was propositioned by a black man. He offered her a hundred pounds. "Not a chance", she said. "I know about you lot." She offered him oral sex instead. "Don't be silly", he said. "I can do that myself."

Charlotte, predictably, squealed with laughter, but Root was disgusted. He took me to one side. 'Sorry about that, lad. The BBC, do you see? I'll ask her to moderate her language.' I'd been a little surprised myself, I must say. Lindi had not seemed to be the one likely to come out with anything so crude. Root patted me encouragingly on the back. 'Right, lad! You're next. Off with the clothes.'

While I undressed, Root continued with his boastful limbering up, blowing out his chest, standing like a pelican first on one leg and then the other, touching his toes and performing a series of press-ups and squat-thrusts. Now that the moment had come, I felt disappointingly unaroused. Had not Root been present, of course, I might well have tried to make the most of the situation. Being attended to in private by Lindi would have been delightful.

Root looked me up and down with an expression of wonder on his face. 'Good grief, lad! What a mess.' He shook his head and made contemptuous clicking noises with his tongue. 'Right', he said. 'Truss us, ladies. Go easy with the lad.'

Lindi instructed us to lie on our backs on the floor and raise our knees towards our chests. She tied our knees together, and then she tied our elbows to our knees.

'Is this it?' said Root. 'Is this the bondage, then?'

'I imagine so', I said.

'Would you imagine Anna Ford has anything like this? My guess she hasn't.'

'I expect you're right, Mr Root.'

'Ingrams. Mr Ingrams, if you don't mind. Security, lad.'

'Sorry. I expect you're right, Mr Ingrams.'

'Just as I thought', he said. He chuckled delightedly. 'She'll not have been up at the sharp end like us, she'll have none of our depth of research.' He screwed his head round in my direction. 'Anything happening for you, lad? This bondage, is it working?'

'Not in the least', I said. I was in agony, in fact. I was losing the feeling in my arms and legs, and my back felt as if it was about to snap. At least I'd discovered that I wasn't any sort of masochist. It would have been hard to imagine anything as unpleasurable as this. Or as risky. Stories came to mind of businessmen, chairmen of publicly quoted companies, left like this by absent-minded call-girls, to be found next day by office cleaners. Had it not been for the reassuring presence of Lindi from the BBC I'd have felt alarmingly vulnerable, trussed and helpless as we were. Thank goodness Lindi was here.

'Over-rated, would you say?' asked Root. 'This bondage? Is that our finding in a nutshell? Is that our summing-up? A letter! A letter to Weidenfeld.'

What a professional the man is. Even now, shackled like a pavement entertainer in Leicester Square, he could think only of the book.

'"Dear Weidenfeld,

It's bondage here. Miss Lindi from the BBC has me and the lad trussed like Christmas gooses as I write. Parcelled up like this, with our heads touching our knees, we could be used as hoops, or aimed at skittles in a bowling-alley, or, perfectly balanced on the point of our buttocks as we are, tapped lightly on the head and made to swing backwards and forwards like executive toys.

Has Anna Ford anything like this? Our guess she hasn't. She'll have said 'masturbate' to a few men and made a run for it. She'll not have trussed them.

Yours etc,

Henry Root."'

'Type that up, lad, once we're loose. Copies to Cape and Faber. Options open, that's the name of the game. What's next, then? What's after bondage? Bear in mind we'll not try rubber, lad.' He turned to Lindi. 'What happens now?'

'We'll leave you to it,' said Lindi, 'that's what happens now.'

'Off so soon?' said Root.

'If you've no objection.' She went over to the video-recorder and removed the tape. 'I'll be keeping this, Mr Ingrams,' she said. She put it in her bag. 'Come along Charlotte.' They departed via the lift.

Root spoke. 'We'll need council's opinion on this one, lad. We seem to have scored an own goal here.'

We struggled in silence to release ourselves, but to no avail. Lindi had done a good job.

'Trussed like Norfolk turkeys', said Root. 'And in the ops-room too. We need assistance, lad. I'll summon Mrs Root.'

That suggestion brought me up with such a jolt that I toppled over on my axis, banging my head against the side of Root's desk. The thought of Mrs Root seeing me like this caused me to thrash and beat against my bonds like a dying mackerel in a net. I tried to reason with Root. There must be another way, I said. Better to call the Fire Brigade than Mrs Root, better to call the police, better, even, to starve in here for weeks until loss of weight caused our bonds to slip from our emaciated limbs.

'Don't be silly, lad', said Root. 'She's seen it all before.'

Somehow he managed to turn himself over on his front. Then, on elbows and knees, he slowly snaked his way towards the desk. Hauling himself painfully to his knees, he just managed to operate the intercom with his chin and then to press the knob that made the pass-door swing open. He fell back and rolled over, exhausted by the effort. We lay on our backs, legs in the air, like two dead beetles.

The pass-door swung open.

'Oh I say', said Mrs Root. 'Whatever are you up to now? You have some guests, Mr Root. Lynda Lee-Potter, Jean Rook, someone from the Hickey column and a very nice girl who says she's representing Nigel Dempster.' Over Mrs Root's shoulder could be seen a small crowd of people, laughing and chatting.

'It's the bondage, do you see?' said Root. He beamed politely, over Mrs Root's shoulder, at the nice girl representing Nigel Dempster. 'Good day to you, madam. A slight hiccup here, as you can see for yourself, but the vol-au-vents will be with us in a minute. We're researching here for Lord Weidenfeld of Nicolson. If you'd care to wait outside.' He craned his head in my direction. 'It's the literary lunch, lad. We forgot the literary lunch. Never mind. I'll handle this.' He told Mrs Root to come inside and close the door behind her. 'Don't just stand there, woman. Untie us, for goodness sake. There'll be others arriving in a minute. Frank Delaney. A.N. Wilson. Katie Boyle. Remember Katie Boyle when we get to "B", lad. Boyle, Katie: "Underneath that flawless complexion lies real character." Another of Barry Norman's, unless I'm much mistaken. Close the door, woman! Do you want the world to see us like this?'

Mrs Root at last closed the pass-door, but she seemed in no hurry to release us. She walked over to Root and stared down at him, looking thoughtful. At last she spoke.

'I need a new washing-machine, Mr Root', she said.

Root exploded. He gasped and spluttered. He fought against his bonds. 'That's blackmail!' he raged. 'How dare you, woman! Only one way with a blackmailer. Into the cement-mixer! It will be the cement-mixer for you when we're out of here!'

Blackmail! For some reason it hadn't occurred to me until now that Lindi had taken the tape in order to blackmail us. I suppose I'd thought she'd wanted it simply to protect herself. My brain, my whole being, descended sharply into my bowels. Unless her demands were met, she'd expose us in *The News Of The World*!

'Please yourself', said Mrs Root. She turned away and walked towards the door.

'A moment woman!' cried Root. 'How much would it cost, this washing-machine?'

'About eight hundred pounds,' said Mrs Root. 'A good one, that is. One with four speeds and a spin-drier attached.'

Even in this predicament, trussed like last week's laundry and with half the national press waiting in the passage, Root was disposed to haggle.

'Too much', he said. 'Have you shopped around? Have you consulted *Exchange and Mart*?'

Mrs Root was almost at the door.

'For goodness sake agree!' I said.

'It's blackmail, lad. I'll not give in to blackmail.'

Mrs Root opened the door. She had a word with someone in the passage. She spoke over her shoulder to Root. 'It's *The Daily Telegraph*, Mr Root. Shall I let them in?'

Root, a *Telegraph* reader, knew when he was beaten.

'All right, woman. You win. A new washing-machine it is.'

'I want it in writing, Mr Root', she said. She went to the desk and wrote something on a piece of paper. She untied one of Root's hands, allowing him to add his signature. She untied the rest of him, and then she released me. I couldn't look her in the face. I was into my clothes in a matter of seconds, even though I hardly had the use of my arms and legs. Then I ran to the lift. For the moment I'd had enough.

'Are you off, lad?' called Root. 'What about the literary lunch?'

SATURDAY 14
SUNDAY 15 JULY

A nervy, solitary weekend, brooding distractedly about exposure in the gutter press, trying to convince myself (a) that *The Express* and *Mail*, aiming, quite rightly, to give their readers a sunny, up-beat view of the world, dwelling whenever possible on tug-of-love cats and have-a-go-grannies, seldom if ever blow the whistle on bondage enthusiasts and (b) that Lindi from the BBC had only taken the tape as a precaution, not as a blackmail weapon. By Saturday evening I'd managed to persuade myself that we had little to worry about. How, after all, *could* Lindi blackmail us? All we had to do was ring the agency on Monday morning and find out her address. We'd pay her a visit and if she refused to hand over the tape we'd go to the police. Their involvement would be regrettable, of course, but we hadn't actually broken the law and a few sarcastic observations from Sergeant Pyle and his colleague Mr Pulley would be preferable to exposure in *The News Of The World*.

That comforting thought went out of the window on Sunday morning when I opened *The News Of The World* to find Jackie and her agency excitedly exposed all over two pages. 'This Tsarina of filth', 'This baroness of vice, trading in the weaknesses of others' – that sort of thing. No chance now of getting Lindi's address from her. She'd have bogged off by Monday morning, that was for sure, she wouldn't wait around for a visit from Pyle and Pulley, or their Bayswater representatives. I sat around feeling sick for an hour, but then managed to persuade myself all over again that we had little to worry about. How could Lindi work for the BBC *and* be a blackmailer? It just wasn't conceivable. She must have taken the tape as a joke, or perhaps, as a documentary film-maker herself, she wanted to keep it for her own records. That was perfectly reasonable. A person in her position, a contributor, quite possibly, to *Wildlife On One*, a colleague, in all likelihood, of Attenborough and Leakey, obviously couldn't allow tapes of such a nature to be floating around London. Why hadn't I seen it like this originally? I'd been confused by panic. By Sunday evening I felt quite relaxed; not relaxed enough, however, to meet Ned, who rang up suggesting we have a drink at Boltons. Until I knew I was absolutely in the clear I preferred to stay indoors, inside myself, so to speak, ready to beat back by interior argument any small worries that might come suddenly to mind. Ned's an ass in any case.

MONDAY 16 JULY

Although far from keen to go to work (that I might bump into Mrs Root was a ghastly possibility) I had to discover what was going on, I had to know the worst. Root greeted me cheerfully as I entered the ops-room, which was reassuring.

'You missed the lunch, lad. What a do!'

Nothing too dreadful had happened yet, it seemed.

'It was a success, then?'

'A triumph, lad. I made a speech. Spoke for an hour. The vol-au-vents were a little late but welcome on arrival. My God the Potter woman's got an appetite. She scoffed the lot. Suffered an air-pocket in the colon, of course. It was the vol-au-vents. Had to go in there.' Root nodded towards the bathroom and chuckled at the memory. 'Rocketed in here with her dress over her head. It was the device under the buttocks, do you see? Haven't laughed so much since I caught the Falkender woman.'

So far so good, but I judged it best to subdue all lingering fears by touching, lightly, on the subject of blackmail.

'Blackmail?' cried Root. 'I'll say it was blackmail!' He blew out his cheeks indignantly and banged the desk. 'What an outrage! I wouldn't have expected it.'

My stomach cart-wheeled. My throat went dry. 'Oh hell. You've had a demand?'

'I'll say I've had a demand. Agreed to it too. That's what rankles, lad.' Root groaned and shook his head. 'It should have been the cement-mixer. Straight in. Head-first.'

My brain was spinning. At least he'd paid her, he'd settled the matter already. If he'd paid Lindi off perhaps that would be the end of the matter. 'How much?' I croaked. 'How much did you have to give her?'

'Eight hundred pounds, lad. You were here yourself. You witnessed the negotiations.'

I gasped with relief. He was talking about the washing-machine. There'd been no demand from Lindi.

'You've gone quite pale, lad', said Root. 'I've seen people look better with tubes up their noses. Are you all right? Disappointed at missing the literary lunch, is that it? Don't fret, lad, there'll be others.'

I laughed. I felt quite light-headed with relief. 'No, no,' I said. 'It's not that. We were at cross purposes. I wasn't referring to Mrs Root and the washing-machine. I was talking about Lindi and the tape.'

'I'm with you,' said Root. 'The BBC lady, is that it?'

'That's right. I had this ridiculous idea that she might try to blackmail us.' I chuckled at my own naivity.

'And so she has', said Root. 'And so she has. Note arrived this morning. Here.' He handed me a piece of paper which was lying on his desk. It was badly typed and unsigned. It read:

'Unless you deposit the sum of £25,000 in left-luggage locker number 678 at Victoria Station by mid-day on Monday 16th July the tape will go to the Editor of *The News Of The World*.'

I felt sick and my hands were shaking. I looked at my watch. It was already half-past ten. 'What are we going to do?' I cried.

'*Do*?' said Root. 'Nothing, that's what we're going to do. Can't give in to blackmail, lad. Anyway, I'm all right, I'm laughing. I did the bondage as Richard Ingrams, didn't I? It's his worry, wouldn't you say?'

'But, Mr Root, they'll see in an instant that it isn't Richard Ingrams on the tape. They'll recognise you. You're a well-known personality. They'll know it's you at once.'

Root's jaw dropped. His eyes bulged with surprise. 'My God, lad! You could be right. That's a turn-up!'

'What are we going to *do*!' I shouted. 'We're ruined! The work in progress down the drain!'

'Nonsense, lad!' roared Root. 'Get a grip on yourself. There'll be a solution. There's always a solution.'

I calmed down a bit. Root was a man of the world, Root would protect us. I felt ashamed that I had reacted so unprofessionally. Root was striding up and down, deep in thought. Suddenly he beat himself on the forehead.

'I have it!' he cried. 'I have the solution!'

'What?' I shouted. 'What's the solution?'

'Simple', said Root. 'We kill her!'

Brilliant! 'How, Mr Root? How do we kill her?'

'We get her address from the agency. Go round to her place. "Good-morning, madam". Splat! The chop to the back of the neck. Over in seconds. Moments later she'll be propping up a by-pass. I blame myself. I should have ordered her out of the ops-room as soon as she said she was from the BBC. Come lad, to the telephone! We'll call the agency.'

'Too late, Mr Root. They were exposed yesterday in *The News Of The World*. They'll have closed down by now.'

Root dialled the number anyway. He held on for a bit, and then replaced the receiver. 'You're right, lad. They've had it away on their toes. Can't blame them. Nasty business being exposed in *The News Of The World*.'

Thank God he'd realised that at last.

'Hm. We need a plan, lad. Can't let her get away with this, the lady from the BBC. I could write to Murdoch – a personal friend of mine, do you see? – but before he got the letter we'd be on the front page. Your father wouldn't like that, lad. Trussed like a goose, legs in the air. Not that he's in any position to criticise, of course. Pots and kettles, do you see? Still, we need a plan. Let me think.'

He strode up and down the ops-room, one hand pulling at his chin, muttering to himself as he thought up, and quickly rejected, one scheme after another. Suddenly he let out a great roar of triumph.

'I have it, lad! One of theirs, that's what we need. A hostage, do you see, to hold against their good behaviour. They'd have the tape, we'd have one of their best investigative operatives. Stalemate! We release the hostage when they return the tape. What do you say?'

I thought it was crazy, and said as much. While my respect for Root as a writer was utterly undiminished, I was beginning to have my doubts about his ability to handle things in an emergency. Desperation seemed to have driven him out of his wits. 'We can't go around *kidnapping* people!' I protested. 'That's a serious offence.'

Root looked at me pityingly. 'Of course it is, lad, if you simply walk in, grab someone and hold him to ransom. I'm not suggesting that. I'm not suggesting that you and I hop down to Bouverie Street, scoop up one of theirs and carry him home under the arm like a roll of wall-paper. You quite misunderstand me. *We lure one of theirs here.* It's the new law of tresparse, lad. You've read the new law of tresparse?'

I said I hadn't.

'Nor have I. But I have the gist of it. If one of theirs comes here *uninvited*, he's tresparsing, we can do what we like with him, do you see? Stranger on the premises. Could be a burglar or a pervert. We have our women-folk to think of. No alternative. Into the broom-cupboard with him!' Root growled with pleasure at the prospect and smacked the palm of his left-hand with a ham-like fist.

'Are you *sure*, Mr Root?'

He looked at me in amazement. 'Of course I'm sure! Here's how we do it, lad, how we lure one of theirs here. We ring up their best investigative reporter – Tina Dalgliesh, she'll do, she'll poke her nose in anywhere, drawn to an orgy like a fly to a dog-turd, Tina Dalgliesh – and report illicit happenings here involving high-ups. We'll have to make it sound authentic. We've been to one of these events, we'll say, and were scandalised by what we saw. As public spirited citizens, etc., etc. . . . You get the picture, lad?'

'I think so.' I didn't at all.

'She'll take the bait, I guarantee it. She'll ask for details. This is where our story has to ring true. It's not at all easy to get into these parties, we'll say. You have to have the right introduction. A pass-word must be used. Security's very tight, we say, because of all the high-ups who attend. I tell you, lad, if we get it right, if the details are convincing, it's odds on she'll ring back, inviting herself to the next party. She'll sniff an exclusive, do you see? We'll give it a go. It should be a girl who rings her, a girl would have been more shocked by what she saw. You'd better ring. You sound like a girl. No offence, lad. This is no time to take offence. This will work, I tell you. Trust me.'

I still thought it sounded crazy. As far as I could see we were going to report ourselves for misbehaviour to *The News Of The World*, which was precisely what Lindi was about to do anyway.

'What exactly do I have to do?' I asked.

'There's nothing to it, lad. You ring *The News Of The World* and ask to speak to Tina Dalgliesh. When she comes to the phone you tearfully describe these parties supposedly happening here. You lay it on a bit. You were outraged, you say, at all the high-ups ducking their heads into one another's business parts. Hint that left-wingers were involved. Mention the NUM. *The News Of The World*, quite rightly, is not in business to expose those to the right of centre. Trots, polytechnic teachers, striking miners – that's their game. The Dalgliesh woman will ask you how she can attend one of these parties. It's very difficult, you'll say. Security as tight as a fish's bum. She might have a chance, you'll say, if she rings this number with a story that she was given it by a Major Snipe. She should ask when the next meeting of the Park Walk Angling Society is. That's the pass-word, you'll say, that's our cover. She'll phone, I guarantee it. When she does, I'll take over. It will be up to me to make it sound convincing. She didn't just fall off a Christmas tree, the Dalgliesh woman. I'll have to be good. I'll quizz her. I'll be suspicious. I'll pretend I don't know what she's talking about. In the end I'll invite her to the next party. She'll come, mark my words.'

'She will?'

'I'm certain of it, lad. As soon as she gets out of the lift, I'll explain the form. "It's wife-swapping, madam. Kindly remove your clothes." It's of the essence that she takes her clothes off. She'll comply. This will be a nasty moment from what I hear, but there you are. Then – bang! – into the broom-cupboard with her. We'll have our prisoner, lad.'

'But surely we can't do that? Isn't that illegal? Locking a *News Of The World* reporter in a broom-cupboard?'

I don't pretend to have Root's knowledge of the world, but this sounded barmy.

Root was becoming exasperated by my slowness. 'In the normal course of events, lad, *yes*. Kidnapping even a *News Of The World* reporter might be frowned on in certain circles. But in this case we'd have committed no offence. It's the new law of trespass, don't you see? This hare-eyed woman whom we've never met pitches up uninvited at a meeting of the Park Walk Angling Society and takes her clothes off, scaring the daylights out of everyone. Simple fishing-folk, do you see? Never seen such a thing before. Women and children present. What were we to do? Taking her to be a mad woman on the loose we photograph her upside down and stick her in a cupboard. Protecting ourselves, do you see? Then we ring up *The News Of The World* and threaten to deposit her on the steps of *The Sunday Mirror*. *The Sunday Mirror* would be delighted. Circulation war. Could beat bingo. *The News Of The World* will see reason, mark my words. They'll do business to get the Dalgliesh woman back.'

I was persuaded, finally, that it was a foolproof scheme – breath-taking in its audacity, but with a cast-iron logic of its own. What, in any case, did we have to lose? Taking any sort of retaliatory action would be better than sitting in a puddle of funk waiting to be exposed. My faith in Root's ability to handle things was thoroughly revived.

I went, as instructed, to the telephone and dialled *The News Of The World*'s number. I asked for Tina Dalgliesh. I called myself Charlotte. I said I was unwilling to give my other name – an authentic touch, I thought. When Tina came to the telephone our conversation went as smoothly as Root had said it would. I told her of my mortifying experience at a meeting of The Park Walk Angling Society and she commiserated with me, volunteering to investigate these parties under an alias. I gave her the number to ring and stressed that she must say she got it from Major Snipe. These were clever and dangerous people, I said, who would be quick to smell a rat. Tina said she had done this sort of thing many times before and that there was no need to teach her her business. There was a slightly awkward moment when she asked me for the names of some of the celebrities attending these parties. Thinking very quickly, I said that I'd prefer not to mention actual names on the telephone, but I hinted that many of them would not be unknown at Transport House. She'd be able to see for herself, I said, if she managed to get into one of the parties. She asked how she could contact me, so I gave her my home number. That seemed safe enough. If she did happen to ring I'd say that Charlotte had had an unpleasant experience and had gone away for a short holiday. Tina and I parted on the best of terms, united in our belief that immorality must be stamped out.

Root was generously delighted with my performance. 'You did well, lad. My guess she'll ring within the hour. When she does, I'll say the next meeting's tomorrow. Time is of the essence, do you see? We must have the Dalgliesh woman trussed up in the broom-cupboard by the time our friend from the BBC takes the video to *The News Of The World*.'

'But that could be today!'

'Not a chance, lad. It's the money she wants. She'll extend the deadline. We have a couple of days, that's my guess.'

In fact Tina rang back within half an hour. Root handled the call in a masterly fashion: suspicious at first, verging on the paranoid, only unbending when Tina was able to satisfy him as to her credentials. She would be welcome, he said at last, at the next meeting of the Park Walk Angling Society, which, as luck would have it, was taking place the very next day at twelve noon. He gave her the address and told her to take the basement lift straight to the ninth floor.

'We've got her!' cried Root. 'Says her "husband" is a keen angler. Wants to bring him too. That'll be Trevor Kempson. He'll go into the cupboard too. He's long overdue. A brace of 'em!'

We decided that for authenticity's sake there must be others at the party already misbehaving when Tina and Trevor arrived. Tina and Trevor must take their clothes off voluntarily, said Root, and they certainly wouldn't do this unless the room was already full of naked couples.

'But can they really do that, Mr Root?'

'How can they avoid it, lad?'

'Can't they just see what's happening, then make their excuses and leave?'

'Of course they can't! They've got to hang around a bit to catch the celebrities. Don't forget we've told them there'll be celebrities present. They'll wait for them. And they can't wait with their clothes on, can they? Look suspicious. I tell you, lad, we've got them!'

I was completely convinced. There was no way that this could go wrong. We spent the rest of the morning organising the guest-list. We must have at least four girls on the premises prepared to take their clothes off, said Root. This involved another perusal of *What's On In London* and further calls to the escort agencies. It was an expense, admitted Root, but the atmosphere must be exactly right. Tina and Trevor hadn't come down in the last shower. Two girls were booked from *Aristocats* and two from *Chelsea Girl* – all four to be in the ops-room by noon tomorrow. We needed two extra men, we decided, to bring the numbers up to eight. Before Tina and Trevor spotted the absence of celebrities we'd have them in the broom-cupboard. Root invited the Major from 138 ('Don't mention Greece, lad') and I rang Ned, explaining that this was legitimate research for the book but that he must on no account mention it to Charlotte. 'Stand on me, Kim, lad,' he said. Ned's a fool, but he's good value at a party and quite at ease without his trousers. The ops-room would have to be made more suitable for an orgy, but this could be left, we agreed, until the following day. All the mattresses from the family-quarters would have to be brought in here and arranged invitingly on the floor.

'What's tomorrow, lad?' asked Root.

'Tuesday', I said.

'Excellent! Mrs Root goes to the hairdresser at eleven every Tuesday morning. We'll fetch the mattresses then. Don't want her knowing what we're up to, eh?'

TUESDAY 17 JULY

I woke up in a mood of some excitement, and dressed with care. There was no reason, as far as I could see, why business shouldn't be mixed, discreetly, with a little pleasure, so I wanted to be looking good. Why, once Tina was securely in the broom-cupboard and negotiations for her release under way with *The News Of The World*, shouldn't I get Root's money's worth (or Lord Weidenfeld's rather) with the escort girls? Must a writer always remain chastely objective *vis-à-vis* the roughage of his art? Was it Jean Paul Sartre or Julian Barnes who dubbed Flaubert 'a trembling bourgeois, joking at the edge of a sin he dare not commit'? (Not, I may say, that coupling at an orgy with an escort girl strikes me as being a very great sin.) It was a lovely day, so I decided to walk to work. In the King's Road, I bumped into Charlotte.

'I hear you're giving orgies now', she said. 'It's pathetic, rarely pathetic.' She raked me witheringly and walked on. A lot of people will be looking exceptionally silly when the book comes out, not least Charlotte.

At eleven o'clock Root and I – he dressed for the occasion in his dinner-jacket and with his camera equipment round his neck – went into the family-quarters to fetch the mattresses. As we were heaving Mrs Root's off the bed, she came out of the bathroom.

'Why are you removing my mattress, Mr Root?' she said. 'Are you having an orgy in the ops-room?'

'As a matter of fact we are,' said Root. 'Why aren't you at the hairdresser?'

'I cancelled it. Can I come to the orgy, then? I like a laugh.'

'If you must', said Root. He turned to me and shrugged. 'Nothing else for it, lad. Can't waste time with a family argument. Our guests will be here in an hour.'

I was a bit confused by this development. I hadn't imagined that it would be at a morning orgy that Mrs Root would finally have her way with me (which was clearly her intention) and the prospect brought a distracting dimension to what was meant primarily – notwithstanding my intentions *re* the escort girls – to be work. Nor, it must be said, was an orgy an occasion at which a normal person would expect to realise a fantasy. Perhaps Mrs Root and I would be able to slip off privately to the family-quarters – once our main task had been completed, of course, once Tina and Trevor had been captured. That would be my plan. While Root was negotiating with *The News Of The World* – our prisoners in exchange for the tape – I'd slip into the family-quarters with Mrs Root. Things were going really well.

By twelve o'clock the ops-room had been transformed, and by 12.30 all our guests had arrived except Tina and Trevor, and Mrs Root. The Major turned up in uniform, but was quickly persuaded out of this by the agency girls, who seemed a very sporting lot, particularly after they'd been paid. The effect on them of cash in hand was indeed quite startling. As their bags snapped shut on wads of notes, they lit up as if suddenly plugged into the national grid, grinning viciously like a chorus line with only two minutes to make an impact. Ned behaved extremely well, apart from a slight tendency to address the agency girls on the subject of coffee futures. At least one of the girls was wantonly pretty, with brown impertinent legs and dark delinquent eyes. Had I not been waiting for Mrs Root, I might well have tried to reserve her for myself. I stayed out of temptation's way by opening bottles of Krug (left over from the literary lunch) and handing round nuts. Thanks to the Major (who seemed determined to make up in one morning for his unhappy experience in Greece), and to a lesser extent to Ned, the atmosphere was quite louche enough to satisfy even the most suspicious *News Of The World* reporter without any contribution from me. The only danger seemed to be that such was the keenness with which Ned and the Major had taken to the mattresses (the Major, to my slight, and quite unprofessional, annoyance, now had his head up the dress of the girl with irresponsible legs) the hired help, assuming that their job was done, would bog off before Tina and Trevor arrived.

I was pondering this possibility, and wondering whether to instruct Ned and the Major to slow down a bit (giving the Major a nervous breakdown, perhaps, by suddenly shouting 'Greece!' down his girlfriend's cleavage) when Root took me to one side and stood on tiptoe to hiss into my ear.

'They're here, lad!'

I looked across the room. Stepping out of the lift were the two most disastrously unattractive people I'd ever seen, she lank-haired and squinny-eyed, he heavy and damp-complexioned.

'My God!' said Root. 'If that's *The News Of The World*'s swapping squad it's a miracle they ever get a result.'

'They are rough, Mr Root.'

'*Rough*? I tell you, lad, if they take their clothes off I'll call the cops myself.'

It was indeed a gruesome prospect, but I reminded Root that this was a risk we had to take, that their undressing was of the essence. This was no time to respect our own finer feelings, or those of our other guests.

'You're right, lad. My God, though, I've a mind to send back Weidenfeld's advance – not that we've had it. Remind me to write to

Weidenfeld, lad. "Dear Weidenfeld, *re* the advance, etc." Is it worth it, lad? Is this beyond the call of duty? I put this to you man to man: did Anna Ford expose herself to the wife-swapping squad from *The News Of The World*? Did she ask them to remove their clothes? My guess she didn't, lad.'

'That's not the point, Mr Root', I said. It pleased me that in this emergency it was I who was displaying the more professional attitude. 'The advance is irrelevant. It's the tape that matters now. Unless we recover the tape there'll be no book. They *must* be persuaded out of their clothes.'

'You're right, lad. Leave this to me.'

'Perhaps you shouldn't have the camera with you. The camera might make them nervous.'

'Right again, lad.' He unslung the camera and handed it to me. 'Here goes. My God!' He passed a hand across his eyes and then, with a glass of Krug in either hand, he squared his shoulders and bravely crossed the room to greet the new arrivals. He chatted politely for a while, and then returned to my end of the room.

'Slight problem, lad. They're being leery. Reluctant to remove their clothes. Invited Tina on to the mat, but she demurred. I should have worn the Thruster, do you think? Shall I put the Thruster on?'

'No time for that, Mr Root.' I didn't fancy being left in charge while Root disappeared into the bathroom.

'Perhaps you're right. They're looking restless. Trevor was keen, mind you. Kept eyeing one of the girls. The little blonde sitting on the Major's face. Do you think she's from the BBC, lad? She has the look of someone from the BBC.'

'We can't worry about that now, Mr Root.' I didn't want to be reminded of the BBC. It would be a fine turn-up if, just as we were trying to extricate ourselves from a blackmail threat, we were blackmailed again. 'What are we going to *do*?'

'Force, lad, we'll have to use force.'

'We can't do that. They must undress voluntarily, you said so yourself.'

'Too late to worry about that. Any minute now they'll twig no one else is turning up. Can't risk that. When I shout "now!" you open the broom-cupboard and stand by to take a photograph. Must have a photograph, do you see? For *The Sunday Mirror*. Press that. The flash and focussing are automatic.'

I went and stood by the cupboard with camera cocked, while Root returned to the unattractive couple. There was a sudden cry of 'Now!', a blur of arms and legs and both were on their backs, grunting with surprise. With a knee planted heavily on either chest, Root skinned them as expertly as eels in the old days. 'Smile please!' he cried, and I had them both on film. 'And again! It's for *The Sunday Mirror,* madam. Over you go! The moon-shot, lad!' Tina squealed and got a cuffing. Then, with one under each arm and to a smattering of applause (our other guests clearly took this to be the cabaret), Root ran across the room and tossed them, protesting feebly, into the broom-cupboard, opened by me.

'Got them!' he cried. 'To the telephone, lad! We'll ring *The News Of The World*.'

Mention of *The News Of The World* had an electrifying effect on the escort girls. Spinning in small demented circles, like rats in a behavioural experiment, they were into their clothes and on their way to the lift in thirty seconds flat, leaving Ned and the Major floundering in a confused heap on the mattresses, groping each other and empty air.

'Here I say what's going on actually?' said Ned. 'Why have the totties left?'

'We've just captured two *News Of The World* reporters', I said.

'Have you by Jove?' said the Major, 'well done indeed,' but Ned went a funny colour and started to get dressed.

'Think I'll toddle along actually do you see?' he said.

Root, meanwhile, was dialling *The News Of The World*. He asked to speak to the editor.

'This will be good', he said. 'This will shake them! Hullo. Is that the editor? We have two of yours locked in the broom-cupboard my old turkey, what do you say to that? Why? I'll tell you why. They walked in here and took their clothes off, that's why. We're simple fishing-folk here, do you see? Not used to two of yours striding in here and taking their clothes off, I can tell you. Who? Tina Dalgliesh and Trevor Kempson, that's who.' He turned to me, covering the receiver. 'They don't believe it.' He chuckled happily. 'The editor's gone to investigate. He's got a shock coming to him! Oh dear, oh dear. *The Sunday Mirror* will love this.' The editor was back on the line. Root listened. 'What!' He slammed the receiver down. 'Trevor and the Dalgliesh woman are in Wales', he said. 'Both of them. That's one in the eye for us, lad. Who have we captured, then?'

He hurried across the room to the broom-cupboard and hauled the prisoners out.

'Right, you monkeys! What's your game? Be so good as to identify yourselves.'

The man cleared his throat and then, considering his condition, spoke with some dignity, I thought.

'Detective Sergeant Smiley, "B" Division, sir.'

'Bit of a turn-up, lad', said Root.

D/S Smiley gestured towards his colleague, who was hastily getting dressed. 'WPC Harris', he said. 'Following information supplied to us by *The News Of The World re* the activities of "The Park Walk Angling Society", it is my duty to arrest you for a number of offences, including, but by no means confined to, indecent assault on two police officers in the course of their investigations.'

'Bagged a couple from "B" Division, lad. That's the size of it, do you see? Leave this to me.'

'I must warn you', said D/S Smiley, 'that anything you say may be taken down and used in evidence against you.'

'Ten thou to you and I'll forget this ever happened', said Root.

'We'll add that to the charges, sir. Attempted bribery. Talking of which, sir, I'm instructed to return the ten pounds you conveyed to Sir Kenneth Newman on the 22nd June.'

'Another own goal, lad.'

'As soon as I've recovered my clothes, I must ask you to accompany me to Chelsea Police Station.'

D/S Smiley got dressed and then led Root towards the lift. As the lift door began to close, Root was struck by a sudden thought.

'Have we finished "A" yet, lad?'

'I believe we have, Mr Root.'

'It's on to "B" then. Must have order, do you see? Must be systematic. Booth, Joanna. The little blonde from North London. The face of 1985, unless I'm much mistaken.'

As he disappeared from sight, Mrs Root entered from the family-quarters. She looked really great in a bottle-green ball-gown split to the waist.

'Hullo, love', she said. 'Where is everyone? Where's Mr Root?'

'He's been arrested', I said. I desired her keenly. She was large and over-flowing. I wanted to paddle around on top of her like a water-bed. I was ashamed of myself for having had intentions towards the escort girl with delinquent legs.

'Bound to happen sooner or later', said Mrs Root. 'Here, you better have this.' She handed me a package.

'What's is it?'

'The video, love. You and Mr Root trussed in the ops-room.'

'But . . .'

'It was just a joke, love. Lindi and I would never . . .'

'You *know* Lindi?'

'Known her for years, love. Pottery class.'

'But you don't go to pottery class.'

'That's true.' She winked. 'Oh – the Major's here, I see. Still, he won't notice anything in his condition.' She winked again, and smiled mysteriously.

This was it, the moment I'd been waiting for. I was alone at last with Mrs Root. And that wasn't all. I had the video, and I had Root's tapes. I'd be able to finish the book and deliver it to Weidenfeld. I'd take the credit. I'd be rich and celebrated. I'd be back to back with Anna Ford.

'There's something you can do for me', said Mrs Root.

She didn't have to spell it out. 'He won't notice anything in his condition', she'd said. That could only mean one thing. 'Whatever you want', I said. I loosened my belt and let my trousers slip teasingly to the floor.

'You can say something nasty about Susan Hampshire', she said.

'Of course!'

'And now we can enjoy ourselves!'

She gave me a brilliant smile and took my hand. I stepped out of my trousers and kicked them away. I pulled her gently towards the mattresses.

'Just a minute', she said. She withdrew her hand and walked across the room. She opened the pass-door to the family-quarters.

'Come in, love', she said. 'The coast's clear.'

Kevin the hairdresser entered. Mrs Root turned to me. 'Leave us alone, will you, love?'

INDEX